Memoirs of a Spiritual Outsider

Suzanne Clores

Foreword by Rebecca Walker

Conari Press
Berkeley, California

To my family

Conari Press books are distributed by Publishers Group West.
Cover photography: © Kamil Vojnar/Photonica
Cover author photo: Nancy Opitz
Cover and book design: Claudia Smelser
Cover art direction: Ame Beanland

LIBRARY OF CONGRESS CATALOGING-IN-PUBLICATION DATA

Clores, Suzanne.
    Memoirs of a spiritual outsider / Suzanne Clores.
    ISBN: 1-57324-172-5
    1. Clores, Suzanne. 2. Spiritual biography—United States. I. Title.
    BL73.C57 A3 2000
    291.4'092—dc21

                                                            00-009140

Printed in the United States of America on recycled paper.

00 01 02 03 PHOENIX 10 9 8 7 6 5 4 3 2 1

Contents

Praise for *Suzanne Clores*

"This 'spiritual outsider' chose a difficult path to discovering the mystic hidden deep within herself. Searching for an authentic spiritual life that would lead her to the Divine, she found the truth: The Divine dwelling within the Self only gives itself to those who surrender, who trust, who commit themselves whole-heartedly to it."
　　—Wayne Teasdale, author of *The Mystic Heart*

"Suzanne Clores' special talent—especially impressive given her birthright of generational 'twentysomething' cynicism—is to enter into various sacred and spiritual worlds with an astonishing innocence, opening doors for the reader to experience each one as if for the first time. I laughed out loud more than once, seeing myself through her eyes, yet never felt disrespected. A charming read."
　　—Vicki Noble, co-creator of *Motherpeace*

Finding God

by Rebecca Walker,
author of *White, Black, and Jewish*
and founder of 3rd Wave

I have never looked for God. Never found myself in a church, mosque, or synagogue, crying into my hands, kneeling in a pew, gazing at the cross, longing for salvation. Religion was never where I turned to be soothed, was not where I looked to know peace, connection, transcendence.

Without knowing it, I have always been a spiritual outsider. By birth, by breeding. When I was born my parents were baptist-pagan and jewish-lawyer, and raised me without the Holy Book, but with hundreds of others. Volumes by Marquez, Baldwin, Tillie Olsen. *Letters from a Birmingham Jail, Diary of Anne Frank, Life of Gandhi. Siddhartha.* They had faith I would find my way, that a relationship to the Divine was obvious, all around me. I would not need the Guide, with all of its pitfalls and problematics.

As a child I loved my cat, to lie down next to my mother's warm brown body, to wear my father's dirty T-shirts that smelled of him. I liked my mother's rose bushes, the dogwood tree she planted, the magnolia trees in the South I visited on summer holidays. I loved lakes, the ocean. I loved the older women in my life who brushed my hair and took me shopping at theater supply stores, letting me choose feathers and glitter and purple cloth to make a magic cape.

God did not live outside of me when I was a child. God did not look down on me, blessing and correcting. I ran free; that was where God was, that was where my joy was, that was when life was magical and good. I did not know I was a spiritual outsider, a seeker on a path strewn with dahlias, petunias, hydrangeas inherited from my mother and all the other mothers before her. In college, I had a crisis of faith. I was anxious all the time. I couldn't figure out what was to become of me. I was fighting against an institution that did not know my name and did not wish to. I felt alone. I wondered how to cope. I could not engage faith because it had never failed me; I had not ever had to reach for it, it was so much a part of me.

I read *Peace Is Every Step* and found that there was a way to breathe, to see, to believe that there was good underneath, there was a flower in every pile of garbage, a mound of garbage in every bunch of flowers. This felt right to me, and so I kept reading everything I could find by Thich Nhat Hahn and then other Buddhist writers. I learned to meditate, and then I saw that I was on a path again and this time I had more tools. I had breathing and meditating and seeing beauty in what was ugly and ugliness in what was beautiful and being kind to people and loving them even when they hurt me.

But even then, when people would ask me what religion I was and I would look at them blankly and say, "None," and when people said, "Oh she doesn't believe in God," and I said, "Yes yes I do" but then couldn't explain that my God didn't look like that God in the books, even then I did not know I was a spiritual outsider, because my friend Matt waited for hours to get tickets to see the Dalai Lama and my professors whom I loved taught me about African American altars that traced back to Africa, and because I knew, fundamentally, that I was okay, that I was being held in the universe's embrace.

We are all spiritual outsiders.

As an adult, two of the people closest to me came out of religion, and came to me for refuge from that place. Both were driven nearly insane by a God who did not love them, a God who lived in their minds as a demon, lashing out at them, beating them with great stripes on their psyches, sending them literally to their knees. They spoke of a God I did not know, one that had never lodged in my mind, for if it had a part of me surely would have died. I would not have seen the flowers, would not have felt the wind, would not have known to love as God the women who took me with them, to love that generous, yielding, sweet smelling place.

We are all spiritual outsiders because we all must seek, must all find for ourselves that which is called God. This book is Suzanne's story of seeking. It is a map of her journey of looking and finding, finding and looking some more. It is a wise book. It captures a land I see myself and all of my friends exploring as we quietly shed what is not essential and allow ourselves to gravitate toward that which clarifies and heals.

As the world spins more and more out of control, we are called upon to get to the quick of it, to waste no time, to find out how to love ourselves and each other with a fierce determination. Suzanne is trying to do this. This book is her record. It exists to affirm and enrich our travels.

Paradise
Lost

No one told me that my twenties, like my adolescence, would be years of major transition. That the instability at the beginning of adulthood attacks the psyche the way rampant acne and the wrong jeans threaten puberty. The advice everyone gives a twenty-three-year-old college graduate is, "The world is your oyster." I'd taken a couple of extra years to graduate, so I was certain, with adulthood right around the corner, that the pearls of success and security followed close behind.

It took a while before I understood the slipperiness of my twenty-three-year-old puberty. It was invisible to the outside world. Technically, I was a grown-up, with my own job and an apartment on 14th Street that I shared with my boyfriend of one year. New York City—my oyster—would provide me with the life education I needed, I reasoned, just as the college campus had offered its dining halls, health services, bookstores, and social opportunities. I'd found the book *Zen and the Art of Motorcycle Maintenance* the very first day of freshman year and walked around with the pink paperback for a month. The story of transcendence was a security blanket. Certainly I'd find an equivalent talisman any day now—it could be another book, a piece of jewelry, a drug, a scene, a friend. Soon, I'd find it: the key to living life soulfully.

Until I found it, though, I lived one day at a time in New York City. My boyfriend and I did couple-ish things: we cooked dinner together on weekends and decorated our spare, loud, one-bedroom apartment with purple velvet curtains and kitschy religious candles from the 99-cent store. My job as an events coordinator at a nonprofit organization challenged me enough so that I overlooked the pittance I was paid. But life felt stilted, crammed into the realms of domestic and professional life. I grew disenchanted and incapable of living one day at a time. Something basic was missing, some larger purpose beyond working at an interesting job, living with an interesting guy. Where was the key? I had no trajectory, no sense of direction, though I *was* moving.

Every morning when I awoke, questions flooded my mind. Where am I going? What should I be doing and thinking about? Does anyone feel the same way I do? The questions recurred, like mantras that didn't help, while I was reading the paper on the subway, dressing for a party, doing laundry. I was sliding into a vortex of insecurity, yet to the naked eye, my life looked fine. I functioned, even flourished. People around me confirmed my normalcy. Coworkers insisted my performance made me an asset, family applauded my finding a job in the recession, my boyfriend returned my love. But I felt lost.

When I tried telling older people that I felt a black hole widening, they seemed acquainted with that vacant space. They grinned smugly, shaking their heads. "I'd never live my twenties over again, even if I had the chance." Why not?, I wondered. Their commiseration did not offer a helpful analysis. On the one hand, I was grateful for the acknowledgment that life was "hard" when first breaking through the shell of college and parental support. On the other, the acknowledgment fell short. Exactly what was so hard about life's mission at twenty-three? These people—survivors of their twenties—seemed to assume that the very real absence of knowledge, experience, and wisdom was just part of "the age." Part of paying the dues of life. I knew I wouldn't feel lost forever, but with each moment, the gap between stability and shaky reality grew larger, invoking a slow terror.

As the gap insidiously grew into crisis, I tried filling it with work. Forty hours a week grew into sixty. Broke and burned out, I quit within a year. I became a temp, a hired gun, adding the insult of professional displacement to my personal anguish. I was professionally marginal, living on the fringe. Angst-ridden, I watched other people my age for some kind of clue and saw similar displeasure with the way they lived their lives. Acquaintances swung from extreme bliss at "being on their own" to discontent once they realized that entry-level pay sucked. But it wasn't just material disappointment. It was personal. Theirs did not comfort my isolation. I tried bonding with folks in bars after work, stood among the frustrated behind Stairmasters at the gyms, spent listless evenings in front of television. *Friends* and *Beverly Hills 90210* featured good-looking people stuck in similar, though more comical and sexy, predicaments. Perhaps this was a generational malaise, I reasoned. A malady specific to the millions of GenX-ers who supposedly can call in sick, toast an English muffin, and channel surf while logging online, but can't get it together to vote on election day. Our "whatever" attitude, social analysts proposed, was a direct result of mass media influence, the growing presence of technology, working parents, and general faithlessness in government and society. But I *had* voted—at eighteen and at twenty-two—and I didn't even have an e-mail account yet. So was mine a generational problem? *Friends* and *90210* never said. I stuffed my feelings behind an attitude of irony, where I hoped they wouldn't bother me.

Then one day, while standing in Columbus Circle at dusk, I thought I was going to die. The treachery of the five-lane intersection was not the culprit. Standing on the curb, I felt my understanding of the moment, the city, and the universe slide out from under me. I began thinking of my mortality, my survival, and my beliefs. What were they? Did I have any? I didn't seem to be living by any. Except for my beliefs in morning coffee, screening phone calls, and not fighting with loved ones. In the event that I lost everything—job, family, lover, physical health, safety—who or what would I depend on? My heart raced. I started to sweat. I thought I was going to die. The panic attack told me I was working with a larger, fiercer monster than generational malaise.

I am not about to write about how God was missing from my life. But I will acknowledge the space that religion, if you were raised with it like I was, purports to fill and what happens when you remove it from your daily life and consciousness.

Ten years earlier, at thirteen, I had experienced a similar crack in stability. Just before high school was to begin, I underwent a "What's it all about?" phase like most restless teens. I wanted answers to large life questions—why are we here, why do some suffer and others flourish, where do we *really* go when we die— and sought a place to ask these questions. Thinking the answers were available beyond the walls of the tiny town where I lived, I transferred from my local public school to an enormous regional Catholic girls' school. The ride on the yellow schoolbus, packed full with dozens of others also on their way to learn about God, became my daily journey to find the answers. Certain they lay outside of my town, outside of me, I endured the ugly brown polyester uniform and convinced myself this was a great idea, a new experience, the right direction. I was wrong.

By the time I maneuvered a switch back to public school two years later, I had completely lost faith in religion and my future as a girl. Catholic school kept my questions at bay, like those velvet ropes that prevent museumgoers from getting too close to the art. Girls shuffled through grades, smiling, pleasing, and obeying, thinking me odd for asking for proof of the afterlife. I determined that religion was a hoax, that there were no answers, and that people simply lived in darkness. This change of heart was my first life crisis.

I'd been raised Catholic but never actually paid attention in catechism. I just assumed that what was being taught went along with what I'd already figured out: Christ was holy because he knew he was doomed from the start and yet he persevered, giving everyone those messages about life and love he knew were true. *Holy,* at least my definition of it, was another word for "brave": sticking with what you know is true in the face of all doubt and scorn. At twelve, I admired anyone who showed an ounce of bravery. This was the extent to which I identified with the religion I knew as Catholicism: it was a religion of bravery for all involved.

But then, at Catholic high school, I was exposed to the true Catholic doctrine. Church history started to sink in—the great schism, the purchasing of indulgences. Truthfully, I didn't really care that Catholicism's history wasn't perfect. I was more alarmed that the system of belief I'd relied on differed so vastly from the religion I was now made to understand was Catholicism. This Catholic school version wasn't about Jesus' bravery. It was about our sinning nature, which shrank both the scope of Catholicism and my world. Now there were only two constructs into which I could fit: sinner and forgiven sinner. *Sinner.* The word tantalized me. What did it mean? "One who had faults." I began counting how many times we uttered it in Mass. Too many.

Equally unsettling was women's contribution to the "sinner" label. Eve, the original sinner, evoked in my teenage mind a glamorous disobedience with her apple-eating. My developing self-esteem understood that her behavior wielded power, but what kind? Instructors told us her weakness of will caused contemporary human suffering, only relievable through Jesus' grace. But the story was surely saying something else. We never learned what that was.

The only woman born without the scar of original sin was the Virgin Mary, we learned. This was the woman, our instructors told us, whom we needed to emulate. She didn't deliver messages in the same way as God or Christ, but she offered a model to which we should at least try to aspire, despite our own scarred births.

Armed with Louis Vuitton handbags and protective clouds of Poison perfume, the girls at school tried defying authority in small ways in order to assert their individuality. In turn, little traps were set up around the building to catch our disobedience. I called it the "nun patrol": the nuns stood on selected corners pulling us aside for rolling the regulation skirt up above the knees, or for wearing too much hairspray, or for chewing gum. If caught, we were sent to the office, written a demerit, assigned a Hail Mary or two in the chapel, and made to pay a few dollars for our sins.

I sensed that most girls in the school knew the whole thing was just smoke and mirrors—a bad card trick. Prayer couldn't quell the need to express oneself, not in this day and age. Such punishments may have hurt in the 1950s, but for New Jersey girls in the 1980s, they were a joke. Word got around quickly among the student body that violating these policies was the way to rebel, if you had any ounce of bravery in you at all. Why we were rebelling, though, was never said. A larger purpose did not exist. A revolution was not taking place.

Girls sensed the discrepancy between men's and women's power in the Catholic construct, but didn't bother, or weren't sure how, to take apart the argument. I was among them. I couldn't figure out if my fury should be directed at Catholicism, or at myself for not fitting in. It was the time in life when I was first discovering my independence, my sexuality, my identity as a young woman. Yet I was in a place where there were only three models into which one could fit: Evil Eve, who questioned authority and ruined paradise for everyone; Mother Mary, who'd been chosen for her perfection; or, least appealing of all, the nuns. Between trying to identify with any of these confusing female models and wrestling the inescapable sinner label, I was left without any inspiration to be brave. I felt totally abandoned.

Determined to face life bravely with my own capabilities, I transferred, finding public high school a faster ride than Catholic school. Liberated from the pursuit of large, philosophical issues of faith and existence, I felt an unspoken camaraderie among schoolmates who were not plagued with images of women they were supposed to either emulate or castigate. I blended into secular student life. Catholicism and its trappings quickly faded from memory. I was a free woman.

The absence of religion in my life throughout high school did not plague me. Even through college, I steered clear of its theory and practice in my personal life. I didn't need some abstract force of God dictating my decisions. I had literature, pop culture, social politics, and my academic load with which to grow. I had myself. I spent college balanced and pleased, most of the time. Except for whenever Catholicism or church or religion was mentioned, and then I felt the sting of a fight unresolved.

One day, in front of the student center, near the end of the autumn semester, a small, young blond woman approached as though she knew me.

"Hey there, excuse me, where did you get your hair cut?" Her voice had a southern swing. I barely turned my head.

"You know, you look just like Jodie Foster. Did anyone ever tell you that?"

"No."

"Well, you do. Your hair is really cute. Do you think my hair would look cute like that?" She tossed it and it moved in a unified bounce.

"Sure."

She smiled at me, mouth agape as though we were fated to meet. Whipping out a leather-bound organizer with a small gold cross in the corner, she quickly flipped to the white pad inside with a little pencil tucked next to it. In a moment it was in her hand and she was expertly scribbling digits.

"Well here's my number. What's yours?" she asked, handing me the paper and waiting patiently for me to rattle off my number. I looked at the phone number she gave me and the loopy cursive name written beneath it: "Cindy."

Her openness and lack of concern for proper campus attitude intrigued me. I gave her my number.

"I'd really like to get my hair cut like yours. Maybe you'll come with me to get it cut on Sunday?"

I wasn't doing anything Sunday. "Maybe," I said.

She beamed. " And maybe you can sleep over Saturday night and come with me to church in the morning. Then we can go downtown to that neat neighborhood, Greenwich Village. Have you been there?"

"Sure, but. . . ." I was thinking about what she'd said about church.

"Well, I just love it there, especially the places that sell all of that silver jewelry like the kind you're wearing. I just love those rings." She touched my knuckles on the hand that could not quite pocket the paper on which she'd written her number. I didn't want it anymore, or her compliments.

"So I'll call you," she said, walking away. "And don't forget, my name's Cindy."

Even if I wanted to forget, which I did, Cindy did not let me. I spent a lot of time dodging her calls, and when unsuccessful, trying to get off the phone. She wanted me to sleep over on Saturday nights and attend church with her the following morning, on the way to doing something else, of course. If I wasn't declining her invitations with absurd lies about "swimming practice" on Saturday nights, I was manufacturing Sunday morning plans. Finally I asked her why she was so insistent on my sleeping over.

"I just thought it would be nice for you to meet all of my friends. You'd really like them. We all live together and go to the same church. It's really fun."

Then I told her I didn't want to go to church. That I wasn't religious.

"It's not really about religion," she said quickly. "It's about Jesus."

I paused. She smiled.

"But don't worry, everyone I live with is really cool," she assured me.

It didn't sound cool. It sounded like she lived in a Christian flophouse. She and her friends had all moved to the Northeast from Atlanta for college. They were part of a youth group for Jesus. She painted a picture of their lives, and it sounded as though their holiday season would be filled with tree decorating, caroling, and Bible reading with new recruits like me. If the image she sketched hadn't been so neatly packaged with a bow on top, the gathering might have appealed to me in some small way. I was lonely, uncertain of what I believed underneath my veneer of indifference. Cindy made no mention of Eve or Mary or nuns. In fact, she said nothing of female identity, which annoyed me. She seemed happy with Jesus, living within a patriarchal religion, letting it define who she was as a young woman in exchange for friends, community, and mission. Cynical, I looked for a weak link in her happiness.

She told me how living with friends had buffered the insecurity and hardship in her own life. Ah ha, I thought. Hardship. Her friends had really supported her since she'd broken up with her boyfriend. What happened? I asked.

"Poor thing," she answered, as though talking about a wayward child. "He just up and left the church before we all moved up here. He pinned a note to the door of the porch of our youth group, saying he was thinking he might not be Christian after all," she shrugged, detached. "We really could have helped him if he'd stayed. We were the ones who helped him find Jesus in the first place." It was the way that she said "Jesus" so familiarly that bothered me. Like a family member. Like an imaginary friend.

"You can't force God down someone's throat," I told her. "Just because you like vanilla ice cream doesn't mean everyone else has to eat it."

I hung up on her, feeling clever. She didn't call me again. I didn't care; in fact I was relieved. Now I was excused from dealing with my secret jealousy over the fact that Cindy had a spiritual system that spoke to her. That somehow, she was able to let religion into her life and let it help her. I told myself she was just using it as a crutch, that she was so out of touch with reality, her true needs and wants as a woman were probably deeply buried, compromised by the laws of God. I didn't use the experience to address my own scorned feelings—that when I had tried to connect with Catholic teachings in high school, I found I could not.

After Cindy, I resumed a religion-free life, accustomed to the emptiness, the gap. The courage I had shown by leaving my only spiritual construct was beginning to feel burdensome, however. Labeling my Catholic experience as impersonal and unsympathetic to my fledgling female needs was a banner. I was hiding behind it, frightened that finding something new would disappoint me again. I didn't want religion to turn me into a "girl"—someone who didn't think for herself, who did what others told her, who felt shameful about her body. I didn't want my identity as a young woman to feel fulfilled by Jesus or God, or any male-figure, for that matter. Neither my family, my public school, nor my peers raised me to feel that way. My needs as a young woman would define my growth, I had been taught. Because of my bad feelings about religion, however, I started to feel like my spiritual needs were some sign of weakness. Religion as I knew it was a bad place for women, and because I wanted something from it, I was weak.

What did I want? What were my spiritual needs? I didn't dare present these questions in public. Yet an answer came to me from the outside world anyway. It came from an editor of a children's book publisher who had been invited to speak in a publishing class I took during my final semester of college. A nice man, a former divinity student, a fellow expatriate. He seemed as calm and generous as a bonafide priest. We stayed in touch months after the class ended because he mentioned the possibility of available summer internships for students. The summer passed without an internship. Instead he offered me the opportunity to write one of their children's books. "We're doing a series on Native Americans," he told me. "Does that interest you?"

"Sure," I said, though I knew next to nothing about Native Americans.

"You can learn," he answered. And I did learn.

Two distinguishing factors about Native American culture struck me immediately. One was that the foundation of Native American culture, human connection to the Earth, was spiritual. Two was that strong female archetypes were central to this culture's spiritual foundation. Warrior Woman's bravery saved the people from slaughter. White Buffalo Woman's wisdom and resourcefulness fed communities with food and faith. Spider Woman's artistic abilities taught an entire culture to weave. These heroines, and a variety of other female faces, appeared regularly in Native American principles, politics, and social customs. A Cherokee activist I interviewed told me that all native peoples had an understanding of divinity. Creation was divine, and because women were inherently part of creation and therefore sacred, this understanding permeated family, community, government, and future. I found myself wishing for a similar understanding, and for inclusion in a global community that respected all of humanity, both men and women, for their sacredness. Where did my connections to myself as a woman and a spiritual being lie? I began mentally searching my role in society, in family, and in the professional world. Neither gender-based sacredness nor my discarded faith appeared anywhere.

The sad part is that I was in plenty of company. I personally knew faithless dozens like me. People who had opted against churchgoing, who only celebrated high holy days for the sake of family gatherings, and who, in their hearts, felt spiritually bereft. But were there others who, equally disenfranchised, had found some substitute? Another spiritual mythology that understood women to have positive and irreplaceable relevance in this life and others? The thought occurred to me over the course of time, the year between finishing the Native American book and quitting my nonprofit job. I was in a professional haze. My boyfriend and I did our best to support each other, but most of my confusion was spent in silence. I didn't have the words to articulate my crisis. How do you explain the absence of faith?

Right around the same time, I noticed more and more media references to "spirituality," and women's magazines began to pick up on the fuzzy feeling. In 1996, *Self, New Woman,* and *Marie Claire* began regularly featuring sections entitled "Body/Mind," which to me read like a disguise for the word *soul.* Was there a national community these magazines had discovered? Perhaps thousands of other women like me had taken the Body/Mind route outside of large, organized religion and found personal pathways to higher consciousness. Maybe thousands of others had connected with each other, fostered community, explored and examined their beliefs. I felt hopeful. Though I'd never read women's magazines before now, they suddenly held new promise.

The Body/Mind breakthrough implied that women's magazines would address my life beyond helpful beauty tips. After all, Body/Mind broke the code of beauty and fashion and health. I half-expected to see articles about spiritual and other experiences based on personal choice and need rather than social requirements. Taking a personal, exploratory direction made sense, since more and more young women I knew felt empowered to do so in other parts of life. Many decided to postpone college for travel, or marriage for professional growth, or to pursue sexuality in a variety of ways or not at all. Depth, soul searching, connecting inner being with life, was the direction I headed in. So far, I had constructed my outer life out of education, liberal politics, and a hope to do something good in the world in the company of others doing the same. But there was much more I needed to explore. I couldn't wait for "Body/Mind" sections to introduce these soul-searching topics into mainstream discussion. The media had the pipeline to tap into what I suspected many, many women needed.

I began to explore these Body/Mind alternatives, assuming the magazines would continue to guide me step-by-step to spiritual depth. But the articles were superficial and impersonal, and I became discouraged. The articles on women's spirituality limited discussion to getting a great bod from yoga, chasing the blues away with herbal remedies, and decorating the home using Feng Shui. Very few described the roots of these alternatives, the philosophy behind them, or the experience of each practice.

I felt cheated. Though the Body/Mind sections gave introductions to other cultures' spiritual practices, the shallow presentation omitted any chance of me truly learning from Feng Shui philosophy, or the Yogic practice of breathing, or the ancient science of herbology. I wanted to bring a greater understanding of the practices into my life, but it wasn't as easy as buying a lipstick or a bottle of jasmine extract.

To experience the soul behind the Body/Mind movement, I'd have to deeply investigate the alternatives myself. I would need to address my rejection of religion and identify my spiritual needs. That was the problem: I wasn't sure what I needed or wanted. A structure within which to grow? A set of rules? An ideal? I wasn't alone, either. During the next six months, I saw other women groping their way around bookstores, seminars, free orientations, $20 lectures, and six-week classes in the same hapless pattern of exploration. They were seeking something "more"—without any guidance.

It was frustrating to see so many of us in isolated exploration. I found it difficult to discuss spirituality with any acquaintances, new or old. I was too embarrassed to tell seekers that I was seeking too. I recognized my tendency to critique anything spiritual or religious, cut it off once the conversation began, because of a discomfort I could not explain. Part of me felt that spiritual forces belonged on the edge of the universe, far away, where we couldn't see them and therefore didn't need to talk about them. The other part of me wanted to see if it was possible to bring them down to earth in an intelligent way.

I sensed this duality in others who were attending spiritual workshops and lectures. I saw and heard from other angry and confused women. Once, at a lecture on "living spiritually," a woman stood and demanded, "How do you live a spiritual lifestyle when your reality is working for a giant corporation that only cares about money?" She was right. Could only the privileged who didn't need to work explore their inner selves? Others sided with lethargy. They picked up a book here and there, sat in the back of a lecture room, skipped a few sessions of the six-week class on Reiki once they realized the speaker was proselytizing or that the book was too "New Age-y" or detached from reality. I remember smiling once in agreement at a young woman who rolled her eyes at the teacher during a lecture on shamanic journeying. Half the time I felt hopeful, the other half I felt like a foolish fraud. My frustration with this back-and-forth attitude was mirrored everywhere I looked. Clearly, I was not going to find an honest account of a young woman at spiritual peace.

I decided the only way to approach this exploration was to dig beneath the mainstream representation of Body/Mind. I wanted to find authentic spirituality—traditions, philosophies, and practices—that provided sustenance to curious people and that understood women as inherently strong spiritual beings who sought growth and depth. Then I might find other women who had begun to carve out spiritual lives for themselves.

Fortunately for me, I live in the age of the World Wide Web, global markets, and mass telecommunications, so investigating the spiritual beliefs of various cultures was relatively easy. I searched and searched, reading books, renting films, and eventually seeking out practiced masters of the traditions that seemed to call to me in some way. All of the traditions beckoning me had attracted numbers of other women, which indicated to me that a prominent place for women existed in their philosophy and the practice. All encouraged personal exploration. All were loosely structured, and frequently offered guides during the personal growth process if one wanted. Most also fostered a community of people who participated as students, employees, employers, family members, and friends in everyday modern life. This was important to me; I didn't want to fly too far out of the real world just to consult with a seeker who sat atop a grassy hill day after day. Marginalizing myself into some unknown spiritual nook was not my goal. The last thing I needed in my life was a cult. Since I didn't know precisely what I wanted or needed in order to be spiritually conscious, I simply wanted to experience various forms of spiritual strength and meet others who lived with it and grew from it in a normal, everyday way.

The young women who have committed to the six traditions I explored spoke to me openly with complete candor, though many asked me to change their names in order to keep their spiritual identities private. I understood. Spirituality is deeply personal to me, too; I could barely present myself as a person with spiritual interest to their sympathetic ears without feeling naked.

Yet, after I looked into the first tradition, other possible roads I could take to a higher self attracted me. Vulnerability aside, I aggressively sought out as many practices as my heart and mind could handle. I wanted to be thorough, to give myself a fair chance. After all, knowing every option has been par for the course for my generation since we started watching cable. We are a generation of informed channel-flippers, who want to know all the variations on a theme. Dabbling is how we've learned to explore new terrain. Test drives, free samples, the Pepsi Challenge, the shopping mall, the exploratory Level One college courses, the search engine—all of these multiple choices in culture allowed me to confirm my instincts, explore my suspicions, and figure out what I want. Knowing the available spiritual paths and the distance I can go on each one is the equivalent of dating. I wanted to understand the changes that may come into life once I chose a practice, like I learned my boyfriends' sense of humor or taste in music before chosing him as a partner. If a spiritual practice were to enter my life, it would have to be active. I was tired of passivity. The way I looked at it, spirituality was a virtual map of roads and destinations. My soul was the vehicle, but I was a new driver. When considering how best to navigate, I decided hopping a ride with someone else who already found a route lessened the risk of getting lost. How many mystical schools of Sufism are there? What kind of spiritual experience evolves from an African-based belief? The questions flowed.

Speaking practically, exploring six different spiritual paths is not the fastest nor the simplest route to the essence of one's inner being. But taking an assortment of backroads provided me with a variety of experiences, and put me in contact with many women pursuing the same end: individual connection with God. Each woman developed her own standards of spirituality by combining unknown, ancient spiritual systems with her own personal beliefs and modern life. Most impressively, each woman I met was able to move beyond the first and perhaps greatest obstacle—doubt—and approach the endlessly demanding feat of keeping her desire and passion alive and in focus.

I personally found doubt the most debilitating aspect of my search. Learning any spiritual practice is overwhelming in itself, but the constant surges of doubt and disbelief in the existence and function of a higher self is just plain discouraging. During these periods of confusion, a passage I read in one of the 80 million books written by brilliant, realized people who have progressed far in their spiritual education kept me on track: "Spiritual life is easily the most complex aspect of human existence. Politics and art are not rivals, because all great traditions include them as subsets of themselves." I suspect the author was talking about the task of keeping the elusive, capricious reality of spiritual practice visible. I knew from experience that a spiritual focus was easily lost in what I conventionally knew as life.

As it was in the beginning, this is still my problem. At no point did I ever feel that my work was done, that I knew absolutely what I believed and could commit myself to one such path without a struggle. But I came away with support much greater than had been available to me before my search. I am still making the transition.

CHAPTER ONE

Weekend Wicca

Wicca (a word that has many possible origins—one is the Old English root *wic,* meaning "to turn, twist, or shape")—is a religious practice based in part on the remnants of an archaic nature religion of Britain: paganism. The word *pagan* has Latin roots and once meant "country dweller," but now refers to a group of people who follow an Earth-based belief system. Pagans, or neopagans, worship a goddess and a god. A large number of witches are pagans, though not all pagans are witches.

Despite its mysterious image as both satanic and chic, Wicca is a *bona fide* spiritual practice. It is not satanic. Its negative reputation stems from attitudes developed during the Inquisition in medieval Europe, when many thousands of women were tortured for practicing midwifery, herbology, and other pagan healing practices. Wicca today attracts people who feel more comfortable with either a duotheistic or female concept of divinity than with a traditional male God. Many women who embrace Wicca focus solely on the Goddess, while more traditional witches embrace both male and female aspects of divinity. Witches either work alone or gather in covens to perform or create rituals, practice divination (methods of looking into the future), and spell-casting to bring about changes in their own lives. Witches recognize the divine forces of the universe within themselves and within all of creation. They often are extremely private about their practice.

Even before I began this quest, the thought of witches instantly brought Halloween to mind. Oh sure, there was the powerfully ugly villainness in *The Wizard of Oz,* who proved that witches could do very bad things any time of the year. And Samantha and Sabrina, the housewife and teenager with their own TV shows, demonstrated that witches could walk through daily life as domestic partners and high school nerds. But my impression of a witch as a real woman, one who secretly possessed powers to communicate with supernatural forces and invoke the dead, arose from Halloween and its lore. Tradition said Halloween was the day witches came out of their homes, flew on their broomsticks, and cackled in the night. Somewhere along the way I learned that witches could blend with the forces of nature on All Hallow's Eve (*Hallow* means "Holy" or "Saintly" in Old English; the day originally honored the dead). Witches were mysterious, wise, and dangerous. In stories like "Hansel and Gretel" and even *Macbeth,* witches lived alone in the woods awaiting foolish children or predicting the future of human affairs. Although the only witches I ever saw were trick-or-treaters dressed in pointy black hats and wearing too much of their mothers' makeup, I still believed another secret truth that was not fully represented in the spooky folklore that bound witches and Halloween together.

While it remains one of the few "holidays" in our culture that isn't well known for its religious significance, Halloween seemed to the carry the weight of *some* kind of commemoration to me. But then, I had a closer affiliation with Halloween than the average person: October 31 was *supposed* to be my birthday. When I arrived two days later—a foreshadowing of the late sleeper I was to become—my Irish-Catholic grandmother insisted my in-utero self was waiting to be born on November 2, All Souls' Day. All Souls' Day is the Catholic feast day that remembers the un-saintly, the imperfect, the everyday people of the past as they move from this world into the beyond. Grandma's reverence for the day had little to do with my birthday experience of it, which over the years grew to resemble New Year's Eve. I didn't know that the trilogy— Halloween, All Saints' Day, and All Souls' Day—*did* mark a New Year according to the beliefs of Wicca. We didn't learn that in Catholic school. And my grandmother, though she probably knew, kept quiet about it.

To Catholics, All Souls' Day is a solemn feast day. As a young Catholic, I thought this yearly memory of souls was the most decent day on the Catholic calendar and was more inclusive than other holy days. It reached out to more people than the Feast of the Immaculate Conception or even Christmas. All Souls' Day called to all persons beyond Jesus, Mary, or any of the saints, and extended respect to non-Catholics as well. All Souls' Day was a chance to remember *all* dead people and hope for their peace in the afterlife.

In a high school history class, I learned that November 2 is known as the Day of the Dead in Mexico, where it is widely celebrated. People flock to cemeteries with food and wine. They meet their living relatives around the graves of dead ones. Some towns have parades, and people make and sell tiny skeletons, whittled of wood and molded of clay, or baked skull cakes and miniature candied corpses in assorted celebratory poses: smiling, lavishly dressed, playing the guitar. When I asked the nun about this day's origin, she said it was a leftover pagan tradition from before Mexico became Catholic. She spoke with a tone of disgust as the word *pagan* slithered through her teeth. Needless to say, I felt included in her disgust. Without even doing anything, I shared a bond with paganism by birth.

Religion had very little influence on my life once I realized the choice was mine to make. Yet every November 2, strangely, I felt an internal pull toward the calm atmosphere of the cemetery. It was as if All Souls' Day acknowledged a commemoration of— maybe even a belief in—a spirit world I could make my own.

In autumn 1996 I decided to revisit the nun's word of disgust— *pagan*—on my own. A few days before Halloween, I bumbled into a magic shop in the East Village of New York City. Friends who went there to buy gothic-looking candlesticks and other housewares that would look fashionable on a mantle had told me about it. They'd mentioned it was a store and center for "pagans," so of course I walked through the store and checked out the folks inside, thinking I might find myself among my own. When a thin, serious-faced man asked if he could help me, I asked him for the book that would best explain the pagan holiday the Day of the Dead. He immediately pulled what looked like a paperback encyclopedia off the shelf. It was entitled *Drawing Down the Moon: Witches, Druids, Goddess-Worshippers, and Other Religious Pagans in America Today* and proudly displayed an eerie photograph on the cover: a beach at night lit with a circle of red candles and a silhouette of a woman, her hands raised to the sky, dancing in and out of the flames. I bought it.

For the next three days I read through the 580 pages. In the index I looked first for Day of the Dead, then All Souls' Day, but neither was listed. Finally, I settled for Halloween. It said, "One of the greater Sabbats." (What was a Sabbat, I wondered?) "Samhain (Halloween . . .); the Celtic New Year, the day when the walls between the worlds were said to be thinnest and when contact with one's ancestors took place." Ancestors? Lots of information about Halloween speckled the book's pages, but I didn't find any references to Mexico or the Day of the Dead. It didn't matter, though. That Halloween acknowledged "the walls between the worlds"—even celebrated the "other world" and dead ancestors—was enough of a discovery. Proof of an historical link changed my concept of the folklore I'd been carrying around. How much of the Halloween and witchcraft folklore I'd learned was actually fact? I wondered what it would feel like to go to a Wiccan celebration of Samhain instead of a typical Holloween party in the East Village. Curiosity empowered me to pick up the phone and call the magic shop.

"Any special celebrations for Samhain?" I asked, slinging my new vocabulary with confidence.

"You mean *Sow-an?*" came a humored woman's voice on the other end.

"Um, yes," I said, mentally acknowledging her pronunciation.

"Well, the Witches' Ball was last night. Too bad you missed it, it was awesome. Everyone is hung over."

My heart fell. I'd missed it.

"But come down tonight," the voice continued. "There's a Minoan Circle at six o'clock. Bring some kind of food or drink to share. And dress warm." She hung up. I had no idea what *Minoan* meant. Checking my new book, I found no definition. Still, I had an invitation, and I couldn't see turning it down just because of my ignorance.

I stopped at the Farmers' Market at Union Square to find food or drink that I could share with the other Minoans. Most of the vendors had closed down, but the apple carts were still open. I grabbed a bag and paid a lean, gray-haired man wearing a flannel shirt who pranced unself-consciously in a giant, distorted, hand-made mask. He pocketed the dollar and I watched him continue to bounce. This country-dweller's exuberance caused me to wonder what modern-day pagans did to celebrate. It's possible, I thought, that the event I was about to attend might try to make me prance like this vendor. I hurried away, dismissing the thought, wanting to keep an open mind.

I entered the magic shop and the powerful smells of incense greeted me, though I couldn't identify any one scent. This time I looked closely at everything I'd ignored on my first visit. The shop appeared to be one of those "cool" stores, where a whole fashionable scene took place separately from the business. A steady, roving crowd of visitors and salespeople evoked the mood of a private club. Canisters full of herbs stacked on the far wall, a glass display case showing tools and symbols, and bookshelves stocked with esoteric reading held mysterious secrets and invited intimate browsing.

I had fifteen minutes to browse through the wares: male and female body-shaped candles in assorted colors, little sacks labeled "gris-gris bags," mortars and pestles, incense burners, and sticks of dried sage. The canisters on the wall were filled with earth-toned powders and labeled with names like "Mugwort" and "Dragon Powder." In the display case were neatly arranged shiny sterling silver daggers, pentagrams, and chalices. Two entire walls were stocked floor to ceiling with books. The extensive collection had odd spellings of subjects I recognized but now felt mystified by:

Faeries, Magick, Vodou. They had entire sections on Trance, Shamanism, Goddess cultures in Crete and Malta, the Minoans, the Greek Goddesses, the difference between white magic and black magic. From one of these books I learned that the Minoans were members of an ancient culture who worshiped the Goddess on the Greek island of Crete, but I couldn't help but feel slightly daunted at how much I didn't know. Concern for my own well-being ticked like a bomb in my head.

Did I really know what I was getting into? Like girls who hitchhike out of a sense of adventure, would I know harm if it pulled over in a pickup and patted the seat, inviting me to jump in and sit? These were real witches. But what did *real* mean? Witches, the stereotype goes, were mysteriously powerful women connected to dark truths, who could raise the dead and communicate their request for power. They could fly, too, I remembered. What was I looking for anyway—a group to show me how to talk to the dead? Power? How much control I would have over that experience, even if I found it, was unclear.

○ ○ ○

Particularly threatening, as I scanned books with such titles as *The White Goddess* and *The Book of Black Magic and Ceremonial Magic,* was the line between white and black magic. I had no idea where that line lay, or even if there was one. Any kind of black magic I'd ever heard about was safely couched in a movie plot. But looking around the shop now, smelling the powerful incense, I reconsidered evil's existence. Was it possible that people walk around practicing evil in the name of witchcraft? The idea was almost laughable. Did witchcraft like this—organized, urbane, hip, available for purchase—affect anything in the world beside a small, believing community? I was poised to find out, but I started to rethink my being there at all.

Before I had a chance to back out, a stocky man with wild hair and horn-rimmed glasses pointed to my apples and asked if I was there for the Minoan Circle. I nodded, and he returned the nod with a strange air of respect. He walked me to what looked like an infrequently used back door, which led out to a garden. "There you are," he said stopping at the door, motioning with his hand. I walked outside. The sun had gone down and the air had gotten cold.

The garden was small and dingy, with a few stunted New York City trees, some shrubbery, empty flowerbeds, and dirt where grass may have otherwise grown. Still, it was a garden. A high fence, behind which stood blank walls of apartment buildings guaranteeing seclusion, closed it in. Three young women greeted me. I told them my name.

"Are you here for the Minoan Circle?" one of them asked as she pulled down her jeans and casually stepped out of them. Standing in her underwear, she reached behind her to where a charcoal gray robe hung on the fence.

"Uh-huh," I said, trying to hide my surprise.

"Don't mind me," she said, now arranging her necklace to sit straight before pulling the robe over her head. "I'm changing for ritual."

I showed her that I'd brought some apples, and she told me to put them on the altar, pointing to a circle of chairs surrounding a little table. It had other things on it—a funky goblet, a bottle of wine, a tin incense burner, a handful of votive candles, and a blunt, harmless-looking dagger. The display had dignity, legitimizing the power of each object. At the same time, the arrangement of objects was modest compared to any other religious altar I could recall. It was not even remotely sacrificial, though I still feared what was to come.

Next to the altar a shallow pit surrounded by rocks awaited a fire. Circling the altar and firepit were white plastic chairs. The ceremonial set-up—its dependence on the outdoors, the attendees, and the objects they brought—obviously followed a different charter than the one with which I was familiar. Partially I was reminded of little girls setting up a tea party, the honor and care for the event becoming more apparent now than it ever had been when I was five. Still, I felt out of place. "Need help with the fire?" I asked two short-haired, husky women breaking up sticks and crumpling newspaper, laying it carefully into the pit.

"No," said the one with the dark hair.

"Are a lot of people coming?" I asked, figuring she was just shy with new Minoans.

"A decent amount," she answered curtly. We three sat there in silence. Why weren't they talking and why wouldn't they let me help? Maybe they knew I didn't belong. The blonde left to get coffee, leaving just the two of us. I was fidgety.

"Will there be any men coming?" I tried again, speaking louder, leaning forward, hoping she'd address me more directly. The dark-haired woman stopped what she was doing and looked up at me for the first time.

"No men. It's a Minoan Circle. All women," she said.

"Oh," I said.

A trickle of women, long-haired, wide-smiling, brimming with enthusiasm, poked their heads into the garden one by one. An atmosphere of excitement grew with every passing moment, relieving me of my awkward self-consciousness. The fire finally sparked and the fire-builder stood up proudly, wandered to the corner, and picked up a drum. I looked back at the gate. Women were arriving in droves now, laughing and hugging each other. Now that the garden was lit by the blazing fire, I saw that all the women wore ceremonial cloaks of dark purple, charcoal grey, and black, resembling priestly adornment for an occasion of great importance. These were women well versed in witchcraft, ready to take part in a ceremony that could, for all I knew, last all night.

It only hit me then, as the mood in the garden escalated, that what was about to occur was a formal holy day service. Perhaps this was the Celtic New Year celebration itself. What was I doing here? I didn't know. Wishing I'd been better prepared, I stood up abruptly, hoping to make my getaway discreetly. I figured I'd slip out before the drums got any louder, and I told myself that I'd return for a more amateur event. I was too late. Before I could take a single step toward the door, a powerful looking woman in a black robe strode quickly into the garden. The gate door closed behind her. Through the window, one of the shopkeepers waved out to us in the garden, visibly sliding the bolt into the lock. The night was about to begin.

I took my seat next to a beautiful Peruvian woman, and we introduced ourselves. Her name was Sunshine Eagle. We sat quietly together in front of the fire, which was in full blaze and crackling in the autumn air. Sunshine Eagle pulled out a foot-long stick of hand-wrapped sage, lit it, and waved it around in slow, circular motions. Smiling easily, she watched the others in the garden. Her calm presence allayed my nervousness about spending the evening with witches.

A middle-aged woman with curly gray locks had brought sparkling shellac to spray in everyone's hair. She waved it in the air until a few interested parties lined up. The two short-haired women who built the fire rolled their eyes and continued playing the drums they held between their knees. I sat doing nothing.

Walking across the garden, a woman wearing large plastic-framed glasses carried a long, wide wooden box full of straw and dried corn into the corner. She asked others who were chattering and rolling cigarettes to help decorate. "Let's get this place looking festive, for Goddess' sake!" she yelled. Someone started carving jack-o'-lanterns, another started throwing them around, shrieking things like, "Ooooooooohhh, isn't it scary!" An elegant looking blond woman began dancing, gyrating, to the drums beside the fire. Everyone seemed to be doing something but me. I was relieved at their respect for my privacy, and watched silently as this collection of women in robes transformed into a pack of wild girls.

The drums stopped abruptly and the garden simmered down when the High Priestess stood. Her hair was sandy and thin, and it rested on her broad shoulders easily. She was not tall but walked with tremendous confidence. When she spoke, she used normal, everyday sentences. She was probably about thirty, and appeared very comfortable in her role.

"Welcome everyone, to this Minoan Circle. In the tradition of our Greek sisters we'll be honoring the feminine divine—all aspects of the Goddess—in this Samhain ritual." She explained the significance of Samhain. We were celebrating the end of the season, the passing of autumn into winter, the beginning of a new cycle of life, which always begins with death, dormancy, and the long sleep of the earth. Tonight was an evening to connect with the dead and embrace death into our lives. Her description of the earth's life cycle—and the inevitable process of death—made sense to me. I listened. Her presence was a far cry from a priest standing on a pulpit. I was as far as I could get from Sunday Mass, yet I felt equally, if not more, attuned to worship.

It was time to open the circle, she said. Could the four officers step forward to call the four directions? Four women stepped forward grandly, and in turn shouted to the sky words for the north, the south, the east, and the west. Each direction had its own characteristic, I learned upon hearing the sky-bound messages. North called to darkness, south called to warmth, east called to brightness, and west called to the underworld. The characteristics were metaphors; none was good or bad, more or less powerful. According to the rules of the circle, all forces of nature were equal and necessary in their influence on our lives. They were forces that balanced the universe.

Drums began to pound again. A strange sound shook me, and I glanced around the garden. Every woman had begun to chant, loudly.

> Dark mother scream, dark father howl,
> listen to your children at this sacred hour.

Dark mother? Dark father? Were these satanic parents we beckoned? Everyone else seemed comfortable, and there was nothing evil about chanting in general. Yet, in a bad movie this situation— women in cloaks in a garden at night raising their voices to dark mothers and fathers—would signal an approaching presence of malevolence: the opening of a giant black pit out of which poured flames, foul-smelling vapors, and Christopher Walken. Racking my brain for a more settling and realistic explanation, I recalled a portion of *Drawing Down the Moon* that talked about Carl Jung's theory of archetypes. He said that archetypes were sources of energy rooted in the human psyche. He proposed that mythological gods and goddesses of all ancient cultures—Egypt, Africa, Asia—may have been based on these ancient, nameless energy sources. Farfetched? A little, but it was all I had to get me through the moment without passing out from anxiety. Dark mother, dark father. I didn't know how far Jung's theory went, but I ran with it. I thought of these dark parents as energy sources. We were calling to the unconscious, hidden side of ourselves that, once tapped into, would reveal new truths. This was a chant asking those forces within us to sit up and listen.

Not wanting to wear the mark of the uninitiated, I joined in. We chanted loudly, and began to clap. Some women could not stay seated and leapt up to again decorate the garden, hanging gourds, bunches of straw, dried corn, tossing clusters of leaves and small pumpkins to each other while the chanting continued. I remained seated, remembering myself as a kid in church acting with minimal awareness, sitting, standing, and kneeling along with everyone else while tuning out the liturgy. Such detached behavior was not possible here. Energy was moving around, in and out of people, at all times. It was an emotionally and mentally engaging experience. I was tired after about ten minutes.

But that was just the beginning. The priestess stopped the chanting and started it again, with different words. We took hands, and began moving in a figure eight. The priestess had mentioned that the two sides of the eight represented two interconnected circles, one for the living, the other for the dead. We were symbolically walking from one world to the next. Passing the straight-faced hooded woman representing the underworld, who stood immobile holding a candle on the intersecting points of life and death, I feared for my safety and thought of all the dead people I ever knew. They were mostly elderly aunts and uncles and a grandfather, all of whom had lived long, happy lives. Fortunately, I presumed, they had passed on to a peaceful place. Then I remembered an acquaintance who had been accidentally murdered in a drug disagreement. His name was Tom. I pictured him as he was at every party, dressed in a trademark black raincoat that waved like a cape. He had always arrived on a skateboard. I shivered. There was a chance his spirit was unsettled. Though he was a great guy, I couldn't think of a better reason for a dead person to hold a grudge than being murdered at the age of twenty.

I wondered if my thinking about Tom during this ceremony would call him up. If so, would it be a breach of some kind of larger divine law? Would he be angry? What if he just appeared, either as a ghost or as a crackle in the fire or as a spirit that manifests in the body of one of these women? I'd seen that before—in the movies. What would I do if *anything* happened? If nothing happened? I told myself these fears were ridiculous, but didn't fully believe it. I actually felt quite threatened throughout this ritual, though nothing happened besides my brainwork.

The priestess asked us to form a straight line on the outside of the life circle. This was the ritual that would initiate us into the New Year.

"What happens?" I whispered to the skinny, middle-aged woman next to me.

"You give her your new name," she said quickly, not wanting to miss a verse of the song. I looked at her with confusion. She kept singing.

"I don't have a new name," I said a little louder, over the chanting.

"You can use your old one," she said, "as long as you want to bring it with you into the New Year. You'll be anointed as whoever you want."

One by one the women before me took the hand of the high priestess, walked under the veil that hung from the center tree, exchanged words I could not hear, and then moved on to where the west woman stood again, the area of the garden designated as the Underworld. I was growing tired. Things were getting intense, and I didn't know what the hell to say once it was just me and the priestess talking under the tree. What name would I give? I only had one. Confrontation with the priests—the representative of a supreme force was freaking me out. It seemed like a pledge, a commitment to witchcraft. What would I say?

The High Priestess approached me and took my hand, led me under the tree. She said a long, ancient-sounding verse that made me feel like a knowing participant. A phrase that obligated me to be responsible.

"Do you of your own free will choose to be seen as a daughter of the Goddess, and swear to serve her for a year and a day?" she asked me.

"Yes," I said.

She dipped her finger in a small bottle of oil, frankincense I think, and drew a star on my forehead. "State your name," she asked, her finger still on my forehead.

"Suzanne," I said, and smiled.

She looked at me blankly. After a moment she said, "No, I mean your circle name."

"My circle name?"

"The one you pick for yourself, for the New Year," she prompted, holding back a smile.

"Star," I said quickly, remembering the shape she drew on my forehead. She was satisfied, even a little relieved.

"Star," she affirmed, and reanointed my forehead with oil. "Pass under the veil, Star, under the gaze of the Earth Mother, and enter the Underworld."

She let go of my hand and I proceeded to the Underworld with my new name.

After that there was a dramatic shift in focus, as the women individually turned inward. No one was shrieking, clapping, or acting out any more. Individual witchiness was over. The women united with each other and with the garden, and the garden became a womb. Each witch became introverted and meditative, shut her eyes, trusting that the space and the previous ceremony would hold her like an amniotic sac. All at the same time, we entered our own personal trances,

I had little on which to meditate, I found. To be in both a group trance and an individual trance is not a usual experience. There was no reflex that kicked in and helped me remember what to do, like riding a bike or treading water. An analogous experience might be the experience of being at a rock concert or an event like the Lilith Fair. A big stadium show that demands high levels of audience participation, in which the individual surrenders to the intent of the crowd. I felt the intimacy and joy that comes with being part of a group of unrelated people all doing the same thing. No longer did I feel like an outsider, but rather like a spoke of a wheel, a wheel of a machine, a star in the sky, a part of the whole. It felt sacred—the sisterhood, the commonality that we

were all here, creating a bond over the death of all things past. I felt
an amazing connection to these people I did not know.

Though they were still in trance, most of the women had gathered around the central fire, I noticed suddenly, and were staring at
it intently. All was quiet, and my gaze was captured by the blaze as
well. Some women sat in chairs, others sat on the ground. Each
had lit a votive candle, so I lit my own. It was the moment to feel
my connection to the persons in my life who had died.

Desire to feel the live presence of a dead person had brought
me here. I thought of my grandfather first, but hesitated when his
memory became rich and real. I looked around. Every woman in
the garden had become deeply embroiled in her own emotions.
Some bent over and held their heads in their hands. The two fire-
building women weren't next to each other anymore but in their
own worlds. The dark-haired one was bent on one knee toward
the fire, the blonde stared straight into the flames as if she were
watching a movie. I heard a wail and looked back to see the
underwear woman shuddering; a few others had broken their
trances to hold her while she cried. It was cathartic knowing that I
had found a place where, if I wanted to, I could freak out about
death—grieve for those lost, even contact them—and people
around me would know what to do. But I didn't want to. I wasn't
ready. That one moment of my grandfather's memory felt like a
warning. I didn't know what kind of emotion would flood into
the garden if I opened up.

Three hours after we opened the circle, we finally closed it. I
felt like I had traveled across the country to a secret mountain
society for the night. I joined my fellow coveners at the food table.
Eating the home-cooked dishes, I was about to ask someone more
about the year and a day service to the Goddess when a fierce
pounding on the back door to the garden made everyone look up.

"That's it," the woman who had bolted the door shouted in an
exasperated tone. "The cops called. We're scaring people . . . with
the fire, the chanting." She broke into a laugh. "Leave it to New
Yorkers to complain." Everyone mockingly agreed. I wondered for
a moment if we really were scaring people, or if neighbors just
wanted to get to bed on a Monday night. I could not quite believe

that our behavior actually scared anyone. Drums, chants, candles, and fire. It was all so harmless. Then again, I remembered that I had been terrified three hours ago.

Feasting cut short, we cleaned up quickly and quietly and headed out of the garden, out of the group. Everyone split off and walked in various directions down the street, back into their ordinary lives in Manhattan. No one specifically asked me to come back. They just waved good-bye with a slightly more personal nod and said, "See you at Yule."

○ ○ ○

So now I had a witch name and everything. I had been initiated. But into what, I barely knew. I told a couple of friends about the ceremony; one knew something about witchcraft. Responding to my concern about how this first dose of witchcraft would affect my identity (Was Star my middle name? Did I have to report to the Goddess in some way?), she suggested I talk to a friend of hers who was a witch. Perhaps this woman could answer some of my questions, lend insight, plot my experience on the map of a larger movement.

I had discovered that I was not alone in my interest in witchcraft. A 1981 survey taken by Reverend J. Gordon Melton, director of the Institute for the Study of American Religion, counted 40,000 active neopagans in the United States. The survey was based on ownership of *The Golden Dawn,* a classic pagan work. At the time of his research, ownership of this book was thought to be a reliable indicator of membership in a pagan community, but more recent serious exposure to Wicca has evolved. Several major texts on witchcraft have been published and sold many thousands of copies. The World Wide Web has birthed numerous sites on all aspects of paganism. This lifted my idea of the movement from a small group in the isolated garden to one that included hundreds of thousands of people.

I couldn't get the Minoan Circle ceremony out of my head. Did I even like it? It was definitely interesting and more liberating to me than anything I'd experienced of Catholicism. Perhaps this was because witchcraft did not function according to dogma, but through constant change, my pagan encyclopedia explained. Modern witchcraft (*modern* meaning the second half of the twentieth century) includes a variety of practices.

Drawing Down the Moon's author, Margot Adler, defined modern Wicca followers as "those who seek their inspiration in pre-Christian Sources, European folklore, and mythology. They consider themselves priests and priestesses of an ancient shamanistic nature religion that worships a goddess who is related to the ancient Mother Goddess in her three aspects of Maiden, Mother, and Crone." I had vowed to serve the ancient Mother Goddess, but did I really want to do that? Would I ever feel comfortable calling myself a witch? I couldn't quite imagine getting to that point.

○ ○ ○

I met my friend's witch—I'll call her Arianna—at a kitschy Victorian coffee shop tucked between a bakery and a bar on Bleecker Street. My first glimpse of this woman and her exotic appearance—dark Latina eyes, hair, and complexion, a long velvet dress, and a small suede pouch on a leather rope around her neck—conflicted with my garden-variety notion that witches only looked like witches in ceremony. Arianna looked, if not witchy, then so fashionable, savvy, and confident that one might be led to think of her as possessing witchlike power. The suede pouch was the first item I asked her about, and it led us immediately into the subject of witchcraft.

"I carry this little pouch around my neck to keep my crystals inside. I've been doing so for the last few years." She picked the pouch up carefully and pulled it slightly away from her chest to take a look at it, and hold it out for me to admire. I touched the rounds of the rocks under the velvet.

"It reminds me, every day, of the Goddess," she said.

Though I liked her and her presence at first sight, her continual references to "the Goddess" felt flimsy to me. I wanted to grab on to more than just a glossed-over ideal. She told me briefly of a history that spoke of societies in pre-Christian Europe and the island of Crete off Greece. Their worship of a Great Mother and her consort—a Horned God—dated back to shamanic systems of worship around the world. Many thousands of years ago, when people lived off the land exclusively, a Goddess and a God were the forces that people believed controlled many mysteries of life: the seasons, the crops, the cycles of life and death.

Some scholars say that between 400 B.C.E. and 300 C.E., these societies stopped worshiping both Goddess and God and began worshiping one God—a Father and warrior—who conquered the natural world. The Horned God was demoted to a horned Devil, and the Goddess was vilified. When Christianity came to Europe, Christ was named the Son of God, and his mother, Mary, was used to convert people who still worshiped the Goddess.

The conversion took hundreds of years. Up until the fifteenth century in Europe, women practiced midwifery, herbology, and the art of dispensing healing wisdom to their communities. They traveled from village to village, caring for and curing the sick. Eventually, as trust in Christianity spread and trust in the Goddess waned, a rising male medical establishment removed women from their role as primary healers, placing what was once the life-giving power of the Fertility Goddess into the hands of a male God. In the late fifteenth century, a book entitled *Malleus Maleficarum (The Hammer of Witches),* promoted the idea of Goddess-worshipers as evil. Thousands of women and girls were put to death as a result.

"It didn't happen overnight, you know. It took hundreds of years for people to change," Arianna said seriously. "They took the very gift that we as women were given and turned it into an evil thing."

A fierceness overtook her as she spoke of the massacre. She was angry, as any feminist might be when looking at social inequities between men and women. Yet she also maintained a sense of equanimity about her.

"Look at it this way," she said. "If women were in power until the dawn of Western civilization, when the patriarchs came in, then the past few thousand years of patriarchy are just a drop in the bucket. Patriarchy is just a phase. Eventually, we'll come to our senses and return to a society where women are respected."

I asked if, in her matriarchal scheme of things, she could make sense of the Samhain celebration I had attended. Of course, she said. In pagan cultures, which were agrarian, people accorded worship of nature with the seasons. Each season had a corresponding Sabbat celebrated throughout the year. *Samhain,* a Celtic word, marked the end of harvest, the final reaping of the crops, and the beginning of dormancy. Other holidays were named *Oimelc* (February 1) for the end of the dormant season, *Beltane* (May 1) for the fertility season, and *Lughnasadah* (August 1) for the first fruits. There were eight Sabbats a year, but these four were the big ones.

Samhain for modern witches is less about crops and seasons and more about the end of one aspect of life and the beginning of another. Each individual recognizes the cycles of life and death in her own life, and part of being a witch is preparing for a metaphysical rebirth on the evening of a Sabbat. In Samhain ceremonies on October 31, participants often remember, even summon, the dead. Remembering people who have died acknowledges that the two worlds of life and death can coexist. That the dead are not really gone.

Her thoughts and theories spilled out of her mouth effortlessly. Most powerful was her faith in the fact that this was "the way it was." The truth behind history. When I asked her how she learned about Wicca, she smiled a little sadly and said, "Oh, slowly. Very slowly."

○   ○   ○

Arianna was not raised as a witch. "I was raised to think of witches as hook-nosed, evil temptresses. I thought witchcraft was about casting spells, putting hexes on people. Tarot readers, or anyone practicing divination, I was told, were satanic. My whole life I'd been fed these ideas." In the Latino Catholic neighborhood where she grew up, the psychic readers dotting every corner were fixtures whom Arianna saw as "dissenting" from the acceptable worship of God. Yet she was drawn to these women in their shops, their brightly colored clothes, their small tables with crystals and cards, their beckoning hands. She wanted her own sense of spirituality, one that resembled the empowerment of these women to know other peoples', and presumably their own, futures. "Even as a child, a male-identified God felt unnatural to me," she said.

Catholic education started in the first grade for Arianna, and she shuttled through the rest of a Catholic girl's life without much external rebellion. She was married by the age of twenty-five; marriage was her ticket out of the house. "I didn't have any other options. It was either, 'Marry or be talked about; do it God's way, or be damned.'"

Arianna wanted to live life as a modern woman and study art, but the roles of wife and mother that were expected of her limited the freedom she craved. She cooked and cleaned. After a few years, her position in her marriage reminded her of mother's semi-subservience to her father and brother. She knew this similarity was a bad sign: Arianna's mother had taken her own life when Arianna was twenty-seven years old, in part, she believes, because of her mother's obligation to remain a wife in an unhappy marriage. Arianna remembers her mother's desperate attempt to achieve happiness by emulating the Virgin Mary.

"My mother came from Puerto Rico and lived by the old school. She read the Bible every night. She set up an altar, always focusing on Mary." Arianna explains that within Catholicism, Mary's suffering was a source of pride for women. Reaching out to the Virgin Mary was her mother's way of connecting with female power.

"There was a feminist fire in her. I remember one time hearing her argue with my father. They were screaming at each other, and she grabbed him by the balls and said, 'Just because you have this package between your legs, don't think you are a man.' That made me laugh. I often saw my mother's moods swing from sweet and nurturing to violent rage."

Arianna's mother's efforts to identify with a feminine divine did not save her life. But her struggles triggered an opening in Arianna's consciousness. Just before her mother killed herself, Arianna discovered witchcraft, unexpectedly, when she was sitting on the bed with her husband watching a television program that featured nature worshipers. "My husband, he's South American, and is very devoted to the Native American traditions. What I witnessed on the show was what I'd heard him talk about before—a reverence for the Earth. It was really wild. I saw a group of women standing in a circle. The program identified them as a coven of witches, and suddenly, my previous idea of 'witch' went right out the window—that moment. I realized witchcraft was about the Earth. That the Earth is sacred and alive, and that we, as women in particular, are connected to it."

The idea of connection to the Earth, and to other women, shifted Arianna's understanding of God. God was no longer an unforgiving father, but a feminine power of creation. Her mother's devotion to the Virgin Mary also began to make sense. Mary was not just a mother—but the Divine Mother. The Mother (Creator) of God. A new vocabulary, distilled from the television program, entered her mind that night: ritual, the Earth, witches, the universe, prayer, coven, the Goddess. These words all fit together, but she wasn't yet sure how.

After that night, information about Wicca began surfacing, she said, in small but powerful ways. Through more videotapes and lectures, Arianna learned about the discovery of archaeological ruins, like the Palace of Minos on the Greek island of Crete, from Goddess-inspired cultures. Further, that many people—feminists, anthropologists, even historians—had devoted their careers to the study of an ancient, rich, lost history of women's spiritual significance. A revival was underway. She started reading books by a Wiccan author named Starhawk.

"After I read them, something changed. Things I had always questioned silently suddenly were validated. I began to recognize that I have an inner voice. I always knew it carried some kind of knowledge . . . but I just wasn't able intellectually to express it."

Watching her mother's emotional decline, Arianna realized suppressing her inner voice might cost her her own peace of mind. She'd discovered in Wicca the spiritual freedom that was taboo in her family and community. This freedom would save her from the entrapment her mother, with her altars and prayers to the Blessed Mother, was trying desperately to fight.

She thought about telling her mother about Wicca, as a way to guide her into an understanding of herself as *part of* the divine, not *in service to* its male icons. "But she was so immersed in the male-God religion. I knew it was too late for her to understand. My biggest regret is not having been able to impart my newfound knowledge to her. But I still try to. Every Halloween, when witches gather to speak to the dead at Sabbat, I speak to her. In a quiet way, I tell her, 'I've made it. Be proud of me.'"

Arianna's determination to clear her own path, instead of walking the road her family expected, is in alignment with Wiccan philosophy. The late Aleister Crowley, an influential leader of modern paganism, defined magic as "the Science and Art of causing change to occur in conformity with Will." Because of her pain and regret over her mother's death, Arianna's need for change was urgent. Putting aside her will was not an option worth considering. She struggled with guilt about dismissing the tradition that formed her. Her road was not an easy one. Arianna found serving her own needs as a witch without family, community, or religious support lonely and frightening. Fortunately, the rituals of witchcraft provided her with guidance away from guilt and toward comfort with her individual sense of God.

○ ○ ○

"There is such a thing as black magic," was her answer to the first question I asked when we reached her apartment. "I'm sorry to say that it does exist. But usually you can tell right away who is using their power for evil. They try and pull you in, convert you." A line separating whiteness from blackness—meaning regard for human rights from indifference to human rights—was central in every portrayal I'd ever seen of witchcraft. For instance, in the 1996 film *The Craft,* the older, more experienced witch cautions the younger "good" witch with the words, "Magic is neither black nor white: it is both, like nature is both kind and cruel. The only black or white is in the heart of the witch."

According to Arianna, a fine line between good intentions and delusion exists when it comes to magic. The major distinction is self-involvement. When you become so consumed with your own ability that you literally start to think of yourself as godlike, you are in trouble.

"It's a little confusing," Arianna explained. "On one hand, everyone should think of themselves as God, but there is a responsibility that goes along with that. When temptation to change other people's reality steps in, your own ego can really screw you."

According to Wicca, using power of any kind has effects, as much on the user as on the receiver of the spell. Harm done reverberates, and every witch knows it. "Witches have a saying: Whatever you put out into the world comes back to you not once, not twice, but three times. So if you curse or put bad energy out there, it will return to you three times over. It eats you up from the inside. It rots your soul.

"Of course, we are all human. I get angry sometimes and think: If I could just curse that person—just once. But you must quickly get thoughts like that out of your head. Witchcraft should be used to change your own situation, not other peoples'. That's what witches deem empowering about the Craft."

Arianna has always used white magic, she insists. But its power has never brought her the bright, fluffy joys you might expect from the phrase "white magic." No magic exempts the user from the pain of life. Witches still have to go on job hunts, deal with marital problems, and function in society. Gaining control over herself and the reality she wanted to leave behind, though, are benefits white magic has offered Arianna.

Arianna has an altar where she practices divination and meditates with ritual objects at the most important junctures in her life. Perhaps ten feet in length, it covers nearly a third of her apartment, running along the right-hand wall, beginning just a foot from the front door. A dried flower wreath wrapped into a pentagram is the centerpiece, surrounded by figurines of tiny Greek goddesses, snakes, stones, statuettes, incense, and colored sand. The ritual tools—a chalice, a dagger, a seashell, and a wand—spill across the surface like sea creatures on a beach.

She points to the wand when I ask her which she uses the most in her practice. "That's the one I worked on the most, because it represents the energy I need the most: fire energy."

Beneath all of the decoration, I could still see a skeleton of a stick. About a foot long, the wand was sturdy, dried, with a few nicks tunneled by wood worms. On top sat a glued feather, peppered brown and white. Wrapped around the wand, aqua and purple cotton yarns alternated their colors from the stem of the feather, over stones, to the two ends of the stick. It wasn't just a wand, but a talisman. A talisman, I remembered from my reading, binds energy to an object, which in turn represents a desire. Vodou healers, who make charms and amulets intended to gently influence another's actions, wrap the charms with anything from wire to thread to ensure its intent.

The wand is representative of fire, one of two male elements (the four elements—fire, air, water, and earth—are divided between male and female identities). Fire is the energy of courage, commitment, contacting and developing your strength of will. "Changing habits, forming a good sense of who I am, and being able to defend that, is what I need from male fire energy," Arianna explains. She needs such a symbol, she says, because she lacks an aggressive identity to complement her natural female instinct.

To obtain more fire energy (strength of will), Arianna used witchcraft for a few years after her mother died, first on her own and, then, in hope of increasing her skill and strength, with a coven she joined at the very same magic shop I had visited. The shop provided a sign-up service for individual witches who were interested in practicing with others in a coven. After several years, the practice worked: She was empowered to end her marriage. "It was a long time coming," she said of the final separation. Arianna participated in a powerful springtime ritual that focused on "seeds of change." The coveners each held a seed in their hand and concentrated on a few things in their lives they desperately wanted to change. Then they planted the seeds in the ground. Soon after, Arianna mustered the strength to make a move. She served her husband the divorce papers and her freedom was underway. Meditating on an intention with the support of a group helped Arianna's seed blossom into change.

Oddly, Arianna felt out of place in the coven. Practicing with others did not feel natural to her yet. She still felt new to the tradition, whereas others in the coven seemed almost egotistical in their comfort. Since the witches were not women she had chosen to practice with, she left. The next time she joined a coven, it would be among women with which she had more in common than curiosity and a compatible schedule.

○ ○ ○

Arianna's experience gave me more confidence about revisiting the Wicca community. Perhaps actively practicing Wicca could help me practice my own life in a thoughtful, principled, and fulfilling way. The catalogs for spirituality resorts and socioreligious festivals kept pouring in through my mail, replete with descriptions of community-building functions and photos of happy people whose spiritual lives found validation. Anthropologist Edward Moody, author of *Religious Movements in Contemporary Society,* writes that the growth of magical groups is an "attempt by various people to regain a sense of control over their environment and their lives." I had to agree with him. Since I'd been disenfranchised from the work world, gaining some control over my environment and my life was definitely high on my agenda. In fact, at the moment it was the only reason I was working a lousy temp job at all.

Temping divided me. As a homeless person of the workforce, I found in every American workplace a sedate sense of calm. I heard a corporate purr of content among employees. Whether they were bonded by high income, fashionable outfits, or career aspirations, I didn't know. But the workers I saw were bonded. I was envious, hungry, sitting on the edge of the couch of life, staring at the plastic fruit on the coffee table. I prowled around those office relationships that were based on projects, flirtations, and interoffice envelopes. I perfected that "I'm a temp" detachment that made people forget I was there. Yet I desperately wanted my own inner purr—a company I could believe in, a staff meeting that waited for me before it could begin. After months of looking in the wrong places, it seemed as though what I wanted required magic.

Why not, then, partake in a weekend magical festival? Although my every career instinct—flaky shortcuts will get you nowhere; the desire for spiritual inclusion is just displaced career aspirations; focus on your work, and you will be rewarded—clashed fiercely with my spiritual wondering, I felt reconciling the two was critical. I went back to my trusty pagan encyclopedia, *Drawing Down the Moon,* and read a fabulous description of a festival called "The Rites." The book described it as "one of the best annual pagan gatherings anywhere, and definitely the best festival in the Northeast." The part that made me actually register was the sentence, "Issues of building community are primary." Perhaps if I built a spiritual community, my place in the workworld would emerge.

I received material in the mail soon afterward. The festival combined a commune mentality with pagan philosophies, presented in classes, workshops, work-shifts, and social ceremonies relating to various belief systems: Norse mythology, Native American healing systems, Gardnerian principles of the Craft. I was interested in women's witchcraft, but held off on committing to any one program until I got there. After all, I wasn't really a witch. I just lurked among them.

But I did not want to miss the daily group ritual. Since I would only be at the festival for two days, I would attend the Web Weaving Ritual and the Rites themselves.

I was met at the bus station by someone dispatched from the festival—a long-haired but well-groomed guy from Manhattan named Bill, who drove a silver minivan. It was nighttime, and we sped around the dark roads that passed rolling farmland and pine forests to a Boy Scout camp where the festival was taking place. Cruising down a narrow dirt road for about half an hour, we were finally stopped by a fence-post barricade. Our headlights fell on scurrying figures with long flowing hair and colorful clothes. A few dim flashlights circled like mini–Bat Signals, and then a woman came into view.

"My God, it's Katie!" my driver exclaimed.

"Hiiiiiyeeeeeee," the makeup-free woman sang, poking her head into the window. Unable to contain himself, Bill threw his arms around the woman's neck for a squeeze. "How are you?" he shouted in a caring and concerned tone of voice. "It's been such a long time!"

"It has," Katie laughed, wriggling out of his grasp and beaming her flashlight ahead on the road. "Park right up there. But don't go to check in until you visit the welcoming area. You need to be smudged before entering."

We parked and got out of the car. I followed the elated Bill. I put together that this festival was the kind that attracted folks like Bill and Katie from other festivals around the country. I was walking into a real national community. Maybe this would be my life from now on. I could just temp and go to these festivals on week-ends and holidays. Think how enlightened I'd be, how many peo-ple I'd meet, how much I'd grow.

We followed the happy festival guides up a steep dirt hill. At the top we approached the Welcoming Center—a crowd of peo-ple milling around an archway built of tree branches, lit by burn-ing tiki torches. I copied Bill's every move. A man in a black Grim Reaper's cloak "smudged" us—blew sage smoke on us—one after another, from head to toe. When I asked why we needed smudg-ing, the Reaper answered sagely that Real World Baggage had a way of attaching itself to us outside of the festival grounds. He told me I didn't need my baggage or my everyday mentality here. I was in the Magical World now.

It was just what I wanted to hear. The cold air, the trees, and the dirt were what mattered. I inhaled the sage smoke, and felt it sur-round my senses. I remembered the evening in the Minoan Circle and relaxed. There was nothing to be afraid of; I'd experienced this all before. Heading to the registration hall feeling equipped with my head full of sage, I was directed to my cabin and told to "have fun" with the five hundred other pagans at the camp. Five hundred. Through the dark I walked to my cabin to meet my bunkmates.

Women were everywhere, setting up their belongings on portable vanities and hanging dry cleaning bags full of garments. One top bunk remained empty, but there was very little room left on which to place my things.

"You can put your things over here, I have some room," some-one said. I looked on the top bunk next to me and saw a smiling dark-haired woman, wearing round, plastic-rimmed glasses. She was pointing to the shelf space that she was using herself, conserv-atively. All of her toiletries were consolidated in about two inches of space, leaving several feet for my clothing. "I'm Judy," she said. I put my stuff down and paused for a moment before walking out-side. I considered inviting her to join me. We didn't know each other, and after all, this was the kind of place where you were sup-posed to meet new people, wasn't it? Isn't that why I was really there? To make friends with people who wanted the same sense of consciousness as I? The thought of my participation in a social scene for just that purpose, though, suddenly seemed artificial and far off the mark. My mind froze and my body went on automatic. I smiled at Judy and walked out the door, leaving her sitting on her bed.

Acoustic guitar and what I decided was music from a lute echoed from a cabin down the hill. I trailed a pair of men dressed in cloaks and moccasin boots into the cabin, because they looked young and handsome and, I don't know, witchy. Inside was a coffee bar full of healthy, earthy people in their forties, the event's general age bracket. The cabin air smelled like hot apple cider and cinnamon. People were sitting in chairs and on the floor in a semicircle around a guitar player who strummed and sang. Some sang along. I bought myself a cup of cider and listened to the performer sing a randy old English folk song about a man, his wife, and their sex life. The performer carried a mysterious attitude and wore a cloak and a shark's tooth earring, his jet black hair and dark thick eyebrows permanently furrowed. People in the audience seemed to know him, called out his name in their laughter and comments, and when it was over they clapped for him and he humbly nodded, as if he'd done it all for many years and so had they.

I sipped my cider and listened as people talked. People were having a good time, but did not act particularly pagan, as far as I could see. I started thinking I had just paid 200 bucks to hang out at a large country party where I knew no one, and I felt swindled by my own expectations.

I walked back to my cabin thinking about the fact that I could not really be a passive observer at a place like spirituality camp. Writing it off before giving it a chance defeated my original intent. If I didn't take part, I couldn't possibly feel the effects. I felt uncomfortable "letting go" among these strangers with whom I shared neither age nor experience, but once in my cabin, I planned to attend the Web Weaving Ritual the next afternoon at 2 P.M. in an effort to get my money's worth.

The next morning a woman blew a whistle from the grassy area below the picnic-tabled terrace. "All newcomers gather here for an orientation, if you like!" On the woman's head was a green fast-food services hat with no icon, and pinned to her white sweater was a round green button that said "THE RITES." Finally, I thought. I'm being pulled into the community. We gathered around her.

It was her concern, she said, as it was of all organizers of the Rites, that newcomers know how to take care of themselves here. This place, purposely created for people to explore magic and how it interacts with their lives, overwhelmed the average energetic system. "Please drink extra amounts of water," she warned with the straightest of faces. "The energy this week is going to be very high, as it tends to be in a spiritual community. We want everyone to have fun and to learn, but it's possible that some of you may become overwhelmed. If you do get overwhelmed," she said, "there is a simple solution. Find a tree, in a place where there aren't too many other people around, and give it a hug. Just wrap your arms around that tree and hug it, tell it you want to be grounded, and you'll see . . . the tree will come through for you."

A few people laughed, then stopped when they realized it wasn't a joke.

"If that does not help, and you still feel like you're freaking out, go to the Healer's Hall. It's quiet there, and people will be on duty who will be able to assist you. Other than that, you can always come to see one of us," she motioned to herself. "There will be a few dozen of us around, wearing green hats and white buttons like these. Our job is to bring you down if you're too high, so to speak. Just come on up to us and touch us on the hand, and we'll help you." She gave the crowd of newcomers an earnest glance, making sure we all understood that she meant it.

○ ○ ○

Two o'clock came around quickly. In a giant field stood a twenty-foot pole. From it flowed streamers in pink, orange, purple, blue, red, and gold, all the way down to the ground. Drummers and percussionists appeared in an organized group at the margins of the field, and after a "thump" signaled by the leader, they began to march around the periphery. Some women I'd noticed earlier, dressed in tattered, colorful dancewear, took each other's hands and followed the drummers. Other people latched on, grabbing hands quickly and connecting streams of people. People came running from across the camp. They ran from the picnic tables where we ate our communal meals. They ran up the hill from the Merchant circle, where soap makers, woodcarvers, T-shirt makers, and basket weavers all sold their wares. Someone grabbed my hand, I grabbed Judy's, and we were swept in as if part of a giant wave. The drums beat faster as we ran, following the rest of the line across the dirt paths and onto the field, making an arc and then a continuous circle. Among those who preceded me were couples, families, men, women, and children, middle-aged, adolescent, and elderly people. We were holding hands running in a circle. Waves of giddiness rose in me as our circle leapt around the giant pole. It was ridiculous: five hundred of us paid money and gave up a weekend to play Ring Around the Rosie. Yet the positive bond from the very effort we made rushed through our clasped hands. It felt strong, as if we might accomplish anything together.

The drummers broke off and formed an inner circle. Directing them with head nods was the man with the shark's tooth earring I'd seen perform the night before. He raised his hand and the drumming stopped. The movement of the circle abruptly ceased, and the break in the momentum made us crash into one another. When we settled down, we were instructed to pick up a streamer or two. "These streamers are our tools with which to create community," Shark's Tooth shouted. "As we weave them we will create a net that will bind us together, at this moment, on this day, for the future." Smiles overtook each face as we looked at one another, and a hopeful sensation rippled around the giant circle. Our size, our presence, our being there together sunk in. The drums pounded again and people passed the streamers to the right, above, then below, then above. A multicolored macramé formed, large and beautiful, resembling a giant teepee under which we could sit, intimately connected to this web spun out of desire for spiritual understanding. When the streamers were woven to their very end, the shark's tooth man motioned for us to sit, still holding the ends, bringing the lovely Technicolor canopy to the ground.

"This is our energy," he announced. "This is our community fabric." Faces around the circle looked at once impressed and bemused. As if all of the dressing up and shouting and dancing and clapping were not for a higher purpose until right now, this moment, when suddenly the objectives of the festival and its organizers and the amount of work they put into it became clear. The feeling of creating the web took me by surprise. It was almost fearsome that such simplicity could yield something meaningful—if we all agreed that it was meaningful.

○ ○ ○

Thinking about the experience later, I realized that key to that afternoon's community feeling was synergy. Physically acting out an idea brought about its reality. The web we wove really did form a bond among us. It wasn't an intellectual bond or a personal "validation of faith," necessarily; the experience erased those categories—at least for a moment. I imagined a new, almost physical space had formed within me, widened, since the Minoan Circle had first cracked it open. I wanted to keep it open, foster its existence with another idea or experience before it closed again. But witchcraft didn't seem like the proper system.

The witchcraft I had anticipated—the muttering of spells, the standing on the points of a pentagram—I never found on this trip. Yet I experienced its essence more than I would have if I had followed a book's instructions on how to "invoke the spirit" or "draw down the moon." Those words held a promise, appealed to my sense of identity. I believed that I could perform those rituals, either alone or in a coven or at a festival, if I chose to make witchcraft a part of my life. But the pagan festival, though joyous, did not feel like home.

Something I remember Arianna saying stuck in my mind: "I'm not here to say, 'This is what you should do.' But what I am here to say is, 'A lot of what we're caught up in is crap. And we've got to look within to get out of it.'"

Hers were wise words. Wicca was the first spiritual system that had inspired me to look within myself in a long time. The results did not lead me to commit to a life as a practicing witch. But they did relieve me of that sense of vertigo—confusion and unresolved anger—I had felt whenever I thought about God. Realizing that spirituality does not have to be either dogmatic or nonexistent was empowering. Once I looked beyond the confines of my religious past, I saw a number of paths down which I could walk. I wanted to walk down every one.

CHAPTER TWO

The
Shamans
of Suburbia

A *shaman* was a figure in hunter-gatherer societies found all over the world, tracing back 30,000 years. At the time when human survival was thought to be in the hands of gods, the human soul was the means by which health could be maintained. Shamans were the principal escorts of the human soul. Shamans used trance to enter altered states of consciousness in order to communicate with the gods, access the human soul, and heal patients.

The word *shaman* descends from the Tungus tribe in Siberia, one of the earliest known shamanic cultures. To me, the word evokes a picture of an Indian man dressed in feathers and skins, holding a drum, standing in a desert or a jungle where only the land holds more knowledge than he does. Shamanism, found in indigenous cultures all over the world, is arguably the world's oldest system of healing. It has coexisted with religion in many cultures; the shaman, a person of either gender, may have had other authoritative roles in society but was ultimately known as the chaperone for the soul.

Skilled in negotiating between human beings and spirits, the shaman maintained a three-way connection among individuals, the community, and the dead. Some semblance of the practice has survived, though most shamanic cultures have undergone profound political and religious transitions. Today shamanism exists in America as a healing method that cares for the psyche, the spirit, and the soul. A resurgence of this healing practice has taken place in the United States since the 1960s. Independent shamanic practitioners take on clients much like psychotherapists do, and work with them by accessing other states of consciousness as a means to retrieve information about the their physical, psychological, and spiritual health. This modern healing process is many thousands of years removed from its origins.

I came to be acquainted with the essence of shamanic healing, and began to realize that shamanic healing would address my unexpressed need to feel cared for.

Since my brief exploration of Wicca, I felt less desperate and alone. Months after the Minoan Circle and the pagan festival, the consciousness-altering sensations from the rituals remained within my body, spontaneously recurring like an adrenaline rush brought on by the desire to share the stories with others. The sensations reminded me that extraordinary experiences could happen when people were moved to create them out of hope, passion, and instinct. But I didn't share the stories often. I knew they were uncommon and precious, hard to find in the everyday world. They also didn't fully engage me, infuse me with the juice of commitment. But a dull aching to feel connected to others, beyond idle office chatter, beyond both platonic and romantic friendships, continued to pulse through me like the need for a second cup of coffee. The discrepancy between real-world experience and extraordinary experience was too wide. I craved constant access, as though I were already addicted.

Nothing I'd ever read articulated the addictive feeling, or the subjective intimacy of the feeling, except Carlos Castenada's writing in *The Teachings of Don Juan: The Yaqui Way of Knowledge*. "The states of nonordinary reality don Juan produced in me through the use of hallucinogenic plants," he explains, "helped me arrive at a coherent view of the phenomena I had experienced." The phenomena he had experienced after drinking a plant concoction known to Mexican shamans as *Datura* enabled him to travel to states of mind that seemed related to the light states of trance I had experienced in the Minoan Circle. Out of the real world, almost out of body. And his disappointing reentry into ordinary consciousness paralleled my own feeling of displacement. "The passage from my normal state had taken place almost without my realizing it: I was aware; my thoughts and feelings were a corollary of that awareness; and the passing was smooth and clear. But this second change, the awakening to serious, sober consciousness, was genuinely shocking. I had forgotten I was a man! The sadness of such an irreconcilable situation was so intense that I wept."

Castenada's journeys were infinitely more colorful, frightening, and informative than any trip I had yet taken to higher consciousness. I suspected, however, that all trance was related on some level. At the very least, the Wicca circles primed me for a more intense journey into, as he says, "nonordinary reality."

I should 'fess up. Wicca circles weren't my first introductions to other states of mind. Various drugs I'd used in the past had taken me to some of these states. The visions I had using drugs resembled some of Castenada's descriptions of his altered states. Though I had neither been guided by a shaman like don Juan, nor been half-starved in the desert, I knew that my and Castenada's experiences were related even if worlds apart. I had been left with a jumble of bizarre, psychedelic memories with no correlating context, and no true wisdom. For example, after eating some mushrooms in college, I'd been compelled to taste every rock I could find along the lake where I was staying. I spent several minutes shoving quartz and granite and slate into my mouth until my cheeks bulged. The rocks felt cool in my mouth. I'm eating ancient earth, I'd thought then. That was as profound as the experience got. Without a guide, or any spiritual mission, recreational drug use was an aimless adventure once the novelty wore off. I spit out the rocks. Rock-eating disappointed me, so much so that I continued experimenting with drugs in attempt to find meaning. Those were blurry days.

The flakiness that accompanied pot smoking and the unpredictability of stronger substances eventually got to me. Without anyone to interpret my visions in light of ancient wisdom, I remained at a base level of consciousness. I determined that drug use was too chaotic a road to take to a higher state of mind. The visions seemed pregnant with potential, I thought, if only they could be more organized. A more organized experience, I was certain, would bring me inward to "nonordinary reality." The question was, How to organize?

In revisiting my desire to connect, travel inward, find support, and discover, I realized that don Juan was the key to Castenada's structured discovery. Anthropology and ancient teachings guided him. What could I use to bring myself inward safely and securely? I certainly would not book a trip to Mexico in search of a shaman; it was out of the context of my NYC life, beyond my budget, and too much of a flying emotional leap toward a system that might not pan out the way I hoped. As far as I knew, real shamans didn't even exist anymore. They'd disappeared with the bald eagles and clean water. But my longing grew stronger. As I kept up the grind of my temp jobs, commuting, and life with my boyfriend in our cramped downtown apartment, I dreamed of the desert heat, the earth underfoot, endless space. I wanted an enlarged view, proof that life's events weren't completely random, that my financial responsibilities weren't just keeping me running on a wheel, that my emotional commitments weren't just existing in a vacuum. I wanted to see an organized backdrop behind the face of the modern world, to understand a larger cosmos of living things in which my individual life and all my choices made sense.

When my boyfriend's mom told me about her own intention to visit a shaman, the desert landscape filled my imagination. I pictured myself standing in another world, gazing up at a sky sparkling with images of jaguar heads and Mexican temples of the sun and moon. Was she going to see a *real* shaman? I asked. She was not likely to involve herself with charlatans. "Well," she said hesitantly. "Yes, of sorts." She explained that an amalgamation of the shamanic methods of ancient South America, Southeast Asia, and the Arctic cultures were now flowing through non-Native America. They were being used as healing techniques, like acupuncture or massage therapy or hypnotism—only they were spiritual healing techniques, according to the shamanic vision of the world.

The shaman she would visit was not the elderly Indian man I imagined from movies like *Altered States,* living peacefully in the Mexican highlands, collecting peyote buttons for ritual use. She was an American woman who had studied Amazonian traditions of shamanism when she lived in Brazil. When she returned to the states, she officially became a Peruvian shaman's apprentice and had been practicing for fifteen years. She sounded pretty hardcore to me. From my perspective, one selling point was that she'd used *ayahuasca,* the plant hallucinogen known to shamans in Peru as the sacred Amazon "death vine," but she did not use drugs in her own healing techniques. I admired the fact that she'd taken traditional routes to transcendence, yet decided against a psychedelic healing process.

She ran her practice out of a yoga center in Montclair, New Jersey. At this time I was skeptical of any "new" therapy, especially alternative ones—like Reiki or laying on of hands, systems with processes one could not see—that purported to "heal" the most troubling ailments. But something about this shaman—perhaps that she had the unabashed audacity to call herself a shaman in these skeptical times—disarmed my suspicion enough so that I made an appointment with her. The possibility that this doorway could lead to the world I was trying to find was too tempting to pass up in the name of "better judgment."

Shamanism's resurgence was spurred in part by an anthropologist named Michael Harner, author of *The Way of the Shaman,* who traveled to Peru in 1956 and stayed for four years to study the Jivaro and Conibo peoples. Upon his return to the United States, he studied with shamans from Indian nations in California, Washington state, and South Dakota, inspired by the ancient wisdom they held in common with the Peruvian Indians. In 1969, he returned to Peru to learn the ways of the shaman from the inside, instead of as an anthropologist.

I didn't know if this New Jersey shaman had anything to do with Harner, but I suspected she possessed a unique personal passion—she would have to in order to learn a 30,000-year-old healing system that was not part of her own cultural tradition. Still, I had a few problems. The first was my doubt that any American person not born Native American or raised in a shamanic community could truly understand this delicate work, let alone perform it with any authenticity. The second was whether these healing techniques would transcend the gap between cultures. Could ancient Brazilian secrets be properly appropriated in modern America? Were our needs really the same as those who lived in hunter-gatherer societies in Peru and depended on the earth for sustenance? That the shaman had undergone an intense ancient teaching and initiation surely was no simple task; part of myself insisted that I trust this woman's judgment: the service wouldn't exist if there weren't a need. Perhaps she had taken the shamanic knowledge and adapted it to the needs of people in suburbia for a good reason.

But there was still a third problem: I literally had nothing for her to heal. No chronic physical pains or obvious psychological problems ailed me. Sure, I was a twenty-six-year-old unemployed woman lost in the modern world. Sure, I thirsted for a spiritual direction that didn't fence me in. But would a shaman's talents extend to curing spiritual displacement like penicillin killed antibodies, or like acupuncture cured inner ear infections? Would I know her authenticity without a concrete problem against which to measure it? Should I just expect that after the experience my barren spiritual landscape would become wildly populated? I didn't believe it possible.

As it turned out, pain found me on the very day I was to visit with the shaman. My dog, old and loveable, had been put to sleep that morning, and my sweet Irish grandmother, recently diagnosed with an advanced stage of cancer, had her leg amputated that afternoon. Waves of misery kept me running to the ladies' room in tears, and a giant golf ball of pain amassed in my temples and forehead. I was sure its round ridge was visible in the mirror. This manifestation of grief was tender to the touch, shooting explosive volts of pain through my entire head and neck, as if an alien was thriving on the back of my eye.

I kept my plan to visit the shaman that night. The shamanic center was offering an orientation for newcomers that evening. This was a perfect opportunity for me to dip my toe in without getting too wet. And now I had something very real to heal, although, in all honesty, I was certain nothing could melt away the protrusion behind my eyes but a few days of crying. The wave of sadness throughout the day kept me on the brink of nausea, and I could think of nothing but my dying grandmother and dead dog, the work community I lacked, and the black hole of emptiness I could not seem to shake. Things had gotten desperate: I was going to see a shaman, for God's sake.

The woman who drove my boyfriend's mom and me to the Starseed Healing Center was named Pam. She'd been seeing this shaman for two years and, I noticed, was quite comfortable chatting about subjects relating to healing, spiritual vision, and of course, her results with shamanic techniques. Pam originally discovered the shaman for her teenaged daughter, who suffered from what sounded like the bubonic plague of migraine headaches. Migraines are one of those unsolved mysteries of the medical establishment. In ways that no other professional could, this shaman worked wonders for Pam's daughter. Seeing the results, Pam brought to the shaman her own issues—mostly psychological in nature—that she thought could benefit from shamanic healing. She insisted it was working.

Through the throbbing pain in my own head, I listened skeptically from the backseat. Two years of weekly treatment using "shamanic techniques" coupled with visits to a homeopath was her daughter's healing regimen. But which results derived from which treatments?, I wondered. What *were* the shamanic treatments? Pam hadn't exactly said. Her descriptions were obscure, always ending with mystical phrases like, "because the universe wanted me to understand it that way." I silently fought the encroaching feeling of dread that this evening was headed toward group therapy, and the suburban newcomers would be doing a lot of talking instead of experiencing authentic shamanism, which was the only reason I had forced myself to go. Pam mentioned something about a "shamanic journey" during which the shaman was able to see your illness. But the shaman would never tell you what it was. You'd have to figure it out for yourself. That was the work. "You really have to look your problems right in the face," Pam said. "It gets much worse before it gets better." But the proof was in the pudding, she claimed. Her daughter Gina was in college now, headache-free.

Inside Starseed we removed our shoes and filed into a small room, the three of us and about a dozen other women from surrounding suburban towns. The shaman's name sounded very shaman-like to me: Jyoti Chrystal. Her first name, Jyoti, had been given to her by her guru (she'd been a student of yoga before becoming a shaman's apprentice). Rather than question this dual identity, I decided that since I had already made the trip I should accept what she had to offer without too much skepticism. Questioning wouldn't do me any good now.

She and her husband, Jason, entered the room and sat with us in a circle to explain their six-week course on shamanic journeying, the essence of shamanism, and their plan for the evening.

Jyoti began, "In shamanic cultures, all people and living things have direct connection with the universe. Relationships between peoples are no different from relationships between trees and birds, or rocks and ants, or ocean and sky. Using this connection, this understanding of the intimate connections throughout the universe, shamanic peoples were able to heal their ills."

Jason followed by saying that by learning elements of this understanding during the next six weeks, we'd learn the rudiments of various healing techniques. In particular we would be contacting our power animals. Each individual, he told us, had a power source that appears in the form of an animal. Sometimes people had more than one. He also told us that we would also learn to take two kinds of shamanic journeys.

The shamanic philosophy of an all-inclusive universe sounded plausible to me, even though I was not accustomed to thinking myself spiritually connected to and on the same par as a stone or a puddle of water. But once I agreed to try, the adjustment in thinking came naturally. The more outrageous idea was that I or any mildly curious suburbanite could share and participate in real shamanic healing. Weren't these methods the sacred, exclusive knowledge of indigenous masters? I wanted to think so. Were they meant for the average American to dabble in? Part of me wanted the answer to be no, but then that line of thinking kept shamanic healing sequestered and out of my reality, which would do me no good. Proprietary secrecy so far did not seem a part of the shamanic philosophy. If it was, then Jyoti herself—a worthy recipient of knowledge, but a wealthy, bored housewife during the first years she spent in Brazil—would not have received permission to learn and train. But she had. If anyone could bring the teaching to an average American audience, I decided, she could.

Our group moved into a spacious plant-filled room with high ceilings. We sat on the floor in a circle. Jyoti pulled various instruments off a shelf and handed them to Jason. I examined her as she and Jason sorted through their tools. Her frame was petite and her face serious. She kept her hair shoulder-length and well groomed. Her clothing was loose and woven of natural looking fibers, and she wore a long necklace with a single stone pendant. I liked that she didn't smile during the presentation. It made me pay attention when she spoke.

"People in shamanic communities have methods by which they call on their connection to the universe," she said, stepping into the center of the circle. "The drum is humankind's interpretation of the heartbeat." In her hand she raised a large pan drum for us to see. In her other hand she held a mallet and a rattle. "The rattle is humankind's interpretation of rain." She economized her words, shunning long explanations. When she asked us to close our eyes, I felt relieved. Allowing a healer to guide you feels nice. Breathing deeply and slowly as she instructed, I almost choked on the pain behind my eye. Images of my dog, old and confused, and my grandmother awaiting death flashed behind my eyelids. Then I heard a sound that resembled beans shaking in a jar. Rhythmic patterns repeated, shifting my focus away from the pain and pictures inside my head to the clear, unbothered sound. It came from everywhere and nowhere at the same time. Soon it succeeded in regulating my breathing.

"The rattle is humankind's interpretation of rain," she repeated. "Water is the Earth's cleanser, and we are vessels of the Earth." I imagined myself as a vessel, a container of skin, but did not know what else I held. "The energy we take from the ground enters through our feet. The air we take from the sky enters through our head. We are the conduits between earth and sky. Let the sound of the rain wash through you and be healed."

This was all moving very fast, and if I hadn't been in pain, I would have been extremely skeptical. But because I was debilitated, my capability to question was nil. I could barely remember her brief overview when Jyoti mentioned the process of entering into shamanic trance known as *journeying*. Journeying used presuggested mental images to help you travel deeper into consciousness. Shamans journeyed deep into consciousness to heal clients, and clients could journey if a shaman guided them. Drums and rattles facilitated that process. But she hadn't mentioned she'd be taking us on a journey. Images of water and rain were all she gave us to work with, besides the sound of the rattle. As the sounds and the thoughts of rain swam around behind my eyes, I became slightly aware of Jyoti and her husband moving around the room. The sound of the rattles gained momentum like a freight train, and my sense of the room distorted as the sounds swept in, swept out. Close by, then far away. A tremor of panic gripped me, until even that lost focus, and dissolved. The bits of sound united like raindrops, as if composing a storm, which started to take visual shape behind my eyes.

I slipped into trance within minutes. Rain, she had said. Rain is a cleanser. Rain on the windshield of a car in which I slept in the back seat came in to view, as did rain on the surface of a lake, rain streaming through a thick forest and a panoramic view of a storm over an ocean. Each image lasted longer than the previous one. As though the images were projecting from a camera, a sense of a landscape developed—a whole planet that consisted of bodies of water and thick green jungle. I breathed deeply and felt the throb behind my eye pulse. It felt like a separate eye, a diseased one that did not belong, like the illness that had struck my grandmother. An odd connection between the picture of the disease behind my eye and the picture of the landscape took place: they were coexisting in the same place, like two possible realities. My insides were the landscape, and vice versa. I felt the urge to choose one or the other in which to live out the rest of this time. The landscape won.

I focused on the more pleasant sensations of the landscape: the taste of wet, thick, fresh fog. An enormous jungle on the edge of the ocean suddenly appeared in detail in front of me, as if I was flying through the air. Moisture had turned the sky heavy and gray, but one area of clouds was particularly dark. Upon closer look, I saw it was no cluster of clouds at all, but a creature, not exactly alive, but writhing with life. It was ugly: a kinetic fuzz, an electric toxic mass that had somehow grown out of the atmosphere. I could feel the confused energy it exuded, as well as its density, but noticed it slightly diluting from the downpour. Rain weakened the thing. I knew that if enough rain poured on it, the mass would melt and the landscape would thrive again. This became my mission.

The whole time this scene evolved, I was aware of a split in my consciousness. Half of me was participating in the experience, the other half observing my involvement. It was like watching myself in a dream, only I had more control. The rain pounded on the landscape, into the fuzzy mass. The fuzzy mass magnified, and I saw its squirming blackness up close. The edges broke loose and dripped. Saturated, huge droplets fell one by one into the ocean, disappearing. The storm completely overtook the landscape now, eliminating any chance of impure dirt or debris. I found myself telling the black mass that it didn't have to work so hard to exist anymore, that the landscape would be better off without it. I heard no reply, but within minutes it was gone and the rain had reduced to drizzle.

The rattles quieted to mild stirring, forcing the landscape to fade from my view and shifting the room back into focus. By the time I had fully reentered a normal state of consciousness, the rattles had stopped. When I opened my eyes I noticed immediately that the throb behind my eyes was gone. In the center of the room stood Jyoti and Jason, motionless, rattles in their hands, with a look of completion, as if they'd just finished performing a dance and were now regaining composure. I checked my temple with my hand and felt no tenderness. It had melted with the fuzzy mass. But when I thought about how that was possible, I had trouble finding a reasonable answer.

○ ○ ○

Shortly afterward, I picked up a few books on shamanism; one was Harner's book, *The Way of the Shaman*. In it, he spoke very clearly of two states of consciousness: the ordinary state we know, and the shamanic state I had experienced. In fact, in shamanic philosophy, there are several states of consciousness, each one as legitimate as the other, and often not requiring distinction from each other. If I had lived in a shamanic community, as Harner explained, I might have incorporated the melting of the fuzzy mass into my ordinary consciousness. Perception of two realities is typical of shamanism, he says, and a master shaman is fully aware of the appropriate consciousness for each situation with which he is faced; the master enters into that state of consciousness as needed.

The other book, by Mircea Eliade, a comparative religion scholar, was entitled *Shamanism: Archaic Techniques of Ecstasy.* Across the world, he noted, the function of the shaman is to keep connection with the souls of all creatures, whether human beings, sacrificial animals, streams, bugs, or plants. The shaman, he says, "knows the road of the mystical itinerary and in addition has the ability to control and escort a soul."

Jyoti certainly guided me somewhere, although I had generated the specific landscape and the goings on. Her healing system guided us to individual thresholds: she knew we'd enter a certain "place" using the element of water as a cleanser. Once in that state, we could explore our own sensations. If the skill and talent of a shaman was her ability to bring clients into a state of mind—an inward location—where they could at least contact or identify the source of their trouble, Jyoti had succeeded. Touching a distinct, raw place on my personal spiritual landscape felt to me like traveling to a different planet. Yet I was unclear whether or not it actually happened.

Pam mentioned that if I wanted to, I could speak with her daughter Gina about Jyoti's treatment. I agreed, eager for a point of view from a young woman who had gone the shamanic route. Besides wanting to confirm my own experience, I had many questions about the whole shamanic cosmology and how to relate to it in waking life. The rain, the landscape, for instance. Had she journeyed and seen the lush ocean scenes? Had her journeys led her to spiritual awareness? Did she grow? If any answers to these questions were yes, then perhaps the shamanic world could answer my questions too.

○ ○ ○

When Gina was home on winter break, she invited me to hang out in the basement den of her mother's house in New Jersey. Furnished in pillow couches, soft beige shag rugs, and warm light, the den provided a comfortable space in which to discuss in depth a sensitive subject like shamanic experience. Dressed in a floppy sweater and flowing skirt that complemented the comfort of the room, Gina smiled heartily from her slouched position on the couch and began to talk vaguely about her sessions with Jyoti. She admitted she lacked precise understanding of the exact methods. Most important to Gina was the cure shamanism provided—it had eradicated her chronic migraines. In terms of spiritual meaning, Gina felt her life had changed completely, but did not understand exactly how.

Gina was twenty-two now. She had visited Jyoti as a last resort. She'd been plagued with migraine headaches since age fifteen, and they had all but destroyed her teenage years. "I couldn't really function because it literally hurt my head when I moved. My vision would get blurry. I'd get front temporal pain, get nauseous, and have to go home and just lie around."

She missed ninety days of school her senior year. The rest of the days she was late. Her sophomore and junior years yielded similar patterns of attendance. When the migraines had first appeared during her sophomore year, neither Gina nor Pam expected them to last.

Pam brought Gina to numerous doctors. They attended the Atkins Center, thinking perhaps that the migraines were diet-related. But despite the rigors of an all-protein diet, on which she lost ten pounds in four days, Gina still felt the pounding in her temples. Next Pam feared the condition was brain-related, so they visited every prestigious neurologist in the tri-state area. After eye exams, CT scans, and tumor tests, neurologists still could not connect the problem with a specific cause. Across the board, they recommended painkillers and therapy, assessing her condition as psychological in origin.

Gina and her mother continued to search for a solution. Alternatives such as acupuncture, reflexology, and massage were next. Although Gina was skeptical of their effects, she tried all three alternately three times a week for the relaxation they provided. Several months went by. The headaches remained. Gina continued to miss more school for another year. "I couldn't get out of having headaches because I couldn't think. And I couldn't think because I was so pissed that I had missed most of my life at that point."

Finally, when she turned seventeen, a doctor jokingly suggested Gina try a shaman. Annoyed, Gina ignored the suggestion. To soothe her depression, perhaps the worst of the headaches' companions, Pam took her shopping. "I had on a T-shirt that said 'bookwoman,'" Gina remembers. "This saleslady stopped me because she loved my shirt and wanted to find out where I got it. I was annoyed, and I wasn't really responding but my mom started talking to this woman about my migraines." Gina stops to roll her eyes. "She would do that, talk to everybody and anybody because she figured everyone knew someone with migraines. Anyway, like an hour later, this woman mentioned that she was studying with a shaman, and my mom insisted I go. I went a week later."

There was no way Gina would have been so agreeable had she not been desperate. "It was just time," she explained. "There was nothing left for me to do."

○ ○ ○

Gina's first visit to the shaman was with her mother Pam. They withheld questions when Jyoti laid them down and took them on their first journey together. They assumed it was part of the therapy. "She asked us to close our eyes and relax. She was trying to read us, I guess. Trying to see where we were, what our relationship was like." Gina went a few times with her mother before deciding to go every week, alone, a schedule that would continue for two years.

Two major factors helped convince Gina that this shaman might be the help she sought. One was Jyoti's presence: Gina liked her immediately, found her powerful and gentle at once. She also enjoyed the peace and calm surrounding Jyoti's home healing center when visiting for sessions. The sessions took place in a special room on the top floor of a huge suburban house. The healing room's windowed walls provided a view of the thick green treetops. Gina felt as though she were sitting in a treehouse.

The treatments she underwent varied. "Sometimes Jyoti used stones and placed them on my collarbone, on my forehead and shoulders, hips, and knees. Crystals and other kinds of stones. She also used to blow smoke—I don't know what kind—sweeter than tobacco, kind of spicy-smelling. And she would chant sometimes. She used a combination of tools every week. Or sometimes she would use only one, and I'd get up and feel okay."

The sweet, spicy-smelling smoke was sage, which Jyoti used for smudging. One skill Jyoti learned from the Amazonian shaman involved "reading" the smoke of the sage after she blew it on a client. Smudging a client would rid the negative energy on her body, but reading the sage, as a psychic might read tea leaves, also provided the shaman with vital information.

I was curious about Jyoti's treatment methods. Checking my books by Harner and Eliade, I discovered the significance of stone use. Eliade notes that in South America, among Araucanian shamans—a tribe in which the shamans traditionally are women —striped or colored stones were projected into the patient's body to purify him; if the stone came out covered in blood, it was a sign that the patient was in danger of death. I didn't quite understand how stones were projected into the body, but I guessed it was a sleight-of-hand action. Or perhaps they were spiritually projected. Both Eliade and Harner mention the power of quartz crystals used by shamanic peoples all over the world. The quartz crystal is associated with the sky, light, and celestial vision. It is viewed as one of the few spirit guides (a nonhuman force in the shamanic state of consciousness that is instrumental in curing) that appears the same in both ordinary and nonordinary states of consciousness. In other words, a quartz crystal in this world looks the same in the shamanic world, unlike my sadness in this world, which looked like a black fuzzy mass in the other. This is because a crystal's material and spiritual natures are the same—a special quality. Perhaps, Harner suggests, shamans long ago determined what we know today to be quartz's remarkable electronic properties, and discovered a way in which this energy could work within the body. That Jyoti had used crystals on Gina shows that crystals are still valuable to modern-day shamans for their healing properties.

In the shamanic view, illness is usually due to one or a combination of three causes, Harner writes: soul loss, power animal loss, and power intrusions. Soul loss is when a portion of the person's soul or essence vacates its place in the body. Soul loss is caused by trauma or, traditional shamans believed, theft by an evil spirit. Power animal loss is when a person's animal spirit abandons the body. Everyone has at least one animal spirit. A power animal's role is to protect a person from harm and keep them healthy and well balanced. But one must be aware of their power animal in order for it to stay. Since most people don't work with or visit their animals on a regular basis, a power animal might leave. Power intrusions or, as Jyoti called them, "possessions" are alien power sources that have entered the person's body, thinking the body is their rightful home. Intrusions enter the body through negative thought forms. If a person does not have power (either they have lost an animal or a part of the soul), they are vulnerable to an intrusion that can easily enter and fill the void during these times.

Were Gina's headaches power intrusions? My own grief headache definitely *felt* like a power intrusion. A power intrusion, according to Harner, could be anything from someone else's anger thrust upon you, to grief, to a disease. A power intrusion was any source of focused energy assaulting the patient. According to Harner, if the client has a harmful power intrusion, the shaman sees on the diagnostic journey dangerous-looking insects, serpents, fish, or other reptiles with visible fangs or teeth, creatures looking to cause harm.

Jyoti's methods of healing usually involve a soul retrieval as the first order of business. When a person's soul is intact, their healing has a better of success. Jyoti journeys to the upper, lower, or middle worlds to find the person's lost piece of soul, brings it back, and blows it into the patient's body through the crown of the head.

Perhaps, she says, a soul retrieval is all a patient needs—to feel reconnected with the essence that left their body. If the client has a power intrusion, however, Jyoti will do a depossession, which, in her method of healing, requires a process of "sucking and spitting" the intrusion out of the body.

Gina's memories of her journeys provided me with details about her condition.

"I definitely visited another landscape—I mean in my mind I did, at least. And it was weird because Jyoti would know what was going on in my head, what I was experiencing. She would facilitate my journey with images that were already happening in my mind. I had a lot of spirit guides (helpers in the other reality) around me, Jyoti told me. But in one journey I had frogs—and I hate frogs. I had a whole journey in which there was this frog, and I was petrified of it." Gina claims she doesn't hate frogs much anymore, although anything scaly or slimy freaks her out. Perhaps the frog was evidence of a power intrusion, a creature that once had enough power over her to repulse her, causing her chronic pain. Now that she had recovered, it had lost its effect. Perhaps Jyoti removed it.

"Jyoti never said, 'This is what is wrong with you—this is why you have headache pain.' It was my job to figure it out for myself. Then it was my responsibility to deal with the problem, and I'll be doing that for the rest of my life. But that's the trick of it. Her treatment was just a first step."

The problem, as she called it, stemmed from a gap in her parental support structures from when she was a child. Her father, a drug addict, had abandoned Gina and Pam when Gina was eight, and her grandmother, a surrogate parent while Pam returned to work, died at the time the headaches were at their worst. Her feelings of loss toward her grandmother were linked with the abandonment she still carried with her from her childhood. The sense of loss, combined with anger and fear of being left again, amassed. While those two factors were largely the cause of the headaches, she determined, the repercussions lived on even after the headaches had subsided.

"I have two irrational fears," she said. "Ghosts and aliens. Ghosts especially. I'm afraid of the energy of people that is still around you after they die. I think of ghosts two ways. My irrational fear is that the person behind the sheet is coming to stalk me. I even check my apartment at night before I go to bed. The other way is when I feel presences and see people who literally aren't there—I call them flashes. It started happening about a year after working with Jyoti." Gina didn't know what to make of these flashes, fear of ghosts, and how to put them together with the spirit guides and power animals she was meeting in shamanic states of consciousness. Once she began to heal, she reinstated her old habit of prayer to help her.

"I pray all the time," she said. "To whatever is out there, to God, to the Goddess, the universe. I have rituals that I do, and I believe in reincarnation. I allow my religious views to change all the time." Gina's former experience with religion, as a nonreligious Jew who grew up among orthodox communities in the hotel business her parents ran in the Catskills, was very removed from organized Judaism. Politically, she disdains all organized religion, hates temple, and has no respect for people who partake in religions that threaten you with damnation if you don't convert. But on the personal level, she said, "I always thought religion was just a way to get you through the night."

Trust in something larger, the desire to see the next day. That is the hope Jyoti focused on in Gina's healing. As Jyoti explained in my evening of shamanic orientation, all of us are connected to the universe. With that connection comes a trust that we will survive, and we will have help along the way. When the trust is broken, however, you can lose faith. You can lose a power animal, a part of the soul, attract power intrusion. The shaman has the ability to help reconnect people with power sources they can trust.

Jyoti identified Gina's sources of help in her mother, who raised her, and in her grandmother, who shared the responsibility when Gina's dad left. They frequently talked about the link between grandmother, mother, and daughter as an unbreakable chain.

Just as people are vessels for energy that comes from the Earth, Jyoti said to Gina, women are the vessels through which life appears on the Earth. Gina felt particularly abandoned when her grandmother passed away, an event she was certain contributed to her headaches. Jyoti made clear to Gina that she would always be linked to her grandmother; she just needed to balance her life to remind herself of that truth. Gina took comfort in the knowledge that she could seek such balance, even if it was a continuous process. But to me the knowledge seemed like a poor substitute for the balance itself. Gina had struggled for so long, yet seemed perfectly willing to allow peace of mind to arrive at its own pace. Perhaps the process was peace of mind itself.

I was willing to accept that shamanic techniques would lead me in the right direction, but I wasn't a shaman and lacked the fundamental skills of practice. Accessing another state of consciousness as a patient with Jyoti seemed to happen naturally, but could I do it on my own? Did I need a shaman to shake a rattle and guide me with images? I wanted to be in control of my own experience. In order to touch something private, to access a source of personal information, I felt I had to be alone. It was the only way I'd believe the information was truly mine.

So I decided to learn to journey on my own. While I wasn't about to take off to South America on a quest to become a master shaman, I was certain there was more I could do to get further into the experience. An underlying impulse to connect to the loss of my grandmother and dog also drove me to seek more information. My immediate grief had been resolved, but I still needed a way to compensate for the loss, to be able to understand it and sit with it without feeling like a part of me was gone.

Through word of mouth I was referred to someone in Brooklyn who could teach me shamanic techniques. Her name was Catlin. In her apartment, we sat together in her small living room on a shaggy orange rug. It was a very soothing and comfortable space, with windowsills and ledges decorated with tropical plants in good health, totems and figurines from Mexico and South America. Catlin brought me a glass of water and explained her style of shamanic work. She gave personal instruction on taking shamanic journeys according to Harner's *The Way of the Shaman*.

"Shamanic journeying," she explained, "is transcendence into nonordinary reality of either the lower world or the upper world, in order to retrieve information." Though Catlin had been studying and practicing shamanic methods for more than ten years, she said she would never call herself a shaman. It is an inappropriate title, she continued, for anyone who simply works with shamanic techniques. "Once I was speaking in Europe, and someone introduced me as a shaman to a Native American woman. It was really embarrassing. The Native American woman was understandably offended, for her mother had been a very gifted seer. There was just no comparison between the two of us." Instead of labeling her practice as "shamanism," Catlin prefers to explain her work as "shamanic methods."

Again I worried—was it okay to do such work with people who were not of the culture originally? I decided that authenticity depends on the quality of experience; the proof would be found in whether I felt empowered by treatment, not the impressiveness of someone's credentials. I asked Catlin to begin.

"Today you will be going to the lower world, which you can access through a hole in the ground that is somewhat familiar to you. You crawl into the hole and end up in a landscape of some kind, and from there, you will begin looking for your power animal. The power animal will act as your guide—your confidant—who will answer your questions and show you around the lower world. Eventually they will help when you journey to the upper world."

The lower world, I had already read, was not anything like my Catholic concept of hell, but instead a place connected with the Earth, its energies, and all of its creatures. There I might meet many kinds of animals, plants, and other living organisms. Supposedly I could have an increasing number of relationships in the lower world the more often I went. But the journey worried me. Getting there seemed complicated. When Catlin said that I "would go" to the lower world, it seemed like an awfully long trip to take without a vehicle. What would propel me? How would I know how to do it?

"I know," she said, sensing my apprehension. "It sounds a little like *Alice in Wonderland,* but there is nothing to worry about. Journeying is safer than dreaming because you are awake. You are in complete control of every move you make. If for some reason you are uncomfortable doing something in the lower world, then you simply won't do it." Again, it sounded okay in theory, but the particulars still eluded me. Kind of like planning on driving across the country without a car.

"Here is what will happen," she said. "You will lie down and cover your eyes, and I will beat this drum for ten minutes." Her hands reached down next to her where a pan drum sat. She picked it up and demonstrated how she would beat it, and I was surprised at how rapidly she banged it. The speed of beats was about the same as the frantic beeping that comes with leaving the phone off the hook for too long. The pace made my pulse race instead of relax.

"Now think of a place where you will enter into the lower world... a knob in a tree, through a hole in the bottom of a lake...."

"Okay," I said.

"Where is it?" she asked.

"Through a hole in a giant old oak in the backyard of the house where I grew up."

"Perfect," she said. "You are ready to go."

I lay back on the orange rug and rested my head on the small flat pillow she set for me.

"Now when you go down the hole through the tree, really use your senses. See if you can smell the dirt, the tree roots. Try touching the walls. When you get to a landscape and find an animal, ask it, 'Are you my animal?' It's really important that you find out whether or not it is *your* animal," she cautioned.

I thought of Harner's description of the fanged insects and serpents that might appear in the tunnel, and then a picture of a landscape loaded with critters filled my mind. I wondered if this task of finding my animal would be any less huge than walking into Times Square and making a friend. What if I had no animal? I wanted to ask. What if I was one of those people who were to go through life without any guidance? Is this how I want to find out—stuck in the lower world surrounded by creatures, none of which were my kin? That might cause some kind of psychic schism. I mentioned none of this to Catlin because it seemed ridiculous to express doubt about a cosmology I hadn't even witnessed yet.

"When you hear my drum break into this pattern"—she repeated four sets of seven quick beats—"you'll know that it's time to come back. At the sound of the call back you'll say good-bye to your animal and make your way back to the hole. When you reach the hole, you will crawl back to where you entered, and through the tree to your backyard. By the time I stop drumming, you should be back in this room, ready to open your eyes. Okay?"

"Okay," I consented. The only way to get anywhere was to try.

She tossed me a black hand-sewn bean bag that looked like it had come from Central or South America. "Place that over your eyes," she directed softly, "and let me know when you are ready."

I took a deep breath.

The drum started pounding, immediately, fast and loud, and my heart jumped to the same pace. I was horribly conscious of lying on the floor with a bean bag over my eyes, but I forced the picture of the old oak into my mind, determined to transcend into the lower world no matter how extreme the pressure. Each drumbeat marked precious seconds. I imagined myself squeezing into the hole in the tree. It was a tight fit. Hurry up, I told myself. Transcend, transcend. The inability to move reminded me of a dream in which monsters began to chase me, and I was trying to run away through waist-high mud. Then I remembered Catlin saying, "This is safer than a dream; you are in complete control of what happens," and I relaxed. Only when I stopped pressuring myself to "do something" did my awareness of the room fade and the closeness of the hole surround me.

The hole was cold, dark, and strange, but I ran like a frightened mole, conscious of the world behind me and the underground ahead where I would soon feel safe. The hole twisted and turned, growing darker and creating a great distance between the world of the oak tree ("the middle world," as Catlin called it) and the approaching lower world. At a certain point, I neared a light and knew the lower world was just around the corner, the same way you know when your bus will come or when the traffic light is about to change green.

For a moment, the landscape where I landed seemed like the wrong one. It was a giant plain in Africa. Not at all what I expected, but I realized that I could expect nothing, only act and do. The drumbeats reiterated that there was no time to expect or think. The plain, bathed in mid-afternoon sun, wide and expansive, lured me into exploration. I looked around for an animal and found an antelope peering at me from the tall golden grass. "Are you my animal?" I asked it intuitively. The antelope intuited back that it was, but only for the moment. Follow closely, at your own risk, it said. With that, the antelope took off across the plain, and I wasted no time in running after it, feeling the agility of my body, the sun on my back, my breathing unified with the pounding of the drum. Across the plains and up a rock formation I followed him, and at the top together we both stood still to catch our breath. The drum still audible in the distance kept my heart racing. Our stillness disturbed me. Why are we stopping here? What are we doing on these rocks? What do we do now?

I looked at the antelope to see if he had heard me, even though I hadn't intuited directly to him. It wasn't totally clear to me how this telepathic communication worked. But the antelope was not paying attention to me. He was looking across the plains to a distant ocean, which had not been there before. Uh-oh, I thought. Not an ocean. I saw it as some kind of wall, a block in my navigation plan. The antelope then bounded down the rocks and I followed, but as it headed toward the ocean, I switched direction, heading instead back to the plains, where I thought I might find my true animal. Running not quite as energetically before, I met with more golden grass that grew higher and higher by the moment, obscuring any evidence of a path I could follow. A flash of the fact that path and purpose were not only connected, but one in the same, told me the grass signified a wrong turn. I felt more unfocused with every step, like I was moving backward, away from the little clarity I had started with. Obviously the ocean was where I needed to go. I ran toward the beach in search of the antelope again.

As soon as I reached the smooth wet sand, the antelope appeared out of the grass behind me and shot into the ocean. He swam to where the blue darkened, as if it were perfectly natural for an antelope to swim that far out into the ocean. This doesn't make sense, I thought. This journey is going haywire. How can the antelope just leave me on the shore with no clues or instructions?

How can I continue this journey into the ocean when I know I can't breathe under water? As fear crept in, the reality of my journey loomed larger and clarified the truth: I was afraid to enter the ocean even though the antelope was leading me to do so. I hesitated, the drum pounding behind me, raising my anxiety level. The antelope was way out in the ocean now. I could barely see his antlers anymore; they had faded to a speck on the horizon. Soon I would be all alone.

Before I knew what I was doing, I was in the water, swimming down into the depths of the ocean, lower and lower. Giant sea plants surrounded me as I descended until I felt a thud on my leg, the whap of the tail of a dolphin. Are you my animal? I asked eagerly. The dolphin, like the antelope, didn't exactly say yes or no, but made it clear that it was my temporary guide, and that I should hold on to his tail. I was aware again of the pounding drum as the dolphin soared through the water in a rhythmic motion. The faster we swam, the more liberated I felt, my body rippling through the water as easily as seaweed. Breathing was no trouble. The dolphin was a mammal, and so was I. That fact alone made it possible for me to breathe.

The dolphin finally led me down farther into the dark depths of the ocean, to a rock formation close to the sea floor. Suddenly I was face to face with a giant sea turtle. I didn't even have to ask if it was my animal, I just knew. Without exchanging thoughts, I jumped on the turtle's back and slowly wafted upward, feeling each of her giant, deliberate stokes cleaving our path. Together we traveled leisurely through the sea until again we were on the beach. The beach, I thought. But why? Is the turtle escorting me home?

The question tumbled out, oddly, the words before the thought. "Turtle," I asked, "how will I live my life as a person who needs to have both sides of myself satisfied?" The side that pursues creativity and the side that makes a living, the side that needs to stay in the city with the side that needs to move to the country? I never expected to ask this question, certainly not on the first meeting with Turtle.

"You will do it like I do it," Turtle replied easily. "I am a turtle that lives in the sea, yet I come and exist on land when I need to."

Oh, I thought. That's true. Turtle feels no need to divide its life, because it is already unified. She just goes where she needs to go when she needs to go there. I can do the same, I suppose. Suddenly, life looked a little brighter.

"I want to go back to the ocean," I told Turtle. "Hop on then," she said, and swam me down to the ocean floor. Here I dismounted and picked up the beat of the drum that was still pounding. We began to dance. I hopped from one foot to the other and waved my arms over my head, and the turtle was doing a kind of two-step, which she seemed familiar with, and which actually looked a lot like that smooth Motown dance the Temptations made famous.

Then I asked Turtle, "How will I live with the passing of time? How will I cope with my rate of growth and progress as time passes, and how will I handle the passing of time that brings with it the death of loved ones?"

"You will endure it like I do," Turtle said. "Slowly, and at your own pace. I've been around for hundreds of years, and I live as if I have hundreds more. You do the same," she said, "and you'll be around for hundreds of years."

This cryptic answer sated me at the time. I understood it to mean that time and its passing was relative to my own life. If I would just go at my own pace and take change slowly, I wouldn't have to worry. If I could live as though I had a hundred years, I would somehow have them.

At that moment, I heard the first set of seven short drumbeats, Catlin's middle-world drum telling me that it was time to come back. I did not want to leave Turtle. "It's okay," said Turtle, "I'll swim you back up to the beach." She pushed her head up under my bottom and guided me up through the sea. This time, I cleaved the path through the water. We left each other at the shore and I ran back across the plains to the hole, clambered up inside the tree trunk, through the dark tunnel at light speed, and landed in the living room just after Catlin beat the last count on the drum.

"What happened?" she asked enthusiastically. I told her. "Wow," she said. "On the first journey, many people can't even get down the hole." She explained a few of the stronger images I told her about. Dancing, believe it or not, is a common expression of joy and commemoration between people and their animals when they first meet. Harner even has a whole section in his book called "Dancing Your Animal." Anxiety about which direction to take and about entering the ocean, she said, I brought with me from ordinary reality.

"That's why," she said, "I told you to try and be aware of your senses—your touch and smell and sight. Your senses will help you next time to cut through your fear. The more you go to the lower world, the more you will understand to how to use your instinct."

I felt strangely fulfilled, both in control of my feelings and amply supplied with a sense of love and companionship. I knew I had made an eternal bond with Turtle, which would not, unlike the people around me, die. Yet it still seemed odd that a sense of fulfillment came from a journey to an imagined world.

"Imagined?" Catlin asked. "I'll tell you what a shaman once said to a disbelieving Westerner. Did you see a landscape? Did you run through the landscape? Did you hear the sounds? Did you talk? If all of the answers to these questions are 'yes,' then why do you say you imagined?"

o o o

It was a good question. *Imagined* was the best word I could find to describe the quality of the landscape I visited. To Catlin's ears, however, saying I "imagined" negated the experience. Shamanically, I went to that other place, yet I felt a great distance between being on a beach in my mind, and physically sitting on an orange carpet where another person could see me. The worlds seemed miles, maybe even light years away from each other. I didn't know how to reconcile the experiences.

Something I read in Tom Wolfe's *Electric Kool-Aid Acid Test* came close to explaining the distance I felt between the two worlds. "A person has all sorts of lags built into him. . . . One, the most basic, is the sensory lag, the lag between the time your senses receive something and you are able to react."

I could extend this idea of "lags" to the trouble I was having interpreting experience in the other world. There was a distinct lag in my brain between Turtle time and real time. Undoubtedly the turtle had given me a lot of advice: I heard it myself. But did that information apply to my real life, where time and space and events took place in a linear framework? I was uncertain, because there was no place for the experience in my ordinary life. No words could describe it besides *imagined.*

The confusion is similar to the feeling I get when I think of hugging my grandmother, going to see her again, feeling her presence before truth creeps in to remind me that it is no longer possible, she is gone. We have an inadequate word for the hole that's left where someone used to be: We say that they're *dead.* But the sensations are still alive, the memory and their wisdom still lives; perhaps the person still exists. If Catlin was to ask her question again to fit this scenario, she would say, "Do you feel your grandmother? Do you see her in your mind? Then why do you say she is gone?"

And she is right. The only solution, to make up for the lag in both shamanic journeying and in coping with ordinary-reality death, is to expand my idea of consciousness and reality to include these other aspects of existence. In other words, to accept the fact that my grandmother is still alive on some level; that on some significant plane of existence, the turtle was my guide.

Still hooked on shamanic journeying, I continued my expeditions to the lower world with a tape of continuous drumming that Catlin gave to me. I was excited not to need a human guide and felt liberated by the frontier ahead of me. I eventually learned how to travel to the upper world. The landscapes I visited fleshed out elaborately. I'd connected with many turtles now besides my primary one, and felt like I could have their help if I needed it in the any of the worlds of the shamanic state of consciousness, and even in this ordinary one. The journeys were rich with symbolism. They were therapeutic in their use of images instead of words.

Trips to non-ordinary reality remained non-ordinary. Increasingly, like in dreams, the pictures advanced beyond my understanding of them, challenging my access to their meaning. I preferred working with shamanism's private, individual system of discovery, but practicing alone left me without a guide to consult.

With every journey, details in each of the landscapes changed; more animals appeared with messages, but often I felt I was getting more information and experience than I could handle. I didn't know how to interpret it into daily life. Sometimes the experiences even left me confused. At one point, spending an afternoon in the sand with my turtle, who had laid some eggs, I spotted a crow circling overhead (not a good sign, intuition told me). The crow, menacing and wise, suddenly dove and scooped up one of my eggs, flying off. I'd been robbed.

I jumped out of the trance, startled, feeling tightness in my throat where my breathing had stopped. What should I do? I found myself asking, What could it mean? For two weeks, my day-to-day life was obscured by my obsession with the crime that had taken place in nonordinary reality. I couldn't shake the feeling of violation and retaliation, but by and against whom was unclear. The crow had vanished into the depths of the shamanic universe. When it seemed like my only option was to ask the turtles for help, I became cognizant of my isolation from outside perspectives. My social life, my boyfriend, and my family could not support me on my shamanic escapades. I suddenly felt lonely. Would the shamanic dimension give me enough sustenance in return? The deliciousness in having a secret world was not so delicious anymore.

Sandra Ingerman, an expert on soul retrieval, emphasizes the importance of the emotional and spiritual preparedness of a practitioner. Confronting a blockage or navigating any kind of conflict in the shamanic universe requires psychic competence, something that a practitioner is trained for. Because practitioners can identify harmful symbols during the journey, they can offer support by controlling the journey's destination, including its end and the patient's safety.

Where was my support, now that one of my eggs had been stolen? Had I worked with a practitioner who could interpret, I might have avoided the numb condition I experienced for two weeks after the crime. I might have felt less violated, I might have been instructed to confront some person in my life who was taking something from me, but without an experienced professional, I couldn't even identify the culprit. Of course, the unaddressed discovery wasn't fatal to my well-being, but I did lose time during those two weeks. Each day seemed bleak, I was slightly depressed, like having had a nightmare that you can't shake. Worst of all, I felt disconnected from both the shamanic world and the real world.

Rather than studying regularly with a practitioner and finding a community, I began to reason my way out of the practice. The connection I had established with my turtle was too precious for me to expose it to just anyone. Since I had connected with my power animal and reconciled some of my grief over my grandmother, moving on through the shamanic realm could take a rest. I had found an ancient spiritual system that was without hierarchy, without gender roles, and that took me into the far out regions of my mind, but it was time to reenter the reality I knew better, where people spoke a language I could understand.

CHAPTER 3

Reformed
Yogaphobic

Yoga is a physical, psychological, and spiritual practice that brings the individual into union with her True Self. In my readings and explorations, I learned that the practice originated in India as early as the fourth century B.C. Yoga predates Buddhism, Vedantism, and Hinduism, though its teachings have merged with each over time. The philosophy of yoga maintains the idea that the Self is born perfect and is merely distracted by life. Through practice, the yogi can rejoin with that perfect sense of self.

People who practice yoga (traditionally known as *yogis*) arrange their bodies in challenging physical positions *(asanas)* while controlling their breath in order to keep their minds focused. By following the breath, the yogi stills the mind, connects with the body, and joins with the perfect Self to reach final liberation (known as *mukti*).

In America, yoga is a fashionable celebrity exercise that leaves the body supple, strong, and relaxed. It is a "lifestyle sport" for which J. Crew manufactures special pants. Such were my first encounters with the ancient Indian spiritual practice, but upon further reading, I learned that the mystical discipline has been called by devoted practitioners "the origin of truth, beauty, eternal happiness, and bliss." It carries a transformative power that, once it arrived in the West in the late nineteenth century, developed into different styles of practice throughout the country among people looking for new paths to spiritual truth.

Yoga is an ecstatic practice of unifying with the Absolute; if you're comfortable saying it, with God; or if not, with Self. But not the ordinary self. Yogis believe there are two selves: there is the small self, known as the ego, and the large Self, which is the divine. The practice of yoga aims to melt away the small, ego self, which gets caught up in the affairs of the body and the mind, in order to reveal the True Self, which is divine consciousness. The word *yoga* is Sanskrit for "union" (the root of the word yoga, *yuj,* means "to bind"). The yogi traditionally sought to unify the soul with God by training the mind and the body under the guidance of a guru, who would guide the practitioner past behavior patterns and values that were considered ordinary in the everyday world. In the United States, yoga is known primarily as a physical discipline, what one reporter called "weird aerobics," but the physical exercise is intricately connected to its ancient philosophy.

Scholars believe that the first person to bring yoga publicly to the West was Swami Vivekananda. He attended the World Parliament of Religions in 1893, and there he taught a number of Westerners the rudiments of yoga philosophy. Many Hindus have come to the United States during the twentieth century, spreading Eastern philosophy and practice in various forms. During the 1960s and 1970s, the trend of taking on a guru struck the fancy of many Westerners—including the Beatles—who were looking for new definitions of God. Today yoga is more popular among the non-guru-seeking masses, and has come to be known as an activity that falls somewhere between a stress management practice and a religious experience.

Yoga philosophy has four main categories and several subsets: *Raja yoga* achieves union with the Self by becoming ruler over one's mind; *Jnana yoga* achieves union through knowledge and understanding; *Bhakti yoga* achieves union through devotion; *Karma yoga* achieves union with the Self through deliberate action, or cause and effect; and *Hatha yoga,* a practice that combines all of these categories, is a physical discipline that balances the body with consciousness. In Sanskrit, *Ha* means sun, which refers to the body and its soul, and *tha* means moon, which refers to the waxing and waning nature of consciousness. Hatha yoga, or the yoga of the body and mind, is the doorway through which I entered into understanding this Union.

○ ○ ○

I had two introductions to Hatha yoga. The first one wasn't so positive. Before I was open to spiritual life, both my own or other people's, I thought yoga was an exercise from India. I found a center in Manhattan where I could sample this new workout. Each time I attended a class, I paid my $12 and noticed clannish groups of people hustling in and out of the reception area carrying groceries, swapping chores on a "schedule," or waking up from naps from the back room. Like any New Yorker, I ignored them. But once in a while I wondered, What exactly was I paying to take part in? Like a dog sniffing suitcases at Customs, I'd trained myself to identify religious territory by the slightest whiff. Instinct told me this yoga center was ripe. I was suspicious.

Several floors of classrooms, a kitchen, and a gift shop/library in the sign-in area hosted clusters of people who wore white and light-colored clothing draped over their macrobiotic bodies. They walked and spoke slowly, as though enraptured by some other, more delicate sense of time. Waiting for class to begin, I sat on a bench and flipped through a book on Hindu gods, not quite making the connection between yoga and Hinduism. A man with wide-open, unfocused eyes approached me, displaying an interest level I was not ready for. He asked, "What's that you're reading?" I held the book up for him to see for himself. He nodded and said, "The wise ones," and wandered away. I couldn't imagine where that conversation might have gone. I was grateful he respected my unwillingness to talk. There was a precious tone to his comment, to his manner, that communicated a reverence—if not for these

Hindu gods, then for a "wisdom"—that drew him and the others who spent more than a few hours a week here at the center. What did I not share with everyone else?

Jubilant voices shouting prayers rose from the back room, and the ping of finger cymbals accompanied the song. A strong scent of something edible but indescribable wafted through the sign-in area. The smell was ghee, I learned upon asking, clarified butter used in Indian food. Members of the center cooked dinner together—the center even offered cooking classes—and if I liked, the desk person told me, I could join the members for dinner and chanting, for a fee. What did it mean to be a member? The community feeling I sensed here was certainly warm, but the center was an awkward intersection between a domestic setting and a place of business. I thought to ask about the kind of dinner served, to discern whether diet was restricted, perhaps religious. "Were those onions I smelled?" I asked. "Onions?" the woman behind the desk replied, taken aback. "I don't think so. All of our food gets offered to Lord Krishna first."

Krishna?

I didn't know yet that Lord Krishna was the Christ of Hinduism, or that this yoga center was actually an *ashram,* a spiritual community where people reside, work, and practice spiritual living. But as I cautiously partook in classes, I began connecting signs and symbols in the classroom—an altar stocked with small figurines, a photograph of a smiling Indian man—with a larger religious significance. The bliss on the face of the man in the photograph revealed contentment: he looked wise and thoughtful, clued into a secret truth that could not have come from normal exercise. With a hue of divinity cast over every corner of the center, I felt that I needed to know what yoga was and why we did not address its religious significance bluntly in class.

But I couldn't bring myself to ask. The unresolved query distracted me, as did the slow but strenuous movements. Trying to obey the gentle insistence on relaxation, I couldn't muster the effort to move into the yoga positions with any kind of pleasure. The adrenaline I was used to relying on was replaced by the teacher's sublime coaxing to "relax." My muscles did the opposite. I was tense the entire time. I moved awkwardly. My mind and body wandered to opposite poles, caught between wanting to sleep and wanting to sweat. It was a most unrelaxing experience.

I became obsessed with the instructor's hypnotic voice and her repetition of *inhale, exhale,* the two words constantly repeated throughout class. The more attention given to the breath, the more I began to feel manipulated, hypnotized, gently urged to give over my natural breathing to the suggested rhythm, to the smiling man in the photograph, to Krishna. Without an athletic goal to concentrate on, the mere suggestion of complying with an unseen force gave rise to uncertainty. I felt pressure in my chest. Were they trying to take over the very air that entered my body? Why couldn't they eat onions? My mistrust of the underlying religion, the community I was unknowingly a part of, threatened my breathing, my safety, and my state of existence. My breath became short. I started to choke. I thought I was going to die.

It was the second panic attack I'd ever had. Rather than investigate its cause and address my spiritual anxiety, I dropped yoga and opted for a gym membership instead.

○ ○ ○

Sometimes first impressions are wrong ones. Especially if they are based on too little information, fear, and suspicion. A year after my experience at the ashram, I had begun a spiritual quest and part of me remembered the relaxation of yoga, the gentleness, and the calm instructors with their tight abdominal muscles. Perhaps I could handle the spiritual elements more adeptly now. Having experienced Wicca and shamanic healing techniques, I might be able better to ignore my fears of the spiritual dimensions. I didn't *have* to go there if I didn't want to.

My reentry into the practice coincided with finding a permanent job that I liked. Now I had a job; spiritual fulfillment did not seem so pressing. My newfound employment granted me candidacy to join the ranks of People Who Worked at Places They Liked. I worked hard. I got involved with my coworkers. We became close and family-like. To alleviate the residual stress, I began exercising regularly at a yoga center near my home.

○ ○ ○

The center I chose is snuggled between brownstones and has a local, neighborhood feel. On the sidewalk out front, the swinging gate clinks open nearly seventy-five times a day with a steady stream of practitioners. The double driveway rarely contains a car, but instead displays an arbor of trees to which regulars attach and lock their bicycles. The regulars are neither slow-walking nor sinewy yogis built of muscle and *prana*—the life-force in yogic terms—but freelance workers, graduate students, stay-at-home moms, artists, dancers, and even some nine-to-fivers looking to rejuvenate their bodies and ideas or decompress from their work days. I felt at home with people who came to take a class and then left without greater commitment. The smells of massage oil, incense, and the light sweat of people who shower regularly, try to eat well, and practice yoga anywhere from one to five times a week did not suggest religious devotion to me, but healthy living. To me, the difference was enormous.

The classes were physically challenging. My body lengthened in places I previously thought short, and the slow movement coaxed areas like the collarbone into mobility for the first time. Surprised, I returned each week, then a few times a week, calmly obeying the instructions to inhale and exhale. At this center I felt no need to panic. I did see a shelf with crystals and clay sculptures and a statuette of a winged Indian goddess in a warrior pose (an asana we practiced). But like a child's collection of favorite objects, this menagerie was for show: icons featuring craftsmanship and design rather than religious intent. A photograph of a smiling man hung in the corner, but without a visible community environment echoing his suggestion of wisdom, his smile might as well have been the Cheshire cat's.

This was yoga free of spiritual wisdom, and I liked it. The instructors complemented the secular environment as they demonstrated and explained the asanas as physical poses. The unfamiliar configurations of twisted limbs and inverted angles occupied my attention. Without gatherings for group meals to worry about, or sleepy, slow-walking nappers to avoid, relaxing was easy.

A current of religion may have flowed through here, but I did not experience any sense that I was participating in a larger program than I wanted. I had a sense of control.

The closest we came to spiritual elements in class was the chanting of "*om*," the Sanskrit syllable for the sound of the Absolute, or harmony in the universe. What harm could "*om*," one little syllable, do to disrupt my delicate spiritual comfort? Very little. My Western, nonspiritual mentality could relate to chanting a sound. No commitment. No abstract concepts. It was a simple call to harmony.

I knew I could handle it, so I happily chanted "om" with everyone else. Bit by bit, I became indifferent to other Sanskrit language the teachers used in class, like *kapalabhati* (a type of breathing to clear the lungs), as I parlayed the spiritual meaning into physical experience. The warm volt shooting through my arms during class, for example, was said to be fresh prana, the secret energy locked in each one of my cells, being released as I breathed. To me, the volt was just the sensation of working muscles. Ignoring the spiritual explanation wasn't so hard after all. With a physical act like a chant or a handstand attached to spiritual theory, I could gauge my involvement through the screen of activity. Without the risk of entering a mental vacuum or a spiritual vortex, I remained involved. This was yoga.

One morning I took a class with a new teacher named Emily. Emily opened the class with three "oms," and immediately I knew something new was about to occur. In every other yoga class, our "oms" had the power of a sixth-grade chorus: self-conscious, restrained, fearful of the sound of our own voices. But Emily's "oms" were vibrant, steady, and according to no particular tone. We all joined in. For the first time, the sound *om* resonated as one strong tone. Our collective "om" felt like a call to someone, somewhere, everyone, everywhere. It had a boomerang quality: no matter how much sound I put out, the same amount returned. Its ring filled the room, like the low, frog-like recordings of Buddhist monks, chanting with tuneless omnipotence.

Shortly after our oms, Emily began to chant Sanskrit words in what sounded like a prayer:

Kali Durga, Durga Ma.

We'd never done this before. No one said anything when she paused. I wondered what the hell was going on.

"This is a call and response," she announced, then repeated the phrase again so we could respond in rhythm. She paused, and this time the class repeated. But I didn't.

Kali Durga, Durga Ma.

What was happening? I had already designated this center a safe space, free of religious reference. I had put down roots. I had even accepted the benign "om." Now we were chanting in Sanskrit, introducing a religious element. Was I angry? Not really. I contemplated whether chanting committed me to a system of faith, or if it just reminded me of the discomfort I felt as a child setting foot in a church that did not feel like mine. The rest of the class echoed the chant in shaky, uncertain voices. Everyone was uncertain, waiting for something to secure their voices in comfort. Were we scared? To be so was kind of silly, almost pathetic. I tried to think about what I might lose if I were to join in. Nothing came to mind.

Emily's enthusiasm finally convinced me to join in the chant fearlessly. What also helped was my past record of ventures into spiritual experience. If in some way the chant brought me into a spiritual world I didn't like, or worse, brought me to a state of panic, I could find my way out if I had to. I'd escaped Catholicism, moved skillfully through Wicca and shamanism. Like a spy on assignment in an enemy nation, I could run from yoga if I really had to.

So I pushed forward and joined the chant the next time *Kali Durga, Durga Ma* came around the bend. Panic did not arise, consciousness did not change, but I suddenly became included. It was kind of nice. Afterward, Emily offered us an explanation.

"When we chant to *Kali Durga,* we are chanting to the Earth Mother," she said from her lotus position at the front of the class. "Think of calling to the Earth—the source of the most powerful and fierce energy, which in Sanskrit is called *Shakti.* Even the word, *Shakti,* is fierce sounding. Kali is a twelve-armed goddess, and she carries a weapon in each arm, and she destroys the ego, that which gets in our way of knowing our true Self. She's the keeper of Shakti, and when we call to her, we are calling for Shakti energy in our practice, the kind that will energize us as we work through positions and push our limits."

Something about the word *limits* reverberated. It hadn't occurred to me that yoga could be about pushing limits. Physically, pushing limits on the body made sense, but using physical energy to push limits of the mind was also implied in her explanation. I thought again of the figurines, the photographs of the smiling man, the chanting, and the disruption these yogic elements all caused in my ordinary thinking. Perhaps they intended to push our limits of consciousness. Perhaps not to control, as I feared, but to gently push who we think we really are.

Emily glanced around the room, as if to survey how many people were thinking about physical limits and how many people had gotten her spiritual allusion. She must have sensed some discomfort among us, because she offered her own personal perspective on the spiritual component.

"I have to say that when I first started taking yoga classes, the little figurines of deities on the altar instantly made me uncomfortable. My only other exposure to the deities or gods of the Hindu tradition was through the Hare Krishnas, who I'd seen at airports jumping up and down and chanting with their instruments."

I'd seen Hare Krishnas too. They rode around Manhattan on summer days in a yellow flatbed truck with a crusty P.A. system, chanting, "Hare Krishna," again and again to the people who pointed at and ogled them. I never understood the spiritual aim behind their endeavors, but Emily revealed the beauty about seeing a part of the self in a deity.

"When you think about it, the Hare Krishnas are just trying to bring part of themselves into union with Krishna. There is no reason why you should think of a deity as something outside of yourself. We are lucky to have deities with whom we can identify. They only exist as a part of you."

I'd heard this perspective expressed before elsewhere. Arianna's motivation behind Wicca was to embrace the Goddess as part of herself. Gina's effort to connect with her power animal and spirit guides was to find an inner sense of self that connected to the Universe. Now, it seemed, I could do the same through yoga, if I wanted to, without becoming Hindu. Emily explained how.

"Think of Kali entering your body through the asana. Imagine yourself grounding down through your feet, or your hands, or one foot and one hand or whatever is on the floor, and sipping Shakti from the earth."

We got into position, into a lunge that stretched the back of the thigh and the hamstring. I felt heat in my muscles, from the ankle through the hip.

"As you move using your breath, really feel that heat entering your body. That's Shakti. Let it push your limits," she coached.

The heat turned into physical pain. I tried Emily's suggestion to ground down by pressing my foot into the floor and breathing. The breathing released tension. The heat passed through me. Holding the pose, an image of the Shakti, red lava-like energy, coursed into my body. More pain. I exhaled again, but not as much of the tension left my body this time. I had the urge to move, but was already stretched to full capacity. A feeling of anger came from somewhere inside of me. Then an image of Kali, Earth Mother of fierce power, came into my head. I thought of her, her twelve arms, her weapons, as the part of me who could push the physical limit.

"What's true about energy," Emily had said, "is that you always have an extra inch to give. Even when you think you are completely extended, there is always an inch more."

I moved, breathed, stretched a little further. The picture of Kali faded, the anger died. My body relaxed. I'd had a breakthrough.

The more I practiced, the more I desired a deeper level of understanding. I bought a book, one of two that had appealed to me. I didn't buy the *Bhagavad-Gita,* a story in which Lord Krishna gives the teachings of yoga to Arjuna at the onset of a battle with his friends and relatives. Though part of me wanted to know about the gods, this was too close to a Bible for me: I had boundaries to maintain. I opted for a more direct explanation of yoga in the *Yoga-Sutra,* a 2,000-year-old work written by a philosopher named Patanjali. A sutra, I read, is a scripture. The *Yoga-Sutra* consisted of short phrases that packed deep meaning about yoga as a mystical discipline.

According to the sutras, people are born divine but are igno-
rant of this divinity: life's distractions lead us away from our essential being. We practice yoga to come back into that union, a union
with our True Self, which essentially is a union with God. This use
of the word *God,* though, was tricky. God in this cosmology did
not have a human form, like the Christian God I had known, or
even a superhuman image such as Hindu deities Shiva or Kali,
with whom I'd become acquainted. In yoga philosophy, God was a
special part of the Self, one that has never been touched by human
experience, and has never suffered from the limitations of finite
consciousness. This part of the Self, a pure frontier, could be
accessed through yoga practice. A state of bliss would result from
connecting with that special Self.

Was it true? Was there really a pure frontier of Self, untouched
by human dilemmas, that had always known the answers during
times of confusion, remained clearheaded when frustrated, or
stayed peaceful while angry? Believing this came more easily than
I thought. I barely had to contemplate, because the knowledge
that this was actually true—that the existence of a special Self was
real—already existed within me. I don't know where it came
from, but the moment I read the sutra, the reality was unalterable.

I read through book one, eagerly. The portion of doubt that
advises me to not "believe" in something was suspended because
the sutras were written so competently. Few statements asked me
to make a leap of faith that I could not actually "feel" as well as
understand. For example, the second of Patanjali's sutras defined
yoga as "the restriction of the fluctuations of consciousness." In
other words, keeping the mind focused was the first necessary step
in practicing. In my first yoga class at the ashram, my consciousness
had never stopped fluctuating. From the figurines to the photographs to the food cooking in the back, my experience was
overrun by fluctuations—and it was not a yogic experience. If I
had only abided the constant repetition of *inhale* and *exhale,* and
willingly followed the flow of the breath, I'd have avoided the
panic attack and learned what I now knew was true, according to
the third sutra. "Then the seer [i.e., the Self] abides in its essence."
It was true. Vanishing into the breath, practicing the challenge of

the posture, and accepting the pain as "sensation" allowed the still-ness to replace frenetic worries.

Every sutra I read revealed another truth about yoga, proving to me that contemplation of mysticism and real-life experience could coexist. The twenty-ninth sutra gave foundation to the aspect of limit pushing: "Thence follows the attainment of habitual inward-mindedness and also the disappearance of the obstacles." Inwardmindedness *did* come with more frequent practice. So did relaxation, exhilaration, and bliss. I upped my classes to three times a week, and all obstacles in my life—job stress, relationship prob-lems, personal dissatisfaction—seemed lifted for those hours of class, and even during hours of life away from class.

No doubt about it: I had fallen under a spell, with absolutely no regrets. The best part about practicing yoga was the utter liberation I felt from any notion of a God who existed outside of myself. The more I chanted, processed the philosophy, and acquired physical strength, the easier it was to see how personal energy could lead me closer to this idea of a divine, special Self. The thought of a "special self" made me laugh, when I wasn't in the yoga mind. It reminded me of having an imaginary friend, a security blanket that kept me calm, the power of which no one else could see. I focused on my increasing physical strength, which now launched me into headstands, backbends, and enabled me to press my chin to my shins.

It's hard to explain what happened to my day-to-day life with-out sounding like a kook. In the past, I'd seen infomercials for exercise equipment hosted by workout enthusiasts who carried an intense, almost fanatical excitement. Those individuals always gave me the impression that they'd experienced a serious life change because of the exercise. Though they were trying to sell the change in the form of equipment, their enthusiasm was sincere, if a little garish when combined with a sales pitch. My enthusiasm for yoga felt like it had reached infomercial heights. I didn't publicly become a yoga fanatic, but I did find myself with an extra amount of energy that to friends seemed to qualify me among the happily converted. They were jealous.

Partly I know the change was from the exercise, but it was also from the yoga philosophy. The vision of people as perfect creatures, each of whom could unify with their bliss, was more and more acceptable to me the more I practiced. I didn't have to try very hard to think this way; the vision simply appeared when I woke up in the morning. I began to see potential in other people, especially people in yoga classes who were trying to reach their cores. I practiced almost every day, now, and was on a first-name basis with people at the center. The more classes I took, the longer the feeling of limitlessness stayed with me afterward. One friend told me, "I think I can actually *see* the yoga on you." I saw more and more how no ceiling could keep me from riding the high of yoga. And it really was a high. It was analogous to those water-theme-park rides where you speed on an inner tube down a long, narrow, enclosed metal tunnel, and then suddenly shoot into the air, the light and sky and trees passing by as your body sails, completely severed from any hold. For a minute, just for a minute, you see how it might be possible for human beings to fly. This was as close as I'd ever come to the idea of God. I wanted more.

I wanted to attend the center where Emily became certified. That was the Jivamukti Yoga Center, once a dark, cramped, intense yoga joint on the dingy Lower East Side of Manhattan. Now prosperous, it had moved to a large, light renovated loft space on the upscale Lafayette Street.

A red neon Sanskrit symbol for *OM* hung above the doorway outside. I entered the lobby and waited for the elevator, preparing for maximum exposure to the yoga I had once dismissed but now embraced. The elevator door slid open and an Eastern Hemisphere fantasy world welcomed me.

The first audible sound was a trickle of water. The softer lilt of sitar music rang mellifluously through the air. I stepped onto the bleached wood floors. A spotless, sun-drenched lobby sported a long desk attended by active and attractive, smiling and well-spoken employees. They were registering the line of hipster yogis who had called ahead and *reserved* space in class. Next to the desk was a browsing area of objects for purchase. My eyes fell upon a rotating rack of CDs. It contained an assortment of Sanskrit chants recorded by countless artists, Indian and American alike, mixed with club beats or performed classically with sitar and harmonium, plus contemporary American music that bridged the gap between East and West. Next were racks of special Jivamukti yoga clothing, urbane and comfortable. Figurines of the Hindu gods Hanuman (the monkey god) and Ganesha (the elephant-headed remover of all obstacles) smiled at me from a shelf. I'd come a long way. I found them cute, even collectable. Posters of intricate mandalas, instructional books and videos on the art of yoga, meditation, breathing. Baskets of yoga mats and oblong yoga mat bags—the assortment of products I could buy to set up my own yoga practicing space at home almost made me forget I had come there to exercise and not shop.

Shoes were not permitted beyond the entryway of the center. I walked barefoot down the hall to the dressing room; the sitar faded into the background, and the trickling water grew louder. Across from the dressing room a twenty-foot cantaloupe-colored tile wall shimmered beneath a gentle waterfall. The yoga rooms were named after gods: Vishnu, Shiva, and Brahma. The walls and ceilings pulsated with aqua and plum paint. The altar in the largest classroom had photos of smiling Indian men, figurines of Hindu deities, and also portraits of the Beatles, John F. Kennedy, and Martin Luther King, Jr.: American celebrities who were altarworthy. Post–Krishna prophets.

The entire center anticipated a ceremonial celebration of yoga. The lavish, ornamental design externalized the mystical, and the teachers kept it buzzing with their discussion of the "focus of the month," during their ad lib lectures at the beginning of class. I was enchanted. In spite of the bold, extravagant presentation of yoga, an underlying elegance and grace helped me see the true intent behind the center's vibrancy: to capture, share, and continually create a place where people can explore their divinity in comfort. I sat in half-lotus on a blanket, watching other people like me blow in from their busy days at work. I watched their bodies start to soften as they sat, adjusting to the secular temple.

In addition to absorbing the ambiance of the center, I became aware that the day was former Beatle George Harrison's birthday (it was announced in class). The teacher sat before us in a half-lotus position, and while she prepared to speak, I heard the classic "My Sweet Lord" playing in the other room.

"You may wonder why we play the Beatles during asana class, or even why we have pictures of them on our altar, along with other non-Indian figures," she said after our oms and chanting. No one answered. "It's because these people spoke the truth. They weren't afraid to say what they saw, and they expressed their vision in a positive and beautiful manner. They were able to get out of the way so that the divine could come through them. And that's what we're practicing here in asana class. Getting out of our own way, so that the Source can come through."

Getting out of the way? The Source? No one commented on this, but then, it wasn't the type of class where students had a chance to talk back. It was a little like church. So I just listened.

"Today is George Harrison's birthday, and George is a very spiritual man," our instructor continued. "He changed his career after the Beatles and went further into Eastern thought and spiritual practice. So today we'll be doing asanas to his devotion, which he gave to us through his music. So let's come onto all fours, inhale, now exhale into a Downward Facing Dog. . . . "

While I breathed in Downward Facing Dog, a position where hands and feet are on the ground and hips are in the air so that the body resembles an inverted V, the familiar sound of tabla drums and a sliding sitar blasted into the room. (Jivamukti has an incredible sound system in every yoga room. It's part of the whole "celebration" of asanas.) Instantly my body loosened as the familiar tune of "Love to You," from the *Revolver* album flowed through me. Yoga was taking on the Beatles. The Beatles had said a lot of profound things about love and society. Though I didn't live at the time when they were together, their words were still meaningful. Posing in Downward Facing Dog in a yoga class to the Beatles amused me. What would John Lennon have thought?

I thought about "getting out of the way" and "the Source" while I breathed in and out. After a while, the position grew difficult, and I had to readjust my body, inhale and exhale, in order to connect with the pain. Connecting with pain was a way of getting out of the way, the teacher had said. I could physically feel the rush move through me, and if I rode it, the pain subsided and the taste of limitlessness poured in. This was the Source, the energy, of which she spoke.

My thinking self stopped. The understanding of three of Patanjali's sutras, which I'd read in the *Yoga-Sutras,* that talk about restriction of consciousness came to mind. I didn't ponder them; they just resonated:

"Or restriction is achieved by the controlled expulsion and retention of the breath."

"Or restriction comes about when an object-centered activity has arisen which holds the mind in steadiness."

"Or restriction is achieved by mental activities which are sorrowless and illuminating."

Time stopped. The rhythm of the class, the teacher's guidance into each pose allowed my mind to rest—it was as if I was practicing meditation in motion. I lost all sense of self as I flew from asana to asana. At the end of the class, during final meditation, I felt warmth shooting through my body, rising up my spine through the back of my neck, and from my abdomen through my chest. I felt a pulse in my chest, and identified it as the fourth *chakra* opening. (The *chakras* are seven energy centers in the body that regulate prana. They also correspond with consciousness. The first chakra is found at the base of the spine, and successive chakras move up through the body to the crown of the head.) Yogis recognize the fourth chakra, which is located in the heart, as the emotional center. Having opened my fourth chakra as a result of the asana class, I felt my heart—*really* felt it. It felt red, vulnerable, and passionate. The passion emanated without attachment to anyone. I suddenly had passion for life, for a relationship with the divine consciousness, or the Source. For the rest of the class, this promise seemed possible.

An hour and a half after class began, and many George Harrison songs later, I was completely exhilarated and exhausted. Never had I simultaneously pushed my mental and physical limits so hard. For a while after class I trusted I could look into the world and find what I needed.

○ ○ ○

The young woman who taught class that day was named Uma. She struck me, for a number of reasons, as someone who strove for limitlessness most of the time. The first clue was the way she spoke to us: in quick, inspired sentences from the front of the class. ("Okay, come to a *comfortable* seated position. . . . Turn to *page 3* of your *chant sheets*. . . ."). On a folded blanket, eyes closed, preparing for the beginning of class, she sat with the rest of us blocked out of her consciousness. We were supposed to have our eyes shut, but I kept mine open for a moment to watch her stillness. Her breathing took on a deliberate and regulated pace. She turned inward, and went *somewhere else.* Suddenly her eyes opened, and a crystal clear voice delivered prayer in Sanskrit; the words came up through the base of her body and out of her mouth as if the movement and delivery had very little to do with Uma herself.

She was a small woman with straight brown hair almost as long as her body. Her bright eyes conveyed alertness and a presence that implied she had let singing take her over. Her melody had only three notes. I could practically see the arms of enthusiasm reaching from her voice like light beams from the Sun reaching to Earth. I could hear how far she was reaching to deliver that sound—it came from millions of miles away. The class followed her lead, doing their best to match the intensity Uma had mustered. But we were on a different plane. Uma delivered an intangible sense of strength, intent, and devotion that I found so appealing, I wanted to know where it came from.

We spoke after class. She was young—twenty-three—and a fully commited yogini. She seemed wise beyond her years because she's been continuously searching for God since she was sixteen.

"In high school I became attracted to deities, and bought two little ones at a New Age store. The first one was Tara because my name was Terra—she's a Tibetan Buddhist Goddess. She's the one who takes you over the ocean of *samsara,* the ocean of birth and death. But her name made me feel close to her."

Uma grew up in Northern California and Oregon, and she spoke of her teenage years as a time in her life when everything was sacred. She set up an altar in her room, lit candles constantly, and meditated. Her interest in spiritual things seemed to arise during these transitional years, as she discovered who she was while constantly switching high schools (she'd been to nearly a dozen) up and down the West Coast in search of a scene into which she could fit. She had aspired to be a dancer. The continual impulse to dance led her to modern dance classes and even to a performing arts high school—neither of which satisfied her desire. Her urge to dance was connected to a deeper urge to participate in a larger community of people who recognized divinity in the individual soul.

She found that community upon moving back to California and discovering the Grateful Dead. "That's when things started happening for me. I got really into the hippie scene. . . and once you get into that scene you start to get a little more connected to the Earth," she said. I knew what she meant, only because I'd listened to the Grateful Dead in 1991. Though that era was long past the hippie days, the Grateful Dead were still performing shows and sharing their celebratory vision of life. The roving community of Dead Heads was all Uma needed to get started.

I found it unusual that, at age sixteen, she would connect to a music scene and find both a sense of identity *and* God. But Uma saw the bridge and crossed it full force. She followed an instinct. Instead of moving through high school to college to a career, her life meandered in many directions, all of which had to do with dancing and a deeper desire to connect to her ideals of spiritual fulfillment. Like most sixteen-year-olds, she had a black-and-white sense of passion. But unlike many, she acted on it spiritually.

Uma rarely stayed home with her father and brother. She had a friend whose mother had money with which to indulge Uma's and her own daughter's creativity. They bought art supplies, New Age trinkets, spiritual books, and health food. And pot. Uma fully embraced the iconography of Buddhist and Hindu deities, the ideology of vegetarianism, and the theology of spirit existing everywhere in the universe. Though she was raised as a Catholic, she shunned practicing Catholicism because "she was having a negative trip" with God, and even proclaimed herself an atheist. Interestingly, the contradiction between her Catholic God and her new spiritual freedom did not stop her exploration. By proclaiming herself atheist and separating her spiritual existence from the Catholic doctrine that she formerly knew, she was able to look at other religions without feeling as if she had to give over her soul to them.

Uma wanted to feel the heights one could reach by pursuing a spiritual path. Her friend's mom's music collection contained many Indian chants, and she had pictures of a man named Bhagavan Das. She introduced Uma to the book *Be Here Now*, written by Ram Dass. In the '60s, Ram Dass was a Harvard scientist named Richard Alpert, who, in his scientific experimentation with LSD, found his way to Kathmandu and met Bhagavan Das, another American who in 1964 had explored his own path in India. Uma became absorbed in Ram Dass' book and Bhagavan Das' recording of chants.

She began going to meditation classes, at her friend's mom's suggestion. She heard about a *kirtan*—a gathering of people doing Sanskrit call-and-response chanting and dancing—in Marin County. Bhagavan Das, whose chanting she admired, would be there. Following an inner compulsion, she hitchhiked, took a bus, and walked two miles in the rain in search of the kirtan. "I remember thinking, in the pouring rain, 'This is it. This is my journey. I'm just supposed to be content in the rain and do my chant, my mantra *Om Namah Shivaya* (I surrender to Lord Shiva). And if I get there, I get there.'"

She arrived at the kirtan soaking wet, expecting a spiritually slanted call-and-response dance party. She was shocked to walk in and find Bhagavan Das and the others opening the ceremony with, of all things, the Catholic service of communion. Were they really allowed to do this? With no priest present in a house tucked away in the country, it was hardly a church. Yet here was this group of people celebrating communion, a powerful ritual of the religion she had rejected. For the first time, communion felt cool and fun in this non-Catholic setting; it maintained some aspect of sacredness. The possibility that Catholicism could connect with her new spiritual path strengthened her image of kirtan even more. She became acquainted with Bhagavan Das during the course of the evening, and returned to the kirtan regularly to participate in the chanting and dancing, which sometimes lasted for hours.

Between tripping on acid, chanting, and dancing at the kirtan, Uma embraced an extended high that zigzagged around aspects of higher consciousness. "After a while, I realized I needed to learn more about this. I loved chanting, but what was I chanting about? Who were these deities I was chanting to?"

Accustomed to taking to the road in search of the next step, she sought the information elsewhere. Uma attended a Rainbow Gathering in Arkansas, a giant festival held once a year in different geographical locations, where people of the hippie-ecologist mindset go to live for a week. There, she saw an opportunity to leave all things mainstream behind her, study the Hindu deities, and live a lifestyle completely immersed in God. Taking a drastic step appealed to her. Dressed in a white sari, she left the festival with the Hare Krishnas.

For six months, she was a Hare Krishna. The focus of this lifestyle was the polar opposite of the Grateful Dead party scene she knew. Among the Krishnas there was no sex and no drugs. They never asked abstinence of her, she said; imparting rules on people's behavior was not their focus. Krishnas lived together, supported each other, split up the chores, and prayed. Uma liked learning how to make flower garlands and how to cook. She cleaned most of the time. The rest of the time she prayed in kirtan, chanting estatically to Krishna.

"After an hour you couldn't take it another second, you were going to have to fall down and throw up because you were so exerted, but somehow you kept going," she remembers. The kirtans, she said, were particularly intense when the boys and girls got together. Everyone was celibate. The reserved sexual energy fueled the prayer sessions.

Living nun-like in an extreme Hindu sect in a house of girls in Columbus, Ohio, suited Uma just fine; she never intended to leave. Except for a creeping feeling of repression that surfaced on occasion. "I did feel a little bit like, They don't know who I am. I know I'm more than just cleaning and cooking, I know that there has got to be something else I am supposed to do."

She increasingly tired of just chanting "Hare Krishna." Remembering the chants to Kali Durga and Sita Ram she had learned in Marin County, Uma grew restless with repeating the same words each day. But the Krishnas were opposed to any other deities. "One time we had this food and there was something wrong with it, so it couldn't be offered to Krishna—like there were onions in it or something. It was supposed to be given to this huge group of people, so I suggested, well, offer it to Shiva. And they were like 'Oh, blasphemy,' and I said, 'Shiva has to eat too.'" Everyone was shocked. But Uma, amused, knew this was the beginning of the end.

Their rigidity continued to bother her. One day she called home; Bhagavan Das had left her a message. When Uma called him back, he suggested she leave immediately because they were brainwashing her. She hung up the phone and thought about that possibility. Had she been brainwashed? While she was certain she had not, the suggestion to leave resonated with her, starting a flood of questions. Her questioning soon led to her departure. She traveled to Oklahoma and arrived at her mother's door in a sari and barefoot.

The culture shock from living in an isolated community of extreme Hindus sent Uma reeling. Who was she, and how could she live spiritually without closing herself off from the world? For several months Uma acclimated to ordinary life but continued praying to Krishna, meditating each day, and listening to Bhagavan Das' chants. While she never went as far as to renounce her Krishna influence, she took a stand against the Hare Krishna lifestyle. She began dating again and going to clubs—all of which helped her reestablish herself in the non–Hare Krishna world.

But she was still caught between worlds. Her spiritual path was not merely a phase that she had maxed out on and was now ready to leave behind. She wanted more, the next step. She just didn't know of what, particularly. Finally one day she locked herself in her room, where she stayed for the next three months, chanting, meditating, dreaming, and writing in her journal almost twenty-four hours a day. Bhagavan Das' tapes played again and again. One day, her mother came home with a bus ticket to Marin County and said, "I am sending you to him. Your bus leaves in two hours."

While this announcement came as a shock to Uma, she didn't say she did not want to go. She felt a bit at a loss to not have her own place to call home anymore, but she enjoyed the thought of seeing Bhagavan Das again.

Bhagavan Das became her guru and her lover. She took care of his house, his business affairs, and him, while working minimum-wage jobs and learning from him in a guru/disciple relationship. It was with him that she shed her birthname Terra for Uma Nanda Saraswati, or Goddess of Light. (It is traditional for a teacher to give his student a new name.) They married. Though it wasn't a legal ceremony, to Uma it felt real.

Circumstances drove them to move north, where Uma met Shree Maa, a spiritual teacher whom many consider to be a saint. For a year, she and Bhagavan Das studied with Shree Maa. Uma was thrilled to be studying with someone who was known throughout the world for her good works and intense understanding of God. Further, Shree Maa was a woman who had spent her life serving others spiritually while still maintaining her personal dignity. She served, but she was not a servant.

The ability to serve and share her spiritual energy was important to Uma. "My whole life, I've only wanted to serve in a way that would use all my talents," she remembered.

As Uma learned the difference between serving and being a servant, she did little else but devote her time and energy to Shree Maa. "She taught me everything I know about *puja* (worship). When I finally got to serve her, I got to rub her feet at night, wait on her hand and foot. I'd always wanted to do that—be the right-hand woman." I was confused by Uma's excitement about serving. It was one thing to admire a teacher, but what to make of a woman who admits that she wants to serve during an era when many women strive to be fully liberated from serving anyone but themselves? In part, my entire spiritual quest sought to learn how to serve my own needs, not the needs of others. Was Uma a throwback to another time, or a super-progressive?

I learned that Uma had a very different definition of *service* than the traditional one. Though in many ways ancient, hers was a progressive definition that explained her appearance, her singing, her mission. Her desire to serve was completely rooted in a belief in the Source: the endless resevoir of energy that is our true Self. "We are all just tools, or instruments, of the Source. It's our ego that keeps us from remembering that simple truth. When we serve others, we blend with the Source and we enter into a state of bliss that is our True Self." She said it with knowing confidence; the kind that comes with practicing what you preach.

Uma had learned about service, her True Self, and the various categories of yoga through Shree Maa when she was only twenty. By then she knew serving divinity was her calling. She was willing to devote her life to it, sacrificing everything. She even stopped dancing, her first passion, though that wasn't in Uma's original plans. Shree Maa requested that Uma dance for her upon their first meeting. Obediently Uma began to dance, and Shree Maa stopped her. "You aren't dancing to God," she said. Uma was confused. "You need to learn to sit still," Shree Maa told her. Her dancing was too wrapped up in her ego. Uma stopped dancing altogether. She wanted to be able to dance to the divine, if she was going to dance at all.

Months passed and Uma sat still. Then it came time for her to perform with Bhagavan Das. They traveled to New York, where they performed at the new Jivamukti Yoga Center. Uma danced for a crowd; among them were the center's two founders, David Life and Sharon Gannon. When Sharon saw Uma perform, she immediately approached her. "She said to me, 'Uma, wouldn't it be great if you learned some asanas. Then you could put them into your dancing.' I didn't really understand. I used to think asanas were boring, but Sharon saw how I could devote my dancing to the divine, and take it out of the ego trip I was in. She knew the difference between dancing and saying with your body, 'Look at me,' and doing asanas and using your body to say, 'Look at God.'"

Uma moved to New York and studied in the Jivamukti teacher training program. But it was a traumatic move. She had to leave Bhagavan Das and the life she'd worked hard to carve out in

California. She didn't have a lot of money. And teacher training was very demanding. She had a breakdown. "One day at the center I just flipped. I told Sharon, 'I'm leaving, I can't take it. It's too hard. Bhagavan Das is missing me, I have no money. I'm leaving.'

"And Sharon said to me, 'You can't leave, Uma.' She just said it. 'You can't leave, because if you leave teacher training, you will live to regret it for the rest of your life.' It was so harsh to hear, but she was right. I started crying. I couldn't stop. I lay down in front of the altar and cried, then I moved into this little alcove in the offices and just cried. I cried because just when things are about to happen for me, I run away. I get scared. Now I was scared and I couldn't leave because people around me were saying no, for my own good." For hours Uma cried in the alcove alone, until David Life, the other director of the center, came to see her. He said nothing while she cried, but instead he held her feet. He just held her feet. She began to feel an amazing love from him and she started to calm down.

She stopped crying. He left. She emerged from the crawl space, down from the loft. She knew it was here, among people who supported her, that she could cultivate faith and who she truly was.

Uma fell in love with the way Sharon and David taught. They brought an element of art to the practice of yoga. Their understanding of the mystical, their blending of the yoga teachings with daily life, and their establishment of a yoga center that perpetuated these concepts appeared to Uma to be divine intervention. Jivamukti was the next step of her education.

○ ○ ○

I regularly take Uma's classes. I see each week how she thoroughly embraces the practice of yoga as a divine practice and incorporates her love of dance into the asanas. Teaching is a way to serve using all of her talents, tap into the Source, and simultaneously serve the divine in others.

"It's so amazing to be in a place where you are being lifted up too. That reiterates how we are all divine, and it's not just one main person who is on top and we're all just going to be serving for the rest of our lives, never able to get there. We can all get there. All you have to do is put in a little bit of effort, and you are going to get there."

I hadn't exactly found a spiritual community in yoga like Uma had. I never talked about yoga to anyone at the center. I never shared my feelings about the intense rushes of love and compassion I felt flood my body many times throughout class, or where I thought it came from, or what or who I thought it was for. No one knew of the gratefulness I left the class with each time. I wanted to share these feelings, tell someone, be able to look at my neighboring yogi or yogini in the eye during the contortion of a standing spinal twist and say something. But what would I say? What did I want them to know? That I thought I could feel God? That I wanted to feel God inside my body, and then outside my body so there was no more difference between being inside and outside and I was just swimming in divine love, breathing it in abundantly and bountifully? Could I tell them that when those surges of happiness coursed through me in such plenty I wanted to, if I could, instill that energy into each and every person's heart personally, directly, blow it through their skin into their souls because, as far as I was concerned, we were all there and willing to concentrate and arrange our bodies in painful positions with fifty other strangers in a plum-colored studio with a killer sound system and the Beatles, all for the promise of the same thing? Could I tell them? I couldn't really find the words. After a while I realized it didn't matter.

As a student in the fifty-person classroom, I automatically feel like a star in the Jivamukti universe. I believe it is largely because the environment gives the sense of having personal commitment to your progress as a yogi. Uma's ability to give what I've come to recognize as divine energy (that is, love and encouragement without strings) to a class of strangers creates unprecedented intimacy and an acute sense of awareness. Sometimes the awareness feels like an apocalyptic umbrella over our limited existence on Earth. Other times I feel the warm and womblike intimacy enclosing me in the perfection of creation. I've stopped freaking out about these emotions of the soul. Now I just let them churn like upwelling ocean waves, and I try to ride them as far as I can.

Uma's methods are deliberate. She assists as you try to put your foot behind your head, or reach your arms behind your back into a prayer position. Sitting in a painful position, she tells a story from the *Bhagavad-Gita*. "Dedicate your practice!" Uma shouts at moments of intensity. "Offer it up, approach your life with devotion." She tries to liberate your soul with an intense form of love not usually found in the secular world. It's like having a lover who, regardless of your past, is ready to love you for the rest of your life, on whatever your terms may be.

Jivamukti offered private sessions where, I imagined, the yoga practice got even more intense and the connections were more personal, closer to the guru/disciple relationship. Budgetary restrictions kept me from affording those on a regular basis, so I happily stayed with the classes I could afford. But the whole money thing bugged me. It wasn't so much that classes were expensive. One must pay for quality. In my heart I had trouble with the exchange of money for access to such an intimate experience like this. Sometimes I felt like I was buying love. For money to be my only expression of gratitude, my only contribution into this yoga world, felt imbalanced. One is supposed to give themselves to a community they feel a personal connection to, yet here I was giving nothing but some cash and some heartfelt thank-yous.

I left this quandary aside for the time being, because I liked yoga for all of its benefits to that part of me beyond my body and my mind. Maybe by the time I could comfortably sit in Hanuman Asana (a split pose with hands clasped above head, modeled after the pure devotion Hanuman the monkey God had in his heart for Ram), I'll have found a route through the money/intimacy barrier. Maybe I'll have hurdled the obstacle by practicing pure devotion. I practice at home on days I don't take a class. Each time I feel much closer to the place in my heart that reassures me of divinity, how it is personal and powerful. It reminds me of what church was supposed to be. Union with God.

CHAPTER FOUR

The Veil
of Vodou

My roving eye kept looking for spiritual experiences. I wanted to make sure, as I practiced my yoga asanas, that I would recognize my next step when it came along. Yoga infused me with energy and vision and gave me access to a state beyond myself. For better or for worse, my antenna for elements of power in the universe was fine-tuned and continually looking for a system with high voltage. I wanted my spiritual life to amplify my existence. Yoga fueled a current of calm within me, and I was grateful for the sense of grounding each time I fused my body with the earth, my mind with my breath. But I wasn't positive that the rush of fulfillment was independent of an exercise high, or that I could keep it going on my own if I skipped class for a week. And what about hanging on to the wisdom? Musing over Patanjali's spiritual insights in class seemed like enough at first. Exiting the classroom, though, I wanted an active force at my disposal, not a philosophy. I needed an animate spiritual system that left a trace I could see. Did that exist?

I was aware of one spiritual practice that was legendary for its active power: Vodou. From an art exhibit I once saw on its history, I knew that Vodou's mysterious symbols of divinity were unforgettable. Glimmering flags depicted wise, spectral faces of the *lwa,* the name for the gods and goddesses in the Vodou pantheon. Videos of outdoor ceremonies featured dancers and drummers performing praise to the gods in intricate rhythms. Altars piled high with items of devotion—alcohol, sweets, money, bowls of fruit or cornmeal—were examples of offerings made to the gods and goddesses for their help and protection. Without ever having witnessed its work, I knew Vodou offered more than just its mainstream reputation as either bunk or evil. But my experience of Vodou was limited to looking at objects behind glass in a museum. I didn't know anyone who practiced it. I knew of no stores around Manhattan where I could buy ritual objects or participate in secret garden ceremonies. Though invisible and unfathomable, I knew Vodou existed; perhaps it held unique divine secrets that would aid in my search for spiritual truths.

As a white woman, however, I expected that my access to this tradition might be impeded. I refrained from contacting the Haitian Cultural Center near my home in Brooklyn, partially because I felt like an outsider. Would my interest be ridiculed since I wasn't Haitian or even black? Was I treading on territory that I shouldn't? Was I trying to appropriate something that didn't belong to me? Culturally and racially, the answers to these questions may have been yes, but spiritually, my interest was legitimate. I didn't know if the categories of race, culture, and religion could be separated. I headed to the library.

I found two books: *Working the Spirit: Ceremonies of the African Diaspora* by Joseph M. Murphy and *Mama Lola: Vodou Priestess in Brooklyn* by Karen McCarthy Brown. The first book explained how, during the slave trade, African religion was disseminated to different countries in the Americas and the Caribbean, and how it adapted to the cultures of these different countries. The second book profiled a priestess who had moved to Brooklyn from Haiti and served as a doorway to the divine for the Haitian community.

From both books, I pieced together a composite history of Vodou and its many faces of worship.

Vodou is an African-based spiritual system that reveres ancestors and calls on a pantheon of deities to assist its practitioners at times of need. It is accessible to the devoted practitioner at any time, and can be used either alone or in a group. The Vodou is the spirit of the universe, manifesting in many forms of deity. It can be called into existence by skilled practitioners—both men and women—with the help of ancestral contact. Traditionally the practitioner calls to deities with prayer, dance, drums, and community involvement. Often the practitioner seeks the assistance of a priest or priestess. As with any priesthood, intimate contact with the lwa enables priests and priestesses, who have equal authority, to conduct religious services, dispense spiritual advice, and work with individuals as they develop their own relationships with deities. In the United States, hundreds of thousands of people practice different forms of Vodou. Primarily practiced in black and Hispanic communities, Vodou keeps spirituality and contact with one's ancestors alive in day-to-day life.

○ ○ ○

When Africans arrived in the Americas and the Caribbean in the late 1700s, their religion was suppressed and vilified by white colonists. Slave owners forced African religion underground, along with most of the rest of African culture. Because of this oppression, African religion in its many forms—Vodou, Santeria, Candomblé—acquired a reputation that was shrouded in mystery and fear. Decades of false imagery created by white media and literature that labeled Vodou in particular "evil" and "dangerous" sustained the negative stereotypes. In spite of the bad press, according to each book I read, Vodou exists in black communities in most cities in the United States.

When, in the late 1700s, different tribes were brought to Haiti from a large area in Africa, each tribe had distinct deities, dances, and drum rhythms specific to its regional religion. Upon arrival, the tribes lost their individual identities when the prevailing

French Catholics tried to convert the African people. The diverse African religions merged with each other and combined with aspects of Catholicism, creating what Americans call "voodoo" or Vodou. This merging, or synchrotism, kept many aspects of the original tradition alive. The faces and characteristics of the Catholic saints came in handy for cloaking the African lwa.

In fact, Vodou continued to grow in secret in Haiti, gaining more power as people gathered to call on the deities for help from their oppressors. In a remarkable display of faith, in 1791 oppressed slaves in Haiti used Vodou during the only successful slave revolt in the Caribbean. It supposedly began with a Vodou ceremony, a sacrifice of a boar to the African gods, and a vow to overthrow the French. The ensuing twelve-year war of independence against the French colonists, won in 1804, established the image of Vodou as a dangerous force to be reckoned with.

As with any source of power, particularly religious, mystery is a potent tool of manipulation. The same faith with which Haitian people liberated themselves was turned against them 150 years later by tyrannical leader Jean-Claude Duvalier. In order to enforce total loyalty to his regime, "Papa Doc" Duvalier appointed Vodou priests to his secret police and used the already established respect for Vodou against the citizens. Many Haitian artists and intellectuals fled to the United States. A form of Haitian Vodou already existed in the United States; freed slaves from the first rebellion in Haiti had emigrated to cities like New Orleans, where they enjoyed relative freedom to practice their religion. This second exodus added to the ranks of Vodou practitioners.

O   O   O

Prior to reading these two serious, accurate books, I had been a victim of anti-Vodou hype. My impressions of Vodou were based on feature films like *Serpent and the Rainbow* and *Angel Heart,* which used Vodou to tell horror stories. Intellectually, anyone would say that trying to understand Vodou from cinematic portrayals was about as ridiculous as basing one's understanding of U.S. politics on *Wag the Dog* and *Saving Private Ryan*. Yet, the cheesy images of Vodou that proliferate—heartless animal sacrifices, the taking over of individual souls—perpetuate its dangerous myths rather than lead to the integrity that lies behind the belief in the divine as a precious force in the universe.

Vodou's survival under oppression spoke to my own spiritual crisis. Since I had cast out Catholicism, the primary urge to be part of a spiritual community survived within me, but the tenacity with which African slaves clung to Vodou in secret demonstrated a faith that was not part of my experience. Africans subverted their practice in order to continue it; while the practice reformed, it never died.

Curious to see the practice in action, I watched a documentary, called *Divine Horsemen,* which depicts Haitian Vodou in the '40s. I witnessed how the Vodou ceremony, through possession, brought divine forces directly into the body. Possession occurred when people drummed, danced, and performed specific rituals to call on deities to possess their spirits. Captured on this video was the spirit Chango, the god of fire, as he exuberantly took over a man's dancing. The man's entire body took on a circular movement, his feet stepped faster, his eyes rolled backward, and his face intensified as the spirit "rode his soul." The dancing man completely surrendered his body to the force, knowing the outcome was unpredictable. He trusted the ceremony, the priests, and the will of the gods.

Baptist, Spiritualist, and other Christian churches have milder variations of possession, moments where persons are "touched by the Holy Spirit," but I was inclined to discount the Christian experience as ritualized, vague, and even illegitimate, maybe because I'd never felt the Holy Spirit in my own Catholic experience. The Holy Spirit, as it had been presented to me, did not have a face. The African deities, on the other hand, portrayed specific characteristics of men and women. They understood human needs for money, protection from harm, and living or job arrangements. Perhaps they could help me more than could the Holy Spirit, a faceless force to whom I couldn't fathom explaining anything about my life, my family, my friends, my romance, or my job. The Vodou pantheon seemed to be a key instrument of survival that was missing from life.

Would Vodou work for me, with my preexisting instruments of survival—higher education, the capacity to work full-time and build a career, a secure home with a live-in boyfriend? Perhaps the gods' influence was not so strong for an individual like me. I had no history of prioritizing faith, and my culture separated religion from law. Tapping into the pantheon properly seemed reliant on my creating a space for the essential tools—the understanding of the rituals, the ceremonies, and the lwa. I still wondered who each of the lwa were, exactly, and knew if I were to have a relationship with Vodou, I needed to learn much more about them.

Each book I investigated listed seven main African powers, although numerous deities exist in the variety of Vodou pantheons from country to country. These seven powers remained constant in some form within each country's practice.

1. Ellegua is the god of the crossroads. He helps in indecision and brings one from the physical world to the spiritual world.

2. Obatala is the god of the mind, who helps maintain self-discipline and avoid greed and debilitating excesses.

3. Chango protects from cowardice, fire hazards, and watches over abandoned children.

4. Oya is the goddess of the winds, who assists in times of change and transformation.

5. Oshun is the goddess of beauty and plenty.

6. Ogun is the god of action and confrontation.

7. Yemaya is the goddess of the sea and hope.

I took to the description of Yemaya immediately. Her qualities of endless bounty, healing, and wealth were associated with the depths of the sea, the source of all earthly needs. The Catholic personage she hid behind was Mary, but I had a very different picture of the all-loving Blessed Mother than I did of Yemaya. Yemaya sounded assertive and alive, and in a primordial way, a provider of life. Mary was immaculate. Yemaya maintained contact with the aspects of life, death, and the beyond. Mary, as I had learned about her, deferred such power to her son. Yemaya seemed full of promise, Mary was untouchable. I thought on some level that if I asked Yemaya for something, she would hear me and help.

How could I bring her into my life? I wondered. A lwa was not a person, yet I found myself wanting to emulate Yemaya's qualities. My desire to associate with her physically, somehow, reminded me of the time when, on "dress-down" days, every freshman girl in my Catholic high school started dressing like Madonna. The hallway connecting the girls' school to the boys' school was jammed with thirteen-year-old bodies wrapped in white lace. They wore shirts that showed the belly and skirts slit to the thigh. This adolescent fashion mistake was not so much a movement to land a boyfriend as it was an expression of brimming sexual identity. To some extent, my desire to embody some aspect of Yemaya was similar. Spirituality is as private as is sexuality in mainstream culture, and as lacking in positive female role models. Not to bestow the title of "role model" onto Madonna with too much seriousness, but my search for female strength looked for an equivalent to Madonna's fearless expression of sexuality. Perhaps Yemaya was it.

Yemaya serendipitously appeared to me within a week, in a specialty gift shop that sold Haitian Vodou flags. I saw her portrait on a beaded flag sparkling from the wall where she hung. She floated as a silver and purple mermaid over a blue ocean; her head was huge; she had streaming gold hair and a smiling face. The purple, silver, blue, black, and white beads created a dazzling portrait, and though I couldn't afford the $1,000 flag, I tried to internalize the image by standing in front of it for a long time.

I took Yemaya into my consciousness and walked around for a few days trying to look at the world through her eyes, but I soon encountered a problem. In the back of my Catholic mind, the first commandment—"I am the Lord thy God, thou should have no other Gods before me"—evoked feelings of disloyalty. Though I'd been an inactive Catholic for years, the teachings remained a part of me. Technically, I wasn't supposed to want any other kind of connection to any deities, because they were all false. But alongside my sense of betrayal I felt a sting of resentment at this commandment. Its mere inflexibility as a *commandment* bothered me. In my early days of Catholic high school, in church history class, I'd asked whether I should apply that commandment to Jesus, and the answers were always the same:

"No dear, Moses brought those commandments from the Lord God *himself.* "

"Oh," I responded, "then why am I listening to what Jesus says, if there is only one God?"

"*Because* dear, Jesus *is* God."

But I thought there was only *one* Lord God, and I should have no others but him, I argued. I questioned this principle—that God was all three aspects: Father, Son, and Holy Spirit—at least once a week. I didn't understand the Catholic mystery, that Jesus was both an aspect of God and a person. I couldn't take the information at face value; I needed proof beyond the instructor's shallow explanation.

"See class, Jesus was the man-i-fest-a-tion of God on Earth. . . . That's why he died on the cross for us, and was resurrected, because he was the Son of God. . . and he did that for us. . . so that we could be saved too. . . and enter the kingdom of heaven. . . like the saints. . . ."

I'd heard it so many times. The doctrine echoed in my mind endlessly, but I still came up short: What I lost when I left Catholicism behind was not only a system of beliefs, but support for my floundering faith and a structure for its growth. Even with Wicca, shamanism, and yoga behind me, I *still* didn't feel like I had the right combination of support and structure. Vodou seemed to provide both. The mysterious gods with their open ears would hear my needs with intimate understanding. All I had to do was call, and learning to call them would provide me with a structure. It was perfect. I had prepared for Vodou intellectually about as much as I could. The time was ripe for practical experience.

○ ○ ○

Don't laugh, but I went online in search of Vodou, trusting in the safe distance of cyberspace. The Web was a perfect vehicle for a spiritual search, in that it provided barriers from too much intimacy too quickly. Why hadn't I thought of it before? I could have conferred with more witches, probably found some real shamans, maybe even corresponded with a few gurus—all in the anonymity that was my greatest protection.

Surfing the religion pages, I let my hand click the box "African Religions," in hope of discovering something sincere behind the electronic doorway—photographs of practitioners in action, an invitation to a ceremony, a Mambo (priestess) advertising her services. More choices appeared, none of which, pleasantly, resembled dead-end roads of horror-show hype. History, New Orleans, Home Practice, Chat. I went straight to the chat room. Confident in my ability to decipher the "real" from the "fake," I smirked as I clicked past an argument about reggae music and the similarities between Jamaican and Haitian culture. One of the arguers, a Mambo, accused the other of making anti-Haitian, anti-Vodou, and anti-woman remarks. I moved on quickly, not wanting to get involved in anything negative, real *or* fake. If there were hostile conversations surrounding Vodou, whether physical or cyber, I'd be wise to steer clear of the parties involved.

Somewhere in the morass of pages and postings, I glanced at an announcement for an upcoming ceremony, to be held in New York, devoted to Yemaya. The prospect of Yemaya's accessibility excited me. I mused for a few moments at how the Vodou gods had already infiltrated life on the Internet. Perhaps the secret-shrouded deities really were available to those who looked. I began to think that Vodou experience might not be so hard to access all.

Copying the contact e-mail address, I sent out word of my interest. The return note came within a few hours, enthusiastic at my prospective involvement. But one thing, the message said: Let's meet first. This gave me pause. Meet? Why did they want to meet first? The Wiccan magic shop didn't care who came to their ceremonies. It was every witch for herself. I wrote back, asking why. The anonymous organizer replied that they liked to screen everyone before admitting them to the group activities. After all, this was the Internet. There were a lot of freaks out there. Meeting first was a way to ensure everyone's good intentions. I sighed a sigh of relief. Of course. Good intentions.

A part of me couldn't help but wonder, though, if the position of a suspicious newcomer was the position I wanted to start from. In our correspondence, the anonymous organizer seemed incredibly helpful, recommending books I could read first, hinting at the kind of spiritual work they conducted at their gatherings (they included shamanic journeying—which told me they did not exclusively work with Vodou). But a protective quality saturated her responses. Each was directly tied to my questions—they never offered additional information about how many people were involved, how they conducted their meetings, what was their purpose. Suddenly I became suspicious, and when they asked me if I wanted to continue our conversation over the phone, I declined, not wanting to give out my phone number to folks who already didn't trust me. I did agree to meet, however, since Yemaya had prompted me to initiate this communication in the first place. She was the ever-giving, bountiful supplier of all one would ever need. Perhaps it was best not to look for hidden meanings, and just focus on the experience I sought.

The meeting took place on a Sunday, over brunch in an out-of-the-way diner in the Bronx. As soon as I walked in, I recognized the entire group immediately. They sat at a corner booth talking enigmatically, with active gestures and loud, attention-getting voices that clashed with the gentle murmur of coffee-drinking senior citizens. I drew two conclusions from this first impression: The first was that my interest as a white person in Vodou was not uncommon. They were all white. The second was that experiencing Vodou with other white people would not bring me to the source I sought. For a tradition as secretive and misunderstood as Vodou, nothing less than a family heritage would transmit the essence I understood as the nature behind Vodou. Of course, snap judgments like these are sometimes faulty, but I couldn't ignore this hunch.

I walked over and introduced myself, making a mental note for the future that meeting a spiritual group over the Internet was probably not a good idea. The method left too much room for error. Spiritual practice, I was learning, has so much to do with gut instinct, and technology, despite all its wonders, does not allow very well for gut instinct. How could I successfully gauge a group of people and their most personal, private practices from a computer screen? Looking at each of them, white women and a few men in their early thirties, they appeared as dislocated as I felt. I sat down and proceeded to get to know these people over the course of the next two hours, already knowing that I would not attend their ceremony for Yemaya. This was not how I wanted to enter into Vodou.

Though I had made my decision to say hello and leave quickly, enacting it took hours. I did not intend to spend the entire afternoon in conversation with complete strangers. Twenty-five minutes, enough time for a cup of coffee and a half-cup refill, was my original plan. But somehow, I felt that extricating myself might seem offensive to these people who had begun to tell me their stories. Each person spoke in circles, talking about their most personal memories of being persecuted as a child in grade school, or misunderstood by friends, abused by family or lovers. Time ran away with the situation, and I learned way too much. Nearly every person in the group had been stalked. Almost all of them had possessed firearms for protection at one time or another. I didn't know what to say, but I stayed longer, quietly sipping coffee, not wanting to offend or disrespect, but also wanting desperately to escape. At one point a man in the group said to me, "What's great about our group is that we really look out for each other. If something happens to one of us, it happens to all of us. That is to say, if one of us is in trouble in the middle of the night, we all get a phone call, and are expected to help. Okay?"

Okay, I thought. Time to leave. I said good-bye, thanked them, and told them I'd have to think about becoming more involved. They must have sensed my discomfort, because their parting words of advice were, "Don't let fear guide you."

Was it fear that kept me there or that made me leave? I'll admit to being a little skittish with these folks. But how else to feel when, at the first meeting, swapping stories about being stalked and resorting to weapons was the table talk? I could have told them about the cap gun I once had fired, my sole foray into the world of firearms, but we didn't seem to have too much else in common. I figured we probably weren't compatible spiritually, either.

I steered clear of aggressively seeking out Vodou people for a while. Not that I let this impression taint my hope to connect with Vodou in a positive way, but the experience made me aware of my own vulnerability. Since I was not Haitian and had no immediate cultural connection to this tradition, it would take longer to find my way of connecting. I was sure I'd find it, though.

People who have joined cults had previously provoked my criticism, but after this experience, I better understood the compulsion to connect with a cult's security and the promise of comfort that could get in the way of someone from keeping their own needs first in mind. For someone who wants to belong, wants a connection to a higher power so badly, a group of people committed to the same goal can offer many attractive hooks: a mission, a community of people, a structure. Cults have distinctive features. Usually they offer a set of ideas, values, and social structures that set a very clear barrier to other social liaisons outside of the group. Membership within a cult is restrictive. They proceed less on principle than on rules of thought, rules of behavior to others, rules of self-denial or indulgence. A spiritual group, on the other hand, determines membership by a personal and individual understanding of principles, usually of positive affection and love. Membership and growth within a spiritual group is not based on rules, like being available to help in a crisis no matter what. In a spiritual group, signs and badges of growth are internal, principles are so broad there is no determination of power, and ideas of reality are not based on personality, but the part of the being that lies behind personality.

Though the lines between cult and spiritual group *sound* clear, I could see how they might easily blur when a person wants to become a part of something larger than herself. I wouldn't say that I felt I was in the presence of a cult in the diner. I will say, however, that my initial impressions and growing discomfort were impossible to ignore. Discomfort and caution saved me, but in another situation, intrigue and hope might have played a larger role. The hunger for a spiritual path can be so strong that for the promise of being fed you can easily compromise what you seek.

After this experience, I had trouble imagining Vodou existing in a real place—one that I might visit without any kind of commitment from my end or suspicion from the other. I had read about the religion being anthropomorphized by its users, and I started entertaining the idea that this religion was avoiding me, its secrets reserved only for people born into it. Then, as I reconciled myself to the possibility of being rejected (yes, really!) by this practice, I remembered someone I used to temp with, who agreed to tell me her experiences.

○ ○ ○

Erika is a black woman who worked with me as a temp at a conservative Jewish organization. Tall, thin, with a striking face that brought your gaze from her eyes straight to her jawline, she repelled with a single look anyone who approached her with anything but respect. She completed her work quickly, had a gentle phone manner, and perfect nails, which were as long, thin, and manicured as she was. She was twenty-eight and was temping in between steadier jobs and her ambitions to act, model, and travel. We bonded over being "in between." Rather than giving in to the insecurity of professional displacement, she mentioned offhandedly that temping served her "larger purpose." Fairly certain she was alluding to something divine, I asked what she meant. "I was not put on this Earth to temp," she said. This comment tipped me off that she was open to talking about spirituality.

Spending eight hours a day around Judaism did not seem to conflict with her own beliefs, a combination of West Indian Vodou, which incorporates the Catholic aspect of God, and Al Islam. The theologies may have clashed in semantics, but Erika did not feel divided in practice. She spent her early years with her grandmother and aunt in New Orleans, who exposed her to Catholic education and a home practice of Caribbean Vodou. During the 1970s, Erika's stepmother took over her care as a teen in Washington D.C., where she lived and participated in the community of the Fourth Temple of the Nation of Islam. "I'm a walking contradiction," she said honestly, smiling at her split spiritual identity. When we met, Erika was saving money for a three-month trip she planned to take at the end of February to Saint Thomas, her favorite of the Virgin Islands. February marks *Carnival* in the Caribbean, when old island traditions of magic combine with Catholic feast days into public parades and celebrations. There, during the weeks of celebration when gods and spiritual worship are on the minds and lips of everyone, Erika feels as if she's "gone home."

I was eager to talk to Erika about her connection to and practice of Caribbean Vodou, particularly because she lived with two religions. If she could reconcile Catholic and Vodou practices with Islamic theories, then maybe I could extend my assortment of spiritual experiences to embrace Vodou as well.

Her Islamic beliefs, she said, did not prevent her from using Caribbean Vodou. The family system of magic belonged to her personally, and was at her access at all times. Caribbean Vodou was independent of religion, as she described it, almost a tool for maintaining control over her personal affairs. Although her knowledge of it was far from thorough, Erika felt free to use what she knew of Vodou when she needed help getting out of an unwanted living situation last year. She had had an aggressive Panamanian roommate whom she did not trust. Part of Erika's reason for resorting to Vodou was that she thought her roommate was using Panamanian Vodou against her.

Erika admits that she could find no visible reason to mistrust her roommate, but she was sensitive to psychic tension and sensed something was amiss. So uncomfortable was she with the living arrangement that Erika asked the roommate to leave several times. The roommate would not go.

Erika consulted a Romanian card reader, about whom she said, "This Romanian woman has gypsy blood and is very up on folklore. She did a general reading for me and said my roommate kept popping up in every single aspect of my life." Erika saw in the cards confirmation of her feelings that her roommate's negativity was harmful. "We concluded that she wanted my life, my bed, and my finances. She was too much of a negative, coveting factor in my life, and I did not want to take a chance." Convinced that the card reading conveyed the truth, Erika agreed with the card reader that she would have to force her roommate out with a housecleaning.

A housecleaning is a process of scouring the house with hot water and a particular recipe of herbs or other ingredients in order to work a spell. Housecleaning was not a completely foreign idea to her. Erika remembers from her childhood the experience of working a spell by deliberately manipulating a physical space or object.

"My stepmother is a feeler. She feels a lot of things, and she sees a lot of things." By things, Erika meant forces that are not ordinarily visible. "Once when I was about six, she got into a really big argument with a coworker of hers. She came home and took my crayons. She drew a face of the coworker in black ink. And then she took my red crayon and started dotting the face. And she lit candles. She gave me a crayon and said, 'Help.' We held hands, she lit the candle, and then she said something. And I started to dot the face with her. Simultaneously, this person was out to dinner with another coworker of my stepmom's, who reported the next day that the woman broke out in hives in the middle of the meal." Erika's memory of this spell remained with her as an example of how to solve problems.

Since the childhood experience, Erika had learned a bit more about Vodou. She knew the lwa were protectors of the people, benevolent and loving unless required to defend their devotee. In the case of her roommate, Erika felt it necessary to resort to their protection but wanted to justify her actions. Taking action against another person with Vodou, she knew, was a serious act of aggression.

"I'm not a suspicious person, I'm not a cowardly person, but I do believe there are things I don't know about," she said firmly. Quelling the fear that her roommate had ill intent and well-developed Vodou skills, Erika set her mind to respond with only enough force to drive her roommate away, not to harm her.

There were several steps to a housecleaning, Erika learned. Advisers told her to first go to a West Indian herbal store, not uncommon in Brooklyn, and buy some sage. They told her to pile it high in an ashtray, light it, and walk around the house, into every room, along each wall to the corner of the room. Then walk down the stairs, take it all the way out of the house, and dump it in the street. This procedure would rid the atmosphere of any lingering negativity, and was known as "smudging," the same as in witchcraft and shamanism.

Erika's course of action altered when the store she visited had no sage to sell her. "I asked the woman, 'What's the next best thing—I have to clean my house.' She knew exactly what I was talking about." The storekeeper gave Erika a small six-ounce glass jar that looked as though it was filled with potpourri. The label on it read "Chango." Chango, the god of thunder, lightning, and fire, is known for courage, vigor, and physical strength.

"She told me to add Chango to a gallon of boiling water and clean my house. I asked, 'How exactly, should I clean it?' She said, 'Just clean it. Clean your walls, mop your floors.' Mind you, I have a three-level, two-bedroom house. So you know what I was doing all day on Martin Luther King Day."

To ensure the power of Chango in her home, Erika also bought a Chango candle. It was a reversing candle, meaning whatever psychic attack the assailant launches, lighting the candle and letting it burn will reverse the attack. Reversing the attack with a Chango candle additionally delivers Erika's courage, vigor, lightning, and fire to disrupt the roommate's efforts. "I lit that candle on a Saturday, and it burned and burned for days. The next Saturday, at about 1 o'clock in the afternoon, it had burned itself out. Shortly after it went out, my way started coming through. [My roommate] started saying things like, 'I'm moving everything out,' and now, finally, she's gone."

While she says she doesn't totally believe the force of the candle and the housecleaning drove her roommate away, Erika would like to believe it helped a little bit. "That's even hard for me to admit, since so much of my past was rooted in Al Islam. But my ancestry is West Indian, and my mother was South American. It's in my blood to believe it."

The fact that West Indian belief systems were lodged somewhere in her personal armory gave Erika the confidence that she could combat the psychic warfare in her home successfully. It was her belief that she could only fight fire with fire, and fortunately, she fostered enough of a personal connection with spirits of protection to do so. Erika's story, coupled with my meeting with the Yemaya group, made me wonder even more just why it was that I sought Vodou. So far people I met were using it for protection. Did I have a secret desire to be able to protect myself spiritually?

Actually, the desire wasn't so secret. Walking around with all of this spiritual hope and desire to find an ongoing connection left me wide open for negative attacks. Nothing horrible had happened—not yet—but I realized my interactions with stressed coworkers, melancholy friends, and the demands of living in an urban center required strength and attention all the time. Not only was my environment barren of spiritual breeding, but living with my mind open to spirituality at all times could actually weaken me, leaving me without defense mechanisms to ward off negative factors in life. I still wanted to develop and pursue a dialogue with my higher self, but I also needed to find a way to fight negative energy when it came along. How would I learn to ward it off without inflicting harm?

○　○　○

A priestess could help me cultivate the power to fight negativity without harming others. From reading Mama Lola's biography, I learned that a priestess is a bit of a community psychologist and personal motivator: the welfare of the client is in her hands. Clients come to a priestess' home for help with problems with love, money, family dysfunction, disease, psychological ailments, and even reversing curses. Clients either pay a fee for these services or barter something the priestess needs, like food or a household item or a favor. A priestess provides help by consulting the lwa, to whom she has direct and intimate access. The trust clients have in the priestess depends on their own belief that Vodou, the greater power, will see justice done, no matter what.

A priestess has direct access to the lwa because it is her livelihood to cultivate a relationship with them. A priestess ideally has enough familiarity with the deities to call on them at will. Often she uses the client's ancestral spirits to obtain results for them, and uses her own ancestral spirits to connect herself. Taking responsibility for guiding the client and using good judgment is part of the priestess' initiation vows. Since there is no "devil" in Vodou, deities might lend justification to anyone to do anything. Still, a priestess' main responsibility is to serve both the client and the gods to the best of her ability. When questioned in an interview about the line between white and black magic, Mama Lola would not reveal just where she drew it but said, "Black magic is not bad, its just stronger than white magic."

I liked the idea of consulting a female authority, a Mambo, who would see me as another woman seeking spiritual solace. She would relate to my various wants and needs, woman to woman. Perhaps she would even provide insight on how to reel in my wandering spiritual desire. At least she might offer a clear version of Vodou for my consideration. What's more, consulting a bonafide authority would eliminate the possibility that I would be spiritually derailed by someone else's agenda. Shunning the Internet, I looked to New Orleans.

New Orleans, known for its tourism around Vodou—shops, trinkets, and lots of stories of Marie Laveau, the famous Vodou queen—provided me with a resource. I scheduled a trip to New Orleans to attend the Jazz Festival, but with a second agenda of hooking up with a priestess. I made several phone calls to the major universities asking for the African Studies departments, and was ultimately led to a Catholic nun who taught African spirituality in literature. A nun, of all people. Could this be a joke? Divine humor intervening in my self-absorbed search? I phoned her, nevertheless, and tried to explain my interest. She listened, gauging the extent of my knowledge. "You need to read," she said. I told her I had read a few books, that I had as decent an understanding as one could get from a book. She paused again for a moment. "Well then, you need to look at Vodou from the perspective of the ancestors."

"What do you mean by ancestors?" I asked. I was thinking she meant particular ancestors appropriate for Vodou devotees to contact, not my own Catholic ones.

Her response sounded as if she was suddenly in a hurry. "If you understand the ancestors, you understand Vodou," she told me. "Oh," I said. She said that I should think about that, and what it could mean, and when I came to New Orleans, I could come and see her and we could talk more about it.

The second person referred to me was a practicing Vodou priestess, Ava Kay Jones, one of the city's authorities on Vodou. She was incredibly busy, I was told, and frequently out of town giving lectures, but she did see clients, and she was the "real thing." I phoned her many times before finally getting a call back from an assistant. I made an appointment to see her, asking for a session, whatever that was.

When I arrived in New Orleans, I went to see the nun first. She invited me to her office at the university. A large, black woman with a warm smile, she was dressed impeccably in a habit and emanated the grace of one who has chosen God out of personal mission. Her appearance and demeanor changed my image of the pale-skinned, shut-down nun who had seemed so impersonal more than ten years ago. Perhaps the difference was merely that I was older now. However, when she looked up and immediately extended her hand, as though to an old friend, I knew my maturity was not the only difference.

Her grip was surprisingly gentle. She had a loud, raspy voice that flowed with ease as she asked me to sit. She joined me, and we looked at each other across the desk. She began to laugh.

"I just want to know," she said, catching her breath, "*what* a young, conservative Catholic white girl from New York is doing here in my office asking me about Vodou?" She started laughing again.

I was dumbstruck. She continued, roaring. "I mean, *what* did your parents think when you told them you were going to New Orleans to see a black nun to talk about Vodou?"

My parents? I thought it was funny that she thought I'd tell my parents of my activities. I was twenty-six years old. But then, remembering my former model, nuns expect young people to have good communication with their parents. It was the "Honor thy father and mother" commandment. Of course I honored my parents. I just didn't tell them about this particular interest.

But she had a point. It was kind of funny. What *was* I doing there in her office? Looking for truth, looking for authenticity. I told her I was looking for real, live young women who were happy with their religions, who did not feel alienated from their practices, who felt like they had personal connections to their own paths, and I had a suspicion that women who practiced Vodou felt that way.

She stopped laughing and listened to me, nodding. "A lot of young Catholic women do not know how to connect to the Lord. In the African religions, as I told you, we work through the saints and the ancestors. All of us have connection to our own deceased in our family. The lwa are aspects of the divine, and we are connected to them through our own deceased, who connect us to the beyond."

So she did mean my personal ancestors. I thought about my Irish Catholic grandmother and how I felt connected to her. If I reached for her memory, would I be able to resuscitate her qualities of patience, honor, and strength? I didn't know. I told the nun that I had an ancestor I felt close to, leaving out that she was a white Irish Catholic lady, though my underlying question was, Does it matter if I'm not of African descent? Without identifying my doubts, she seemed to know I was speaking from the heart.

"We believe that the ancestors watch over us and protect us, act as intermediaries," she explained. "If we remain in connection with them, we have a connection to God."

"What about the saints?" I asked her. After all, this was a nun I was talking to. The saints must play a role in her vision of Vodou, especially since she devoted her life to Catholic practices.

"The saints are the faces of the lwa, to the Africans. Do you know the saints well?"

I told her I didn't, and she looked slightly disappointed.

"Didn't you go to Catholic school?" she asked.

I told her I dropped out. She made a small noise, as though she was beginning to see the particular complexity of my quest. "Well, if you study the saints, you'll understand what aspects the lwa represent. The saints are aspects of the lwa; the two are interchangeable. Our ancestors are intermediaries between them and us. You'll understand better as you begin to figure out your own connections."

A nun advising a Catholic expatriate to go and find her own way was unusual. But to admit that no matter how you slice it, God is the same regardless of the names was truly unprecedented in my experience with Catholicism. Her lack of distinction rolled out a new kind of welcome mat. Up until now, I'd been thinking I had to find the correct religion, one that felt more promising to me as a woman, in order to enter a pathway of spiritual growth. Each new religion became exclusive in my eyes, exceptional from previous traditions I'd explored as if no continuity linked one to the next, no common history associated the practices, understandings, and wisdom. Yet here I stood, back at Catholicism's doorstep, facing a nun who felt comfortable with both traditions, telling me it didn't matter which way I went, finding my own route was what mattered.

I wanted her to address the lack of positive female identity within Catholicism. I could not reconcile it even as I looked into the eyes of a strong Catholic woman. With African spirituality on her side, she had two aspects of God with which to identify. With distant Catholic role models and a pocketful of random experiences from alternative spiritual traditions, I had bitterness. Did it show? I asked if she had advice for any young women seeking truth, connection, and contentment with God that honored their feminine aspects of divinity. She smiled.

"I have some books for you," she said. "But you'll have to come with me to my house to get them." Warmth rushed through me; I was elated to be helped by a nun. I drove with her to the convent.

We drove through the backroads of New Orleans past worn, wooden homes that were warped by heat and humidity. We crossed a bayou, and pulled into a parking lot behind a large red building that looked like a former schoolhouse. Several other elderly black nuns stood outside on the porch. A few sat in lawn chairs, but most of the others carefully made their way down the steps. They each wore plastic rain kerchiefs around their heads. They were on their way crayfishing.

"It's 4 o'clock—looks like the sisters are going to try to beat the rain and go fishing," sister laughed, parking and getting out of the car quickly. All of her movements were quick and direct. We walked up the steps toward the nuns, who carried buckets and nets. She introduced me to each of the sisters and they all nodded, smiled, looking me in the eye. Discomfort with facing an army of old, Southern black nuns on their way fishing reinforced to me that I was out of place. I felt awkward.

The nuns diffused the tension. "Coming along?" one invited.

For a moment I considered accompanying them, because fishing with these nuns might actually teach me a thing or two about spirituality. I couldn't accept, however. Thankfully, Sister declined, saying we had plans. They went on their way, since rain was expected and the crayfishing hour was passing.

At the top of the stairs Sister introduced me to the Mother Superior. Thin and frail, she stood holding on to a post for balance. I put out my hand to shake, but she didn't respond, I concluded, because she was blind. "Mother, Suzanne would like to shake hands," Sister said. Letting go of the post, she grabbed my hand with both of hers, holding me for a moment while looking beyond me. She nodded her head and smiled, reading as much about my intent from the touch of my hand than vision would have permitted. I knew she knew I had come seeking something. By her touch, I knew she thought it was okay. Leaving Mother Superior on the porch, we entered the convent.

Inside Sister offered me an apple. As I crunched it, we walked through the expansive foyer, kept immaculately clean as though expectant of guests. On the far side of the house, she turned on the light in a small room that looked like it hadn't seen a visitor in several years. "In here is the history of our order of nuns. Feel free to look while I go find you those books."

She left me alone to browse. China cabinets contained honors and documents praising various nuns for their good works. Opaque, nylon curtains draped the windows, allowing only a crack of light to illuminate the wall of photographs. The photographs had names of women who had been nuns in this order since the late nineteenth century. Some of their faces were serious and thoughtful, others glee-filled. Most were black. A sense of heritage in my gender flooded through me. Even though I was barely Catholic and far from black, I still felt connected to these holy women.

One woman's photo from the mid-1800s was faded slightly. Upon closer examination, I saw that her skin was much lighter than the other nuns'. Sister returned, noticing my scrutiny. "That was Henriette Laveau," she said. I looked at her with surprise. Did she mean a relative of Marie Laveau, the famous Vodou queen?

She nodded, "And her skin wasn't much darker than yours." I wanted to know more, the connection between Henriette and Marie, the connection between Catholic practice there at the convent, and Vodou that was obviously within their knowledge and history. But Sister was not forthcoming about the information, and I didn't want to pry. African spirituality was obviously close to her heart. She, and perhaps the other sisters, did not experience conflict wearing a habit and practicing Catholic tradition.

She smiled and handed me a purple book called *Jambalaya,* by Luisah Teish. "This," she said, "will tell you about African spirituality. A lot of the questions you have about practice will be answered in there. After you read it, if you want to know more," she looked me in the eye now, "you can come back. You can come back and even stay with me, anytime."

I took her words as a kind of assignment, to go home, read the book, ponder my own connections and bring my thoughtful questions back to her. We left the convent and drove back to the place where I was staying. She seemed very open to my questions now. I asked how she became a nun. She laughed and told me her story. She grew up in rural Louisiana, where her mother was what's known as "a treater," or a community healer. People came to see her when they weren't well, and her mother helped them. Sister didn't tell me how. But her memories of her mother as one who healed were positive. "My mother worked with God through the ancestors. I knew from a young age I wanted to serve God. But I wanted to do it in a way that the world saw as legitimate." She opted for Catholicism, already a staple. I realized Sister truly knew the meaning of New Orleans Vodou and wanted to share its beauty in spirit any way that she could.

When she dropped me off, she gave me a last bit of advice. "Honor yourself as you find your own path," she said. I took her words to mean that I should take my time, figure out what it was that I truly sought, and examine my soul. I thanked her, not mentioning how weary I grew of looking.

"You *will* find it," she proclaimed. "I know, as sure as you are getting out of my car, after coming all the way from New York to talk about the African deities, that you will find it."

I could practically hear her laughing as she drove away.

The fact that a nun had actually condoned my personal exploration encouraged me. Rather than feeling sucked back in to the tradition from which I came, her words felt like approval from the Catholicism I had abandoned. Not that I needed approval.

○ ○ ○

The priestess Ava Kay Jones was my next stop, and I looked forward to deepening the dimension Sister gave me. Perhaps Ava Kay would show me exactly *how* to nurture my relationship with my ancestors, to call the deities, maybe even understand the saints. Not to discount Sister's good advice about confronting my needs on my own, but I thought I still needed an intermediary. Ava Kay might show me how to make my needs known to the pantheon. Really *do* it the *right* way. Make it all stick.

Worry crept in, though. What if Ava Kay couldn't show me how to contact the lwa for myself? What if contacting the lwa was unteachable, something I had to automatically know as a result of culture or upbringing? I imagined a priestess of Vodou, like any spiritual guide, would usher me toward divine contact if she gauged me spiritually prepared. But what if she judged me as miles from preparation, if I had come all this way in search of an authentic gateway only to find that the gates were shut? Worse, what if the gates were open, but she was protective of her knowledge and of the tradition? I'd feel rejected, cast out, undeserving, and worse, foolish. I thought about the biblical promise, "Seek and ye shall find." Although all religious proverbs encourage the individual to follow God, none seem to talk about the pain and fear of rejection involved. Here I was seeking, hoping to find in the face of so many forces that could deny me.

I didn't know what to expect when I rang the doorbell of Ava Kay's orange house. I hoped she wouldn't see me and laugh like the sister had. She answered the door dressed in loose white clothing, a cloth expertly positioned on her head, symbolizing her priestess status. She looked me in the eye and held a straight face. Greeting me heartily and guiding me into her home, I decided that she must be the friendliest Vodou priestess one could ever meet. Excusing the boxes and bags piled neatly around the main room, she offered me a chair, one of a few pieces of disarranged furniture. I liked that she was unconcerned with showing herself as she was—in transition from a move. She disappeared into the kitchen to get me a glass of water and to talk to one of her assistants, a tall handsome man, about the packages that needed to be brought to the post office. She was a priestess, and she was a businesswoman.

My concern about access to the lwa subsided once inside. Her presence, and my sitting in it, reinforced the truth of this scenario: she agreed to see me as a client, she would do for me what she could. If it was within her power to help me, to teach me, her word and reputation would ensure that she do so. A large area on the floor behind the front door was clear of boxes and clutter, but for a small colorful carpet, a few candles, a carved coconut bowl, a bottle of rum, a crooked stick. It was an altar. Vodou altars usually honor one lwa at a time; I thought this one might be to Legba. Legba, or Ellegua, the god of the crossroads, monitored the doorway to the spiritual world and therefore must be called on first before calling on any of the other gods. His was the most common altar in a home; he monitored getting through the doorway. Calling to Legba was a bit like making the sign of the cross before praying in Catholic Church. The Mass never began and never ended without it.

Ava Kay's combination of home and workplace merged gracefully. I felt welcomed as an outsider. Books piled high in the corner where they didn't fit into the shelf, the relaxing scent of coconut oil, and the air conditioner blowing at a low cool created an atmosphere of thoughtful meditation that anyone would appreciate, no matter what their level of spiritual accomplishment. Across a small desk in the corner, yellow packages stuffed full of materials awaited a trip to the post office. Walls were spare, left until the time when the perfect decoration might be hung. Ava didn't appear to have a lot of time for those things. Her life was a full schedule of speaking engagements, dance performances, spots on the Discovery channel, and panel discussions on the modern state of Vodou.

But she had a huge amount of time for clients. She sat with me at a large desk piled with books and papers, and engaged me in pleasant conversation. She was trying to get to know me, get an idea of my life in New York my friends and family. Slowly through conversation she drew me out, to the point where I had to put my issues on the table. I told her about my work life; she sensed correctly how the stress took its toll. I told her about the consistency of my relationship, and she nodded, acknowledging how important it was to have a good man around. I dodged telling her about my spiritual displacement, however. Exposing my panic attacks, the black hole feeling, and the inability to feel grounded despite the structures of my life would make me too vulnerable. I wanted answers, to know how these feelings could exist when the rest of life seemed status quo, but embarrassment prevented me from asking.

"So what can I do for you?" she finally asked. My mind raced through the Vodou flashcards: Did I need a spell? An entire ceremony? I had no idea how Vodou would help me connect to a higher self or provide an antidote to my despair. From afar, I'd thought its animation would infuse me. Sitting here with a priestess, however, I grew increasingly aware of my inner limpness. I asked for a reading regarding my work issues, since we had not discussed any spiritual material yet. If it was true that spiritual life encompassed the whole self, the focus of the reading did not matter: spiritual clues to my wants and needs would surface.

Ava Kay arranged herself in her seat, and informed me that she used the Tarot deck as a tool to interpret larger themes in people's lives. She shuffled the deck, and began speaking quietly, whispering names, some of which I recognized: Legba, Ogun, Oya, Chango, Obatala. She was calling the spirits to assist her in the interpretation of my cards. Not only were the lwa invited, but she asked for assistance from the saints, Jesus Christ, my ancestors, and then repeated my full name, first, middle, last. With a look of honor and intensity, as though nothing else was on her mind, she called to every deity and spirit known in Vodou, important personages in Catholicism, and my personal ancestry. So this is how to ask for guidance, I thought. Open one door and invite every positive force in while asking for their guidance. The sensation of being cared for, by Ava Kay and what she knew, the lwa she had connections to, and the security that she had in their power to help me, lifted me out of the tortured helpless feeling I had come to know so well.

The cards I expected to see when she turned over the Tarot deck—goddesses in various poses symbolizing virtues and vitality—did not appear. One by one, she turned over pictures I could not identify. On top of the arrangement, a card showing a person bound and gagged, tied to a tree, surrounded by swords, completely alone, stood menacingly. Oh my God, I thought. That's me. Ava Kay sat for a moment not saying anything.

"The good news," she began, "is that no one else is binding this character." I waited for her to explain more. "But it speaks of prison of self—temporary prison of self," she corrected, and looked at me. "You lack the confidence to make a change, the mental baggage that you're carrying is akin to fear."

I was bound by my own perception of spirituality. She said nothing of career, but it didn't matter. This was the root of all of my problems. The reasons repeated in my head again and again. It all made sense. But what was I afraid of? Being manipulated? Disappointed? Betrayed by religion? Probably. It had happened once when I was a teen, why wouldn't it happen again?

She read on. "You are trying to stave off competition and doubt. This is a card," she pointed to a set of scales, "that says you are trying to balance too many things at once—you are in a juggling act. Duality. You seek the balance, but you must first learn *how* to balance."

Yes, I thought urgently, I must learn how. "How do I learn how?" I asked. She nodded sagely, and turned over another card.

"Deal with the Goddess within yourself," she replied, indicating its message.

Words escaped me. Wasn't I dealing with the Goddess within? Isn't that what this whole journey was about? In Ava Kay's presence, with my cards on the table, I knew the answers to my own queries. I was looking, certainly, but I wasn't looking within.

Ava Kay had told me in our conversation that she was a priestess of Oya, the goddess of the winds of change. As she gave me her interpretation, I felt her intensity build up. "These readings are not to freak you out," she comforted, stacking the cards up again. "I know, just from talking to you, that you are going to undo this binding." Her words transmitted a power I could feel myself absorbing, like a dry sponge in need of moisture. It was as though Oya herself had come to bring us the message.

I asked her to suggest methods of change that would help me unbind myself. I wanted to end the duality, untie the ropes, and move forward. Now that she spoke of freedom from doubt and ongoing guidance, I wanted the tools.

"You've got to cultivate security," she answered simply. "You've got to do it yourself. Each day, every day. You were raised Catholic? Here's what you do. You repeat Psalm 23, 'The lord is my shepherd, and I shall not want' . . . and you mean it." She looked me in the eye to see if I understood how much I should mean it. "Say it with purpose, with meaning, and ask for it to be true. You say that in times of great need, *and* in times of peace.

"When you don't know, when you're at a loss for what to do, something else you can say that my own reverend gave me is, 'I am one with the clear, unclouded mind of Jesus Christ. I think clearly and I act wisely.'

At the end of our conversation, she made a potion for me—a potion for, among other things, protection and "uncrossing," so that I could uncross the hex I had on myself. On a pink instructional sheet she gave me, the power of thinking and praying was described as it works in Vodou. The more you mean it, the more results you will see. The most important process, after anointing myself with the potion. was the repetition of Psalm 23: The lord is my shepherd, I shall not want. . . .

○   ○   ○

That was as close as I came to Vodou.

More than with any of the other spiritual systems I examined, with Vodou, I had ended up back on my Catholic doorstep. How did it feel? Not like relief, like I had come home after a long trip, or as Dorothy explains in *The Wizard of Oz,* "I learned that if I can't find what I'm looking for in my own backyard, maybe I never really lost it to begin with." I felt grateful, in a way, that Ava

Kay had actually given me a tool. Something to hold, a charm for my mind. I trusted that it would work for me, not because it was Catholic, and not because it was Vodou-affiliated, even though it wasn't the Vodou I had anticipated. I trusted it would work because I trusted Ava Kay. I looked into her eyes, saw her wisdom, heard her words, and believed that she knew how to move the spirit. She knew how it moved, what made it stop, and what made it go.

I had to face it. Race and culture separated me from the Vodou fantasy. Enjoying connection to the lwa and the rich Vodou mythology was possible, but clearly the feeling of connection to my ancestors and any pantheon of spirits beyond would have to come from me; I couldn't expect a tradition to provide me with the actual contact. I took the advice from the priestess and the nun, and set myself in the direction of cultivating my own direct line.

CHAPTER FIVE

Sufi Living

Sufism is an ancient school of divine wisdom. In the West, Sufism is best known in its Middle Eastern form, as the mystical aspect of the Islamic religion. However, Sufism predates Islam and has existed in different names and forms for thousands of years. *Sufism Reoriented* is a contemporary, American form of this ancient school of wisdom, refashioned by an Indian spiritual teacher called Meher Baba. Meher Baba renewed the core spiritual principles of Sufism in ways that harmonize with contemporary American life and allow for intimate, individual pursuit. Sufism Reoriented assumes that divinity is present in everyone's inner core, and can be awakened and actualized through a life of love and service under the guidance of an illumined teacher.

Sufi teachings were first brought to America by Hazrat Inayat Khan in 1910. He handed his teachings to a Western disciple, a woman named Rabia Martin in 1927. Eventually she handed her Sufi group over to Meher Baba, an Indian spiritual teacher. The Sufism Reoriented community is small—500–600 people are actively associated—in the United States, but there are about 5,000 people who are "lovers," as they call themselves, of Meher Baba.

Sufism Reoriented students believe that Meher Baba is the *Avatar* or incarnation of God on Earth (also the World Teacher or Messiah) and are devoted to him and to his principles. The student is inspired to pursue an individual relationship with the *Murshid* or teacher who directs Sufism Reoriented. A school-like structure of classes and workshops and a shared path of spiritual learning in the form of cooperative living and shared work projects engage the student. Most individuals are expected to lead active, productive lives in the everyday world as part of their participation in Sufism. They aspire to unite with God (self) through love and service to his creation.

The word *Sufi,* if familiar at all, may conjure up vaguely Middle Eastern associations of "whirling dervishes," wailing Pakistani singers, and mysterious monasteries in the mountains of Afghanistan. But, as I came to know, Sufism could be almost anything. One academic told me Sufism is like water: It can take the shape of any container, but it does not become the container. Just as water, according to the conditions around it, can exist as frozen ice, as flowing stream, or as vapor, and still be water in essence, Sufism is adaptable. Some forms of Sufism are crystallized and rigidly disciplined; other forms are elusive, like vapor; and others are always flowing and changing, like a river on its way to the sea.

Sufism's mystical nature has kept its essence shrouded behind poetry, art, and musical traditions for centuries. Unlike my investigation of yoga, in which visible, accessible students practiced in studios, or Vodou, its tradition ensconced in New Orleans culture, Sufism was well hidden in daily American culture. In fact, such mystery may have carried it from one form to another throughout time.

The word *Sufi* has had different meanings in different languages and cultures. In ancient Greece, it meant "wisdom" *(Sophia),* and it was taught by Pythagoras, Socrates, and Plato as the love of wisdom *(philo-sophy).* In the Middle East, *Sufi* was connected to the word for "purity" *(safa);* the "Brothers of Purity" were among the

Essenes, a Jewish spiritual community at the time of Jesus. With the coming of the prophet Mohammed, *Sufi* became identified with the Arabic word for "wool" *(soof),* because of the woolen cloaks worn by Sufi travelers, who adopted their ancient teachings to Muslim styles of worship. Even though Sufism continually adapted itself to cultural influences, the essence of Sufi belief remained intact.

Sufis say that God can be known directly, not as a remote, impersonal Force, but as the intimate essence of love at the core of our being, our True Self. Sufis say that the purpose of life is to know God, to rejoice in God, to become God. The Sufi path is through the heart. Sufis celebrate and serve the beauty of God's world, and by doing so ignite the flames of ecstatic love for God that melt the boundaries of the individual ego or personality. "Sufism" is the process of embracing love's transforming flame; the Sufi is a drop, joyously dissolving into love's ocean.

Despite an exotic Middle Eastern history that I thought had sequestered Sufism, I found a new form of Sufism percolating in everyday American culture. It was small and personal, without a public front for me to easily access and understand. Yet because I had begun using prayer to find a personal connection with the larger universe, my spiritual intellect stirred when I first learned of its teachings.

I knew nothing about Sufism until one of my more outrageous friends gave me a typically off-the-wall birthday present: a CD of the Muslim Sufi singer, Nusrat Fateh Ali Khan. I wasn't sure what to expect of the music judging from the CD's curious design: a deep-focus, full-color photograph of a rose in bloom, glistening with dewdrops and anatomical accuracy. The flower's exotic exuberance almost embarrassed me, as though the photographer had peeked in on some private, nearly sexual moment of the rose. At the same time, the image evoked a deep sense of beauty. These dual impressions of beauty and voyeurism hindered my usual ability to anticipate the music. Though I hoped to hear a funky, Peter Gabriel-sponsored artist from another culture, I was less than enthusiastic as I popped the disc into the player. A new-age Yanni type was more typical of the cover.

The Sufi vocalist sang up and down the musical scale, hitting every discordant note on the way to touching the familiar and pleasing ones. Sometimes the singing lapsed rhythmically into chants, replicating a weightless man ascending to higher planes of existence. The melody embraced me: the CD was one of my friend's better choices.

Inspired by the music's Sufi nativity, I ran to my local spirituality bookstore and picked up a magazine entitled *Sufi*. Its appealing, flaming red cover was adorned with a gold image of divine figures sitting in lotus positions and floating through space. The cover implied that Sufis live on another plane, perhaps even another planet. After listening to the ethereal sound of the music, I was almost ready to believe it.

Nusrat Ali Khan's style of singing, I learned from reading an interview in the magazine, was known as a special *Qawwali* tradition of singing. Qawwali is an impassioned, improvised, highly personal form of devotional music of intense longing and love for God. Khan's talent was believed to be a manifestation of divinity moving through him in the form of song. In the interview, Khan himself humbly attributed all of his talent to Allah, the Muslim name for God. His messages of love and unity, his own popularity, wealth, and renown, were all gifts from divinity, he said. As I flipped through the mag, I found myself unusually excited by Khan's devotion to the tradition and his description of personal contact with God. The musicians I knew did not talk about their musical connections to God. The bravery that Khan and apparently other Qawwali singers demonstrated by attributing their talent to a power beyond their own egos was unfamiliarly sexy. Like the sexiness of the rose on the cover of the CD, Khan's singing heralded another standard of beauty. I was drawn to it, this beauty that surpassed body image, youth culture, moral boundaries of promiscuity. It was a beauty that beckoned life.

Before I heard the Nusrat Fateh Ali Khan album, the word *Muslim* if anything evoked both intrigue and caution in me. Intrigue mounted the first time I passed a mosque on the Lower East Side. A deafening bell clamored, followed by droning prayer in Arabic shouted by Muslim men dressed in long robes and small square colorful hats. They fell to their knees. Since I had been uttering Psalm 23, awakening further to prayer, I saw this strict devotion as an acceptable, almost beautiful route to divinity. Opening to prayer each day to receive divinity, just as the rose on the CD bloomed widely beckoning beauty, cast spiritual people in an ultra-human category. Praying people had the habit of devotion, like schools of fish circling into a cone at dusk or geese flying south in a V. Was prayer and devotion an instinct? Seeing it in action, after a while, had a seductive effect on me.

Maybe because I was a woman or a Catholic expatriate, or both, I was wary of the seduction. I never saw any women at these prayer interludes, a fact that stirred my sense of caution like fur bristling on my back. Most news I read of Islamic culture reported alarming oppression of women. I received the same e-mail several times on the Taliban in Pakistan. It described how a mob of Muslim men beat a woman in the street for accidentally showing the bare skin of her arm while driving. An aberration on instinct, for certain. Like the witch burnings in Europe during the Inquisition, such oppression, whether fact or propaganda, punished offenders of the "laws of God." Laws of God gone madly awry. Since I did not share in gender or belief with the said oppressors, a tingle of confusion shimmied up my spine while walking past the men outside the mosques. Were these men capable of such oppression too, even though their devotion was so beautiful from the outside?

Devotion was a continuous thread through Sufism. The *Sufi* articles used terms like "awakened heart" and "the music of the heart," and other very passionate-sounding phrases. They described the famous "whirling dervishes" of Turkey, who use music and dance to spin themselves into ecstasy. The dancing dervishes of Turkey were originally a Sufi school founded by the great poet and teacher Rumi in the 1200s (the word *dervish* refers to a monk or member of a spiritual school). Their hypnotic, spinning movements are said to put the dancers in harmony with the celestial spheres and summon an ecstatic merging with the beauty of divine light that pervades the universe. Through dance, or trance, or chanting or listening to Sufi poetry or Sufi music, a practitioner ideally enters a fiery state of Love so deep, one article said, that everything but God is consumed. I shuddered at the idea of total sublimation to God. Who were these people who allowed themselves to fall so deeply in love? Where did they find the devotion? The trust?

At the same time, if one was going to have a spiritual path at all, a passionate path seemed necessary. I was a perfect example of someone who did not have passion, and therefore did not have a path. But I *wanted* the passion. I wanted to feel it, now that I saw and heard others who were infused with the divine essence. The magazine mentioned some Sufi groups in America. All had Islamic names and seemed firmly rooted in that tradition. I wanted to explore Sufism somehow. But it seemed totally foreign, totally alien to me.

○   ○   ○

One afternoon, out of the blue, I received a message from Mary, a distant cousin from my grandmother's side of the family. Mary wanted me to telephone her. I'd met her maybe once or twice, each time among close to a hundred other relatives at family reunions, wakes, or weddings. All I really knew about her was that she was near fifty, had grown up and stayed in Northern California throughout her college years, disconnected from the majority of my East Coast family. At some point in her adult life she moved to Washington, D.C., where she lived and worked in the fashion industry as a stylist for public figures who appeared on TV. She remained unmarried, a sign of idiosyncrasy in my large Irish-Italian family.

My parents had always classified Mary as a "free spirit," a trait they viewed with both admiration and apprehension. "Cousin Mary went traveling in India," one parent would tell the other, impressed with disbelief. They would speculate that some kind of purpose existed behind her traveling, like a job or a vacation, but they weren't sure. "Cousin Mary is living in Washington, D.C., in a big house with a lot of roommates," they'd told me once when I asked for her story. The word *roommates* confused our nuclear minds. No one besides her own parents had ever been to visit

Mary and her clan. We knew that living with roommates for so long signified a tight bond with good friends, but exactly what kinds of friends they were, no one in the family was completely sure.

"She's part of a collective, where they all contribute to the food and the chores," one aunt clarified years later. "Kind of like a commune, but they aren't hippies or part of a cult or anything. They're very artistic."

"Is she an artist?" I guessed.

"Well . . . she did go to art school," my aunt reasoned.

"Oh," I said, still missing the connection. My aunt really didn't know. Nobody knew, and it didn't matter much until the moment she called.

Mary had heard through family that I'd been exploring various spiritual traditions, and was curious as to which ones I was looking at. "Wicca, shamanism, yoga, Vodou," I told her, wondering what she thought when she heard the eclectic mix. She probably never heard of half of them. She'll probably change the subject. "Hmmm," she said. "How are you finding the experiences?" she asked. The question floored me. This was the first person in my family who had actually asked me about the experiences, and what they meant to me. My boyfriend and I kept our spiritually intimate feelings separate in the name of freedom, but that freedom had erected a barrier. As for my parents, I'd been grateful for their discretion in their inquiries into my spiritual interest. Spiritual commitment had become such a private and personal matter in our family that we no longer had an open dialogue. I didn't encourage otherwise, since I didn't know where this personal tour was heading , and I felt vulnerable. Faith was a dead language with no vocabulary among most people I knew. But here was Mary, an estranged relative, calling me to discuss spiritual experiences. I fumbled for words, for the ability to explain.

"They've been very rewarding, each in their own ways," I answered vaguely. Her silence indicated to me that she was either confused by my answer, or waiting for further details, and a feeling of dread came over me. Where would I begin? I had no idea who she was, really. Would she know what I was talking about when I told her I was just wandering, looking for experience to fill some kind of gap? I may as well have sliced open my back and put my spinal cord on display, the discussion seemed so potentially invasive, even life-threatening. Cautiously, I filled her in—that I had arrived nowhere in particular with any of the practices, yet I felt connected to the process of exploration. She said nothing. I added that I was getting closer to understanding why I might consider one path or another. "Uh-huh," she said. After I finished explaining, I felt even more vulnerable. But screw it, I thought. What else can I possibly explain? The Lord is my shepherd.

"I'm asking," she said finally, "because I've investigated quite a few non-Catholic spiritual systems myself."

I felt as though she were scoping me out. I said nothing.

"So what are you looking at now?" she asked.

I told Mary I now wanted to learn about Sufism, but felt barricaded by the tradition's irrelevance to my life as a non-Muslim. I told her how I hoped to discover spirituality through experience, but that experience had always come through personal connections—a friend of a friend, a coworker's colleague, someone. But this time, I told her, an inside connection to Sufism was nowhere to be found.

After pausing a moment, she said, "I might have an inside connection for you."

"What's that?" I asked.

"Well, I've been a Sufi for twenty-five years."

○ ○ ○

Mary was in no way a Muslim. But she was a Sufi. She practiced an American form of Sufism that had been created by a contemporary spiritual figure. And her first Sufi teacher had been a woman. This was definitely *not* the traditional style of Sufism described in the magazine articles. Mary's brand of American Sufism seemed radically new, yet mention of it was conspicuously absent from any of the books about Sufism that I'd skimmed. How had she found it? And where had it come from?

Mary quickly sketched her own story. When she was in her early twenties, she was attending art school in San Francisco and working part-time for a publishing company. She was deeply in love and engaged to be married. Mary had not been consciously looking for Sufism or any other spiritual path. But she had questions about herself, about love, and about life that had not been answered by her religious upbringing. From time to time, a companion at work would lend her spiritual books, and one of those books turned her whole life inside out.

"It was a collection of talks by a Sufi teacher. His book captured me in a way I had never experienced," she explained. "It awakened me to the idea that there was such a thing as a spiritual path, and that 'love' could be something much more than a romantic relationship. All the issues I was facing, sex and marriage and raising children, were discussed as expressions of a spiritual life," Mary told me. "I had never been touched so deeply by another spiritual book, sermon, or philosophical idea."

Mary fell in love with these ideas, or "principles," as she calls them. But as she moved toward them, she found herself moving away from her partner. "I was engaged; the invitations were out. But I realized that I couldn't marry someone unless we shared a spiritual life together. And we didn't. It was a very painful parting because I did love him. But life was leading me toward a deeper kind of love, which certainly didn't exclude romance, but made it kind of secondary, at least for me at that time. It was like, did I want to swim in a lovely little pool or did I want the ocean? The ocean, I later realized, was called 'divine love.'"

Around the same time, Mary was given a picture of a Christlike Indian guru named Meher Baba. Something about the picture chimed within her; she liked to look at it. Walking by a bookstore one day, she noticed a book with a photo of Meher Baba on its jacket. Baba was holding a young goat, and it made Mary think of Christ with a lamb, a picture of divine love. She was drawn to this image and could not forget it, even though she had abandoned churchgoing long ago. Something about these images of Meher Baba moved outside of her Catholic world and touched the same chord of deep feeling as the Sufi book had.

Several of her friends at the publishing company were followers of Meher Baba, and they invited Mary to come to meetings of their group. The group was called "Sufism Reoriented"—a school of Sufi teaching that had been created by Meher Baba for American seekers. Meher Baba had said that Sufism, with its emphasis on love for God and service to others, was a practical spiritual path for Americans. As a "path of the heart," it was well suited to seekers who led active lives in society and were uncomfortable with traditional Eastern disciplines of meditation, yoga, or isolated monastic routines. In setting up this group, Meher Baba had taken the basic principles of Sufism and adapted ("reoriented") them for use in our modern culture. People spent lots of time together, rather than in isolation.

When she learned of Sufism Reoriented, Mary did not commit to it overnight. She'd been "walking around the temple," as she called her spiritual shopping process, just like I was doing now. However, Sufism Reoriented called for a full-scale commitment. It took Mary three years before she felt ready and able to honor Meher Baba's principles. Her commitment was extremely private and personal. Outside of her parents, no one in our family knew about her involvement. Yet everything in her life was based around this decision—her friends, her job, her lifestyle, her appearance, her thought, her preference for honesty, her relationships with men. She never did marry (though she told me that most Sufis do). And she isn't sorry about how she's chosen to live her life. "I would leave in a minute if I ever stopped growing or stopped being in love with these principles. In nearly thirty years there has never been a second of regret."

Many elements went into Mary's process of making this commitment. Perhaps the most important was meeting the teacher who ran the Sufi group, a remarkable woman named Murshida Ivy Duce, who had been chosen by Meher Baba to lead this new school and had worked closely with him for more than twenty years to establish it. Meeting her was a turning point in Mary's life.

"She was called *Murshida,* which means 'teacher' or 'guide.' She was in her mid-seventies when I first met her, and I think she had more energy and vitality than I'd had in my twenties! She was short, stout, with fine, gray, curly hair and twinkling hazel eyes, always impeccably dressed, like a perfect grandmother. But she was incredibly perceptive, and her personality was very forceful and strong. She'd lived an amazing life all over the world. She served in the Red Cross in France in World War I, she'd had careers in business and law and publishing, and then she married a prominent oil executive and became a Washington hostess, giving dinner parties for kings and ambassadors. But she also had been on her own spiritual search for many years, and after learning about Meher Baba she went to India to meet him. One moment in his presence convinced her that Meher Baba was the God-Man, the very incarnation of God on Earth."

I found Mary's plainspoken acknowledgment of Baba as the modern-day Christ pretty incredible. But Mary did not. I asked my cousin, "Do you believe Meher Baba was Christ?"

"Yes," she answered. No hesitation.

○   ○   ○

Mary had captured my interest with her secret spiritual life. Further, we had a distinct family connection, which allowed me to let my guard down more than I usually did with the other traditions. I wanted to get to know her. In addition to being a blood relative, her interests and understanding of spiritual matters sealed our sense of family. We spoke every few weeks, and when I asked, she told me about Meher Baba. She even sent books. Meher Baba called himself the "Avatar." That is a Sanskrit word that means "descent or incarnation of divinity." When Meher Baba used the word, he capitalized it and was always *The* Avatar. In his definition, there is only one Avatar, one Messiah, one World Messenger who plays the role of Christ again and again. The Avatar returns to Earth every 700–1,400 years to renew the divine message and flood the world with light and grace. Zoroaster was the Avatar. Rama was the Avatar. Krishna was the Avatar. Buddha was the Avatar. Jesus was the Avatar. Mohammed was the Avatar. After a series of intense experiences in his early years in India, Meher Baba knew that he was the Avatar. His messages of love, forgiveness, and awakening are the same as the other prophets. This is why all major religions are so similar in their essence; they are all variations of one teaching, given by the same divine Messenger,

Meher Baba explains in his writings. The incarnation of God takes on the divine message as his identity. Meher Baba said, "I am the Ancient One, the one who lives in every heart."

Mary was giving me a very condensed version of her understanding. She said, "It doesn't matter to me if you believe or accept this or not. You just have to know that *this* school of Sufism flows from Meher Baba's work. There are other Sufi groups that don't recognize Meher Baba, and they do things differently. Everyone in this group is a devotee of Meher Baba, and each of us has had some personal experience to confirm our belief in him."

Okay, that's fine for Mary and other Baba lovers. But if he was the Christ, why hadn't we all heard of him?

Mary explained that, too. During his lifetime, the Avatar renews and revitalizes the spiritual energy of all people and all spiritual paths. His work occurs on many different levels of awareness, and takes hundreds of years to manifest; for example, Christianity did not emerge as a major force in the world until about 300 years after Jesus had lived. Meher Baba lived from 1894 to 1969, and in the thirty-odd years since his passing, his following has grown slowly all over the world. In America, there are about 5,000 people who are "lovers" of Meher Baba. They connect with Baba's guiding presence individually and personally, in much the same way as active Christians connect with Jesus. They may or may not join groups, and most Meher Baba groups are fairly informal and loosely structured, allowing anyone to come and go as they please.

Sufism Reoriented is a subcategory of Meher Baba devotees. The 500–600 members of this group follow a structured path that Meher Baba defined for them. Reading through the guidelines in one of the books Mary sent me, I could see that Meher Baba expected Sufis to be grown-ups, or at least on their way to maturity. "Lovers" were to be free of recreational drugs or other addictive substances, to be working toward freedom from financial debt, and to be free from any preexisting emotional chaos that would better be dealt with in therapy. In addition, he felt that participation in a spiritual path required honesty in all one's dealings; otherwise the goals of a spiritual life could never be achieved. Finally, participation in the everyday work world as a functional human being is expected. There is no room for slacking spiritual wanderers here.

Meher Baba explained that these seemingly strict guidelines are imperative for a member of Sufism Reoriented. Following a spiritual path takes tremendous focus and energy; it cannot be supported amid a life of chaos. Such requirements cut down on the number of shoppers, like myself, who come into Sufism Reoriented for a "try out" period. It is one reason why the population of practitioners has remained so small.

Another reason is that Meher Baba's Sufis keep a very low profile. They do not advertise themselves or seek to convince others about their path. They rarely discuss it at all. No external badges of achievement are pinned to individual participants at any stage of personal development; there are no visible signs or marks of progress. All learning for a Sufi is internal and personal, based on inner feelings and inner knowing. Yet Sufis form a strong community.

This path is not for everybody. Mary told me, "If people find their way to Sufism Reoriented, it is always because Meher Baba brings them. They learn about it through a chance meeting, a random conversation, or a series of coincidences at just the right moment and attribute it to 'synchronicity.' Well, it's really Meher Baba! He said *he* would choose the membership of this school, and he does that in many different ways." Like all of Meher Baba's followers, she speaks of Baba in the present tense. I found this habit alarming, on equal par with the unsettling image of Meher Baba working from the beyond to bring people to his teachings. Not that paranormal solicitation wasn't possible. I just wasn't yet in the habit of acknowledging deceased people's earthly influence. I felt better thinking that it wasn't Meher Baba himself, but the truth behind his teachings that brought people to Sufism Reoriented; though to Sufis his teachings and his person were the same.

Mary and the other members of this school strive to "reorient" their personal lives according to Meher Baba's principles of unselfish love, devotion, and service to others. Their individual relationships with Meher Baba are aided by their association with the Murshid, the living teacher who directs the activities of the group.

"What exactly are the activities of the group?" I asked. What do Sufis do?

o o o

Sufism Reoriented has few external rules, so explaining what Sufis "do" was difficult for Mary. Participation in Sufism Reoriented is a way of life, a practice of approaching all the tasks of everyday life according to what she called "principles of higher love." Mary spoke of the way an artist or a dancer loses herself in her art as an example. "Creative expression is a form of love, and any form of love can lift you out of yourself and free you to know and join a larger design of harmony that is always there." Living as a Sufi does this for Mary, awakening her to deep levels of beauty and joy. "We try to apply that awareness to all the mundane tasks around the house, to relationships, to our jobs, to everything," she said. And to aid in that, members of Sufism Reoriented strive for the same goals under the direction of a Murshid who is considered by the Sufis to be especially enlightened.

The Sufis put these ideas into practice in several ways. They have two main centers, one in Northern California and one in a quiet, suburban neighborhood in Washington, D.C. The one in Washington is a cluster of six or seven private homes, where Mary shares her life with about sixty other Sufis in a spiritual community. Nearly everyone in the group has a full-time career in the Washington area. Many are married. And they all make time to share the work of the household, giving at least sixteen hours a week to the tasks of shared life: meal service, cleaning and household maintenance, gardening, all on the scale of a small, elegant hotel. This work is part of their Sufi practice. One goal of this shared life is to create an atmosphere of harmony. The state of harmony, born of unified purpose, allows Sufis to look past personal ego-patterns that might otherwise block and distort a deeper connection with divinity. This lifestyle releases a flow of love, Sufis say, and a free flow of love is the main objective.

Shared living of this kind, Mary told me, felt like a continual process of unpeeling. In an environment of shared spiritual awareness, crystallized attitudes or understandings constantly crack open and fall away as newer, deeper realizations emerge. The dynamic of living with companions who aspire to the same spiritual ideals helps everyone to discover deeper parts of themselves as they follow their own individual paths within the group. The demands of shared life were not always "fun," Mary said, but there was always a background of joy and a reservoir of love among fellow participants that sustained and nurtured everyone in ways she had never experienced with her own family. All recognized and sympathized with "the process" as it happened within them and around them.

I had a hard time imagining mature adults living happily in what sounded like a spiritual commune.

"Why not come visit and see for yourself?" she asked.

I was excited at first, but torn about entering an active community of devotees when I did not share in their faith. I neither wanted to judge or be judged, but didn't see how I could avoid it on my end. I already had formed an opinion. I did not, would not, believe this man was Christ. Connection to a family member who consciously lived an active spiritual life soothed many of my jagged feelings of isolation. At the same time, I felt disjointed by the fact that Mary had developed a large spiritual family with whom her life was completely integrated. She was living with the type of passion I'd longed for. But now that I stood beside someone thoroughly committed to her spiritual self, and to a spiritual community, I couldn't quite fathom what life was like for her. Was she out of touch with the reality I knew? Would we not understand each other once meeting in person ? Would she, and her group, try to suck me in? The principles and beliefs were already sucking me in, in their complexity.

Mary had told me that the Sufis believed in reincarnation, and on the train ride to D.C. I felt my brain tie into a knot just thinking about it. Even though common spiritual sense told me that this kind of thing—multiple lives—transcended linear thinking, dropping a body at death, then returning into another one at

another time in history reached far beyond the spiritual mathe-
matics I had learned thus far. I saw no wheel turning in time or
space that would dictate just when one life was over and when
another began. Yet I was about to visit a house full of people who
lived with such understanding on a daily basis.

Mary had de-emphasized this, saying that since most people
have no access to knowledge about past lives, it didn't usually
come up in conversation. But the subject tantalizes many people
who are uncommitted spiritually—how else to explain the prolif-
eration of people paying psychics for "past life regressions." I had a
few friends who fell into that racket and were constantly left
wanting more info, more details about their past. I never thought it
helped them much. For most of her companions, Mary said, the
novelty of reincarnation had worn off long ago, perhaps once they
found more grounding aspects of spiritual design on which to
focus. The framework was helpful, she said, in understanding
things that happen to people in life. You can look at everything as a
continuity that started a long time ago and still has a long way to
go. It explains a lot about relationships with family or lovers or
employers: you're nearly always picking up with someone from
where you left off before. There's a hidden history that shapes
many of your feelings and reactions. In other words, I reasoned,
your actions and the situations you find yourself in now are pre-
destined. Was that comforting or disconcerting?

I read the books Mary had sent me on the train, hoping to
absorb Meher Baba's description of life's purpose before I arrived
at the commune. In our essence, according to Meher Baba, each of
us is a "drop" of the ocean of divinity, unconscious that it is part of
this Divine Ocean. Creation exists to develop and mature consciousness sufficiently so that the drop can become fully aware of
its oneness with the Ocean, with God. Baba calls that process the
"journey of the soul," a journey driven by the soul's deep, unconscious yearning to know its true nature. This journey, Meher Baba
says, takes place in three main stages: evolution, reincarnation, and
involution, a trilogy during which we experience ourselves as
everything in creation, from an inanimate stone to a burst of cold
air to a human being.

Unlike Darwinism, which traces the evolution of biological form, Meher Baba's spiritual evolution maps the development of consciousness. Apparently, every one of us evolves towards higher consciousness with each new form of life we take. The evolutionary stage ends when we become human beings and achieve full consciousness.

Then starts the reincarnation stage. Even though consciousness is complete, the soul remains an unknown essence outside of this awareness. Baba says the soul still does not know *itself* because it remains focused outward toward the world. So we reincarnate through many human lifetimes in order to gather all the experience the world has to offer, both positive and negative, rich and poor, strong and weak, male and female, bright and dull, all races, all creeds, all nationalities. It takes millions of lives for the soul to know every aspect of life's totality.

Finally, says Baba, we reach a stage where we've seen it all and done it all, and we begin to question the purpose of existence. Is this all there is? Eventually, we awaken to the internal dimensions of life and realize that the quality of our inner life is more important than outward success, wealth, or even pleasure. We find ourselves interested in spiritual issues, and we begin to sense the light and mystery of divinity around us. We are ready for the third and final stage, involution. We are drawn to find a path that will integrate the diverse experiences of life and deepen our awareness of divinity. There are many such paths, each one emphasizing a different aspect of meditation, service, and devotion. Most of these paths require the help of a guru or spiritual teacher, someone who is *spiritually* older than us, someone who has already "been there and done that" everywhere, reincarnated through millions of lives and started the involution phase. Someone, I reasoned, who would fit the expression I hear now and then: "He is an old soul." What draws us to such a teacher, and ultimately back to what Baba calls God—the place beyond the longing—is the soul's deep longing to know itself.

Reincarnation and consciousness baffled me, but the mention of the soul's longing to know itself rang true with the longing I felt and the compulsion I had to find intimacy. I'd never heard the needs of the soul articulated as such before. With this context, the longing I carried each day, from tradition to tradition, now made sense for the first time. What human being didn't have that longing from time to time? Whose soul really knew its own self? Baba's explanation of path-seeking grounded me. I looked at involution as the center of my quest, whereas the patterns of reincarnation could not be helped. My search was both for a path and that aspect of divinity that would help deepen my awareness. Looking out the Amtrak window, the suburban houses, lawns, parking lots, and supermarkets sped by me and I suddenly felt as if I was moving toward the threshold of Sufism Reoriented—leaving the non-spiritual world and holding a ticket to the truly spiritual arena but not yet entering. I knew I wasn't going to move in with Mary and the rest of the Sufis, so what was I doing? Had I done this before, in other lives? My head was spinning. I had to breathe deeply in order to alleviate the sense of vertigo.

I'll admit, I didn't fully understand this Sufi view on living life while keeping in mind many other lives. The principles seemed heavy duty, and having a family member involved only illuminated their intensity. But mixing my cousin Mary with these concepts— reincarnation, shared living, Meher Baba, the Avatar—brought lightness to these otherwise overwhelming notions. Still, though, I felt spiritually fatigued. The train ride had become a metaphor for my seeking, riding from place to place with a destination in mind but with no plans to stay. I wanted to stay in a system of some kind. Even if I had to create my own spiritual practice, based on limited knowledge, I'd prefer it to hopping haphazardly around the edges of traditions. Withholding my trust exhausted me. It kept the door of my heart shut, prevented me from fully experiencing. Was I giving in? Giving up?

○ ○ ○

At Union Station the platforms held throngs of people awaiting their loved ones. I passed through the atrium of shops and fast-food stands. Outside it poured rain on the capitol. I spotted Mary after a moment, strikingly dressed in an outfit from Bloomingdale's. Her raincoat billowed like a black cape; she looked very cosmopolitan. She stood beneath a black umbrella, smiling contentedly, waiting, assured. "Mary," I called. She air-kissed me and brought me under her umbrella, walked me to the car. Inside it was warm and dry. I was relieved to be off the train, out of my head, and in a new place where I could relax with family.

The first thing Mary told me was that I wouldn't get to meet the Murshid, the teacher who lived among them. He was out of town, at the other center. I was almost relieved—I was not ready to meet an enlightened master. Hearing about him was enough. As we drove through teeming rain past government buildings, Mary told me about the role he played as an American version of a guru. Murshid helped direct the practitioners through their spiritual growth, lived, talked, laughed, and ate with them like a family member. In Sufism of the past, spiritual students often lived with their teachers or very close by. The teacher's home was the students' educational and spiritual center. This modern-day Sufism follows the same practice. The students, on both coasts, can share everyday life with their teacher.

Our relationship with our teacher is closer than a relationship with a parent, more instructive than one with a schoolteacher or counselor, deeper and spiritually more intimate, Mary said, than with a lover or spouse. I suggested the psychotherapist/patient relationship as a model, because the care, insight, and trust exchanged were for the same end: personal growth. Mary shook her head: No, it's much more than that; therapy is a relationship of intimate trust but not necessarily of love. The love must be what enables them to live together, I reasoned. I couldn't imagine sharing a house with my therapist and all of her clients.

Mary and I stopped at a stylish restaurant, where we met Lisa, another woman from the Sufi house, for brunch. Conservatively dressed, like most of the people I'd seen so far in this largely white, affluent part of Washington, D.C., Lisa held a small black umbrella over the bouncy curls of her hair. She was twenty-nine, Mary told me, but a childlike glee showed in her disposition, which made me think she was younger and untouched by life. Besides her inner glow, nothing else about her revealed to me that she was a Sufi. She may as well have been just another well-dressed Sunday bruncher, enjoying a day of rest.

We spent most of brunch talking about Sufi life as women might discuss their domestic relationships over tea. Sharing the upscale salads and egg platters like society women nibbling finger sandwiches, we behaved as though at an exclusive yacht club that was available only to those in the know. I felt like an honored guest. Both women lived at the center, where there were accommodations for married and unmarried Sufi students. Mary lived in a dormitory type of room with several other single women. Lisa shared a small bedroom with a single roommate. Scattered throughout the complex were several married couples in private rooms, including one couple with an adolescent son who lived in one of the houses that made up the "campus." Neither Mary nor Lisa had very much space for personal belongings: a small closet, a bureau, a desk. But the house offered many facilities that could be shared—office space for individuals who worked at home, a library, a television room, spaces for reading and study, a snack area, a room for meditation, parking. One of the residents was a physician who, in addition to his local medical practice, took care of the medical needs of his companions. They had a bookkeeper who tabulated their monthly expenses and rent. Life was organized, but demanding for both Mary and Lisa. Commitments to a sixty-person family, in addition to their full- time careers and personal lives, left them with little reserve time to spend idly. Mary herself had responsibilities to tend to that day, so she left me with Lisa.

When we finished and left the restaurant, I was psyched to start talking about Sufism Reoriented with a contemporary. Lisa and I were about the same age, and though there were great differences in the way we lived our lives, I already felt a kinship between us. She drove a small black Honda wagon, carefully, giving me a tour of the surrounding suburb and telling me about some musicians who lived in the Sufi house who recently released a pop album based on Persian Sufi poetry. This music is an inspiration to everyone in her house, Lisa said.

At the mention of musicians living communally, I couldn't help but recall the first time I entered a slovenly home of Grateful Deadheads in college. Batik tapestries cloaked the walls. The air was sweetened with the scents of patchouli and spilled bong water. Guitar music doodled in the background, while long-haired, tie-dye-clad, stoned people sat around discussing details of Dead shows they'd never even been to. These 1990s' Deadheads were both impressive and unnerving in their obsessive interest. Their commitment served as both therapy and community. They weren't terribly productive people, though. I never did see them in class. Certainly this was different, I reasoned. Lisa and Mary were so *together*. I couldn't imagine them frittering their time lying on the couch with bandmates saying things like, "Dude, chant that again."

Lisa picked up a cassette tape from the stack in front of her car stereo and popped it in. "This is my friend's demo. I want to play you this song that I think will help you understand just what keeps me in Sufism Reoriented."

O O O

As we sped past the suburb, I could pay little attention to Lisa's tour. After a while she stopped talking and disappeared into the music crooning through the car stereo. The tune drew me inward, though the mix of styles was jarring. They used modern instrumentation: guitars, flutes, synthesizers, slide guitar, bass drums, and gentle Middle Eastern percussion in melodies that combined styles of pop, rock, classical, and R&B. The lyrics revealed it as "God" music, nothing I'd ever been able to deal with before. It was a ballad, almost painfully honest, the emotions raw and bare. Lisa stared straight ahead of her, half-smiling, and singing along as she drove. The singer beckoned, "Come to a room, there's a party where dancing and love will be shared. . . . Don't worry if your wine cellar is empty, the whole universe could drink from mine." (Lisa explained that the "wine" he refers to is divine love.)

I'd heard plenty of Christian rock ballads that ask the listener to trust in the heavenly father. They always made me laugh because the Christian message so fundamentally opposes the tenets of rock and roll, and no Christian rocker seemed to get that. Sufi poetry merged a little better with contemporary music. This song spoke of love of a nonsexual nature. It wasn't preachy, just earnest and vulnerable. I could see how deeply it spoke to Lisa, so I tried to enjoy it. We drove for a while and I found the melody, the instrumentation, and even the message of celebration charming.

We stopped in front of a large Georgian mansion on the edge of a park. Lisa waited until the song ended and snapped off the engine. We walked through neatly manicured gardens that featured rows of roses and boughs of delicate irises and tulips on the way to the door. I was impressed not just with the house and grounds, but with Lisa's ability to move between worlds. Helping a curious outsider negotiate into her faith could not have been easy. Yet her manner, her grin, exuded ease.

She led me inside to a sprawling, sparkling white interior, through a giant multiperson kitchen to a sitting room where we settled into white wicker chairs. Statues, photographs, and pencil drawings of Meher Baba surrounded us discreetly: a bust on the mantle, an etching on the coffee table, a print on the wall. Each room I later toured praised him somewhere. I felt a bit as though I were in a rectory or a lay person's convent—some kind of holy residence. The delectable smells of dinner stewing reminded me that I was to dine in this holy home. Curried beef, basmati rice, Greek salad, and pistachio ice cream would feed sixty people in two dinner shifts, at 6 P.M. and 8 P.M. I was the special guest. People milled about, crossing to and from the staircase, the kitchen and backdoor. "Oh yes, hi, we've been hearing about you," they all said when Lisa introduced me as Mary's cousin.

I felt as if I'd walked into a bees' nest or an ant colony, where the subjects all lived among the glory of the queen, happily, voluntarily, in a symbiotic relationship. The importance of Meher Baba to their everyday living was obvious to me. Most people smiled easily, generating a curious state of happiness. The Sufis didn't have a hierarchy in the house. People did not appear to have competitive relationships. Out of habit, I scanned my inner radar for blips on the "cult" screen, but came up with nothing. They didn't want me to "join" them. On the contrary, they only allowed me in because I asked. I'm glad they did. I felt quite comfortable here.

Once Lisa began explaining how her life and feelings were situated around Sufism, I was reassured even more.

She began with a caveat. "In some ways I may be representative of people in Sufism Reoriented, but I really can only speak for myself when I talk about the meaning of these spiritual principles in my life."

She referred to the song we listened to in the car and remarked on its message: the inexhaustible supply of light and ecstatic beauty within. "Slowly I try to bring that idea into daily reality," she smiled. "It can be grueling work."

The work, as she calls it, comes from the demands of shared living, but also from the challenge of remaining centered through the course of her daily life. "It's easy to remember God when relaxing and celebrating. But can you remember God when you've got three people holding on the phone, fifty e-mails coming in, and someone standing at your desk wanting something? Then can you remember?" she asked rhetorically.

There is nothing more precious to Lisa than her Sufi practice. Generally, she does not talk about it. It is personal, disciplined, sacred, and therefore impossible to discuss, to a large extent. "My practice is for me," she explained. "What does it have to do with anything, or anyone else?" Yet, because I asked, she agreed to discuss her experience.

○ ○ ○

Lisa's exposure to Sufism was unconventional compared to those of the women from other traditions I had met. These other women had been driven to find something new in their lives because of a crisis or unhappiness or an urge to change things. But Lisa was born into a Sufi family. She learned of Meher Baba as a child, from her parents. She tells the story of her very first exposure as though it proved Sufism was the path for her.

Her parents were intellectuals at Harvard. Though her mother was Jewish and her father Christian, they both recognized Meher Baba as the Avatar. In 1969, Lisa's parents attended Meher Baba's last public gathering in India. Lisa's mother was pregnant with her.

"My family cherishes that experience in India. It was an explosion of love," Lisa said, as though she herself actually remembered the event. Though unborn, Lisa considers this event an important introduction to this Sufi lifetime.

"I have lots of dear friends who were also in their mothers' wombs at that gathering, but they did not become Sufis. So one doesn't necessarily lead to the other. But for me, I believe all my little cells were irradiated at the event." Lisa's belief that her spiritual direction was set before she emerged from her mother's womb mirrors her understanding of reincarnation. She feels very fortunate that she grew up knowing about Sufism and Meher Baba and did not have to search for them in this lifetime. Lisa had never had the feelings that plagued me or anyone who was searching for a path. Because she'd been raised in a Sufi family, the moment of choice in which one decides, "This is the divine practice for me," seemed to be missing from her experience.

Not entirely, she explained. In college Lisa felt an urge to test her faith. She spent a semester in France, far away from Sufis, family, and all support networks. Until then, an atmosphere of love for Meher Baba had pervaded her life, spontaneously celebrated in her family and among friends with poetry, songs, and plays. During this semester abroad, she hoped to sift out her Sufi influences and discover her true beliefs.

Once isolated, Lisa realized how closely she'd lived to Sufi principles and saw that she could not live without them. Whenever she had some space alone, when she was faced with what to do with time for herself, she longed for Sufism. She pined for the sense of inner happiness that could not be gleaned from socializing or a shopping spree or other types of ego-gratifying pleasure. During this time, she read or listened to tapes of spiritual treatises and found them uniquely calming and inspiring. Once she had made the decision that Sufism grounded her, she was prompted to travel to India with her boyfriend on her winter break. She encountered Sufis and other Baba lovers almost every step of the way. She visited Meherabad, Meher Baba's main center in India, where his tomb is and where his remaining close disciples continue to live and work. There, Lisa confirmed that Sufism and Meher Baba's teachings were not simply a family and community structure in which she felt comfortable. They were her life.

Her boyfriend, who later became her husband, even became a Sufi. Their relationship had begun spirituality-free, but the subject soon came up. He began asking questions about the Meher Baba pictures around her parents' home, then about her spiritual beliefs. His curiosity coalesced into interest and then commitment to Sufism as his own path. "To have a partner who shares the same spiritual practice as you is pretty incredible," she remembered. They married. After six years, as they both neared thirty, life seemed to take each of them in different directions, and they divorced, amicably. I wondered about her early marriage, if its demise shook her beliefs on love of the sexual and marital nature. I imagined it would shake mine. But Lisa has recovered; she assumes she will marry again. She's now dating a non-Sufi. They meditate together, but that's as far as their spiritual practices overlap at present.

Lisa had tested Sufism both in her individual life and in her domestic life. I tried to imagine living in spiritual union with a lover, measuring the dimension of openness against the dynamics of my current relationship. I knew it was possible, as Lisa could attest. At the same time, it seemed unobtainable, since I and my partner were currently spiritually unattached. Individual spiritual consciousness in daily reality was enough of a challenge right now. The idea of mixing sex and spirituality was almost surreal.

O O O

When it came to sex, the stakes were high for a Meher Baba Sufi. I was shocked to find out that in a path that otherwise asks very little of the participants, sex outside of marriage was discouraged. While visiting, I asked about this specific sex principle. Several Sufis shared their own perspectives on people involved in serious spiritual practice. They emphasized that married Sufis had healthy sex lives. It was only casual sex or unmarried sex that were issues.

The central point from Meher Baba's perspective is not that casual sex is "bad" or "wrong." There is no moral judgment in his writings at all, since, from a reincarnational standpoint, everyone has done or will do everything, and no one is ever damned. One of his quotes is, "Sinner and saint are waves on the same ocean." His observation about casual sex is that it tends to separate sex from the rest of life. In casual sex, one's interactions with sexual partners can be limited to the sexual level only. And, he says, life will automatically compensate for that limitation by ensuring that sex partners come together again and again in many lifetimes, until they learn to love and cherish each other in all dimensions of shared life. In that sense, then, casual sexual expression is one of the most binding of human interactions. One may be required to spend several lifetimes of positive, self-sacrificing, and loving interaction with someone who was a one-night-stand 10,000 years ago. From a reincarnational viewpoint, there is no such thing as a one-night-stand! In marriage, on the other hand, one is sharing life fully with a spouse, relating to her or him as a complete human being, not merely as a sexual partner. In marriage, one is bound on all levels at once. In one-night-stands, one is bound only partially over several lifetimes. So one is not bound in the same way.

There are, Lisa explained, other reasons that spiritual aspirants shy away from casual sex, but the bottom line is that sex outside of marriage is definitely out for Sufis.

I was in a committed monogamous relationship, but I didn't know if we would marry. If we were committed, would that meet Meher Baba's standard? He might say, If you're committed, why not demonstrate your commitment by marrying? If you don't marry, are you really, honestly committed? These were issues I would need to think about if I ever considered living the Sufi life.

And if I didn't want to marry?

It was a tall order in this day and age: abstinence. The very idea of eliminating the desire for sex was unimaginable. Sex was everywhere in our culture, in media, in advertising, in school. Yet Baba maintained that one could move beyond the craving for sex and its equally limiting opposite—repression—if one really hungers for divine love. But part of me already felt repressed by having to live in a way that would deny the possibility of sex happening naturally with someone.

Lisa was committed to Baba's understanding. "Yes, our culture is obsessed with sex and eroticism. I think it is because we live in a time of heightened spiritual energy, the time of the Avatar. There is more energy for every kind of human expression now, more beauty and more ugliness than there has been for thousands of years. Some of the sexual expression around us is beautiful and artistic, but so much of it is based on selfishness. It doesn't seem to have much to do with love, with giving, with an elevated expression of the heart, does it?

"Baba's principles are aimed at people who want to follow a spiritual path. That's not very many people," she said, wistfully. "For us, this way feels right, it becomes natural and appropriate. If this is something you're not comfortable with, then our kind of life may not be right for you just now."

She didn't say, "Maybe you'll be ready in some other lifetime," but she was probably thinking it. I told her I understood the logic; it was application that eluded me. What of the sexual revolution and how far we've come, especially as women, in expressing our sexual needs? She sensed my dissatisfaction. "This is not a moral code. There is no gender specificity here." She shrugged. "Of course, I understand how hard it is. Sexuality is built into all of us. It's a heritage of evolution. But in a spiritual school, we're interested in involution and growth toward God. What good is sexual freedom if it means spiritual bondage?" Clearly her understanding of the balance between sex and spirituality was highly evolved.

"This kind of life is only for people who really want it, who find themselves ready for it, who really can't be comfortable living any other way—that's why we don't talk about it much. In many ways, we move against the current of contemporary society. That is one way of saying 'reoriented.' People try to honor the highest understanding of love they know. For some people, wild, unrestrained sex is their highest understanding. To speed their learning, that's probably what they should do. But if your inner life is your main concern and you want more light, you have to try to live a different way, just to see if it's possible. We don't ask anyone else to do it; some of us barely manage it ourselves. But people here are all drawn in that direction, and we're all trying every day. And for most of us it's working."

The shared living, the consultation with the Murshid, the workshops, the activities were all demanding commitments of Sufism Reoriented. But to me, celibacy outside of marriage because of an external principle was the most impressive act of commitment Sufis exercised. Pursuing a vision of intimacy that was not dependent on sexuality required one to have great trust in the quality of surrounding relationships. I had a new way to look at everyone in the house that evening at dinner. I saw their trust, and I saw their love.

o   o   o

At 6 o'clock Mary returned from her daily chores to bring me to the guesthouse for dinner. We crossed the mist-covered yard and passed smaller surrounding homes owned by individual Sufi families. Some Sufis wanted to maintain their own sense of family but desired proximity to the community for shared events like group meditations, special dinners, and musical performances. I followed Mary through the doorway and watched as she greeted everyone with formal familiarity, as though she were returning to her favorite restaurant. Everyone was clean and dressed for dinner. The other Sufis returned smiles, expressing greetings and interest in me: Mary's family, their guest.

"Come this way," someone had said, and led me to the dining area. Two long tables were set up perpendicularly, adorned with white tablecloths, fresh-cut flowers, and name cards. I moved among the small crowd of Sufis who led me toward the buffet. Curried beef, salad, and basmati rice were spooned onto my plate by a man, a Sufi, who was otherwise anonymous. "Is that enough for you?" he asked me. It was plenty, I told him. "Well enjoy," he said sincerely. I carried my plate to the table and sat where my name card assigned me.

Others took their seats next to me. We began a meal. I didn't want to deconstruct the experience too much, since I was thoroughly delighted by the food, the company, and the relaxed atmosphere. But I couldn't help notice how customized etiquette had become actual behavior, and good manners for special occasions were the norm. People passed bread, listened to each other without interruption, laughed. I saw nothing that resembled brewing bitterness between these non-family members who lived communally, shared everything, and forfeited a large part of their personal lives for spiritual community. In addition to scheduling cooking shifts, shopping runs, menu planning, and clean-up crews into their lives as computer programmers, academics, Internet and service professionals, they really enjoyed each other's company.

Later, after collectively shuffling our plates to the kitchen, where we scraped, commented on the deliciousness, and deposited dinnerware into soapy water, we moved around the buffet line again and found dessert—pistachio ice cream, chocolate lace cookies, coffee, and black and herbal teas. I fell into conversation with a young man sitting across from me, and the subject took on a metaphysical dimension. It was the non-Sufi boyfriend of Lisa's younger sister—she also lived in the house. The boyfriend visited from Virginia nearly every weekend. He was welcomed, as I was, and was also intrigued by the Sufi commitment. While everyone at the table had avoided heavy conversation about Sufism, the principles, Meher Baba, or any number of subjects that would have revealed our uncommon ground, this young man steered the conversation right to spiritual foundation. No one stopped him, but everyone listened. He earnestly explained himself as someone without a path, who was caught between the scientific model—"There is no God"—and the spiritual model—"God is in everything." As he spoke, I watched the silent communication between Lisa's sister and he: gestures, looks, and other nonverbal communication. They shared an intimacy that reminded me of a brother and sister. I couldn't help but think, "This young couple isn't having sex." But in the atmosphere, their relationship seemed appropriate. Lisa's sister bit into an apple as she listened to her boyfriend labor intellectually. She looked like a young woman of tremendous patience.

As we all listened to this young man talk about his spiritual dilemma with openness and urgency, I felt an intense connection to him well up in my heart. His words were familiar. I'd just repeated them earlier to myself: How can any of this be true? How can I not feel a personal connection to God all the time, or reconcile it with my intellect? Somehow, though, as I watched the words flow from his mouth, their sadness, their pursuit, I felt comforted. The conflict between the heart and mind possessed this young man in a way he could not see outside of. He was struggling too.

The rest of the Sufis responded to his queries about reincarnation. "I'm depressed," he said, "at the thought of how short life is. That convinces me that there is no order, and no God. That we are simply here by some accident of nature."

"That *is* depressing," a Sufi answered. "I couldn't walk around thinking that way," he said, and everyone laughed. A flicker of understanding crossed the young man's face, as quickly as when you think you see someone you know in a crowd. And then it was gone.

"Why *wouldn't* you think about future lives?" a Sufi asked him. "How can it be that this is the only chance we get? How else could we live a happy, appreciative, thoughtful life without an idea of future chances?" I saw Lisa's sister smile sweetly at him. The mood in the room had quieted with group understanding. The moment passed, taking with it his need to separate the two parts of his mind.

"Well," he said. "I guess I should think about that."

This was the end of the conversation and the end of the evening.

I returned to my hotel feeling supported. Though I was a solo journeyer, I'd met more people who had joined a team, which gave me hope. Since they shared their views, I had a much easier time jumping in and taking part in a God-consciousness, now. I had practiced. As for participating more fully, the example of the people I had met at Sufism Reoriented showed me how a long-term commitment could grow into something beautiful.

I remembered Mary's words, however: one-stop shopping would not hold up in Sufism Reoriented. I wasn't sure if it even held up in other traditions I had experienced, but visiting each practice had at least touched what I could not yet find. The search had not been without its costs. It had become exhausting. Without following through on one system, spiritual growth seemed like an endless and unpredictable pursuit. Until now I kept hoping to find one spiritual system that would feel right to me. But as I lay down to sleep that night and began to think about the apparently peaceful lives lived by the Sufis, I knew that spiritual contentment wasn't just about finding the right tradition. It was about committing to spiritual understanding as a part of life.

I had asked Lisa earlier that day whether a sense of accomplishment accompanied her involvement in Sufism Reoriented. The way I saw it, her act of constantly choosing to participate, releasing whatever temptation or desires impeded her practice, was a life lived with intense discipline and work. The thought of taking credit for acting on spiritual principles almost embarrassed her. "I don't consider it to my credit that I am aware of divine presence. I consider it my privilege to find it more and more around me," she said. She wanted me to understand how little she had to do with the cause and effect of the rewards of committed practice. "It's not me," she insisted. "It's the doing of that total energy in the universe. Certainly I collaborate with it, but it's not something I do alone."

Her answer reoriented my own thinking toward what true devotion must actually feel like.

CHAPTER SIX

Shambhala:
The Battle of
Sitting Still

Shambhala is a contemplative practice that was fash-
ioned for Westerners out of Tibetan Buddhism. It is
a system of meditation in which one sits still for a
period of time each day, systematically clearing their
mind of thoughts so that an inner sensation of wholeness arises
into consciousness. The practitioner tries to maintain this sense of
genuineness in every waking moment. Shambhala calls this
attempt, which has an accompanying set of principles, "the sacred
path of the warrior"—a warrior being a devoted spiritual student.
It was founded by Chögyam Trungpa Rinpoche, a Tibetan teacher
recognized by the Karmapa (Tibetan Holy teacher who performs
the activity of the Buddha). Trungpa came the United States in
1970 to spread his teachings, though they were controversial by
traditional Buddhist standards. Trungpa Rinpoche taught that the
role of the guru was not to exhibit "good" behavior but to prevent his disciples from living in illusion. Unlike other schools and
traditions of Buddhism, which presents a path in the context of

religion, Shambhala's spiritual path of illumination is compatible with any religion, but it is taught as a practice that can stand alone.

The truth, Shambhala teaches, is that the world is a place of goodness, that our basic human nature is "good," and that living according to this goodness in everyday life is possible for the individual and the community. In Tibetan folklore it is said that there is an ancient lost kingdom in Tibet called Shambhala, where people live in harmony and the principles of goodness and bravery create human happiness. Rinpoche established more than 100 meditation centers in the United States, and since 1970, the number of Shambhala practitioners has grown to nearly 10,000. Individuals meditate daily and undergo five levels of instruction that work to still the mind and connect with the heart so that they can see clearly the goodness in all things.

Was I made of warrior material? I didn't know. I wasn't a Sufi. I wasn't a witch or a shamanic practitioner. I practiced yoga, but was far from becoming a yogini (I still couldn't do a full lotus). Forget about committing to a particular lwa. My level of involvement and understanding were not even enough to attend a true Vodou ceremony. But I had worn one shoe of each of these identities. I walked with one foot in each world, creating a distorted sense of time and place. Like the *Brady Bunch*'s Marsha when she signed up for too many clubs in high school, I'd spiritually fractured myself.

Negotiating five separate spiritual systems eroded my focus and left me in a mild state of shock. I'd gone from practicing nothing to dabbling in too many ponds. I'd done the work—I'd mined traditions for their "answers," or at least found pathways to the answers. I had a body of knowledge, drawing on the understanding of fire energy, the wisdom of the turtle, the lwa who fight fear, the universal truth of *om,* and the Sufis' concentration on love.

But changing my behavior based on this body of knowledge was a problem. Ordinarily, when faced with a desire or need for change, I'd make a list—of books I wanted to read, music I wanted to listen to, people I wanted to call. I put some kind of system into action. With my spiritual pursuits, I had made no list. Creating a schedule to "pray Psalm 23" or "journey to the lower world and visit the turtle" seemed forced and reminiscent of religious structure. After all, there were no rules here. Living spiritually, by my set of ideals, would evolve naturally in my behavior. Despite my honest desire to adopt a practice, somehow spiritual living went the way of sporting equipment—to the back of the closet. There it lurked, reminding me that the sport I'd been meaning to try out for some time was still on hold, but would make its way into my life as soon as I pulled that equipment out. My lack of commitment to any one path made me question whether my approach to spiritual consciousness was the same as my approach to one of my fads, like the three weeks I signed up for classes in the Brazilian martial art, capoeira. Did I lack what it took to make a change?

There *were* some spiritual elements that had settled in to my daily life. Nothing terribly concrete. But in concentrated moments, like when sitting still at the kitchen table waiting for the coffee to brew, or when walking to work, I'd think about my place in the larger scheme, how my behavior of the day might effect the way the world worked. If I looked quickly I could see in the faces of the homeless people I passed, in the haze of bus exhaust mimicking clouds in the sky, or during serendipitous encounters with friends on the street, that something larger connected all of us. Chance. Fate. Moments like these smacked of purpose and then floated away. With my indecision about living in a higher consciousness, my "Maybe these moments are significant, maybe they aren't" attitude, these moments in real life felt as arbitrary as staring into a teacup and reading the arrangement of leaves for a clue to my future. Part of me still wanted to have faith, but of which variety I could not choose. I was a spiritual packrat; I'd collected too much information without moving forward. None of my surplus of spiritual hope and ideas spilled over into my daily behavior with enough permanence for me to see. Without knowing how to apply them, nothing would change. How would I learn?

I learned at a Girl Party. Girl parties were a trendy type of gathering a friend of mine had begun throwing in an effort to get back in touch with her *girl* friends, "cool" women she'd extracted from the heap of regular folks in the city. My friend had devoted ten years of her life to the music industry, and the women who were invited to meet at the Irish bar on the Upper West Side arrived decked out far ahead of the fashion curve. I understood their skunk-striped hair, purple leather pants, and disinterest in non-music scene life to be a code to some secret society. A privileged one. I listened. Their convincing talk swindled me into thinking I was getting to know real insiders on the music scene. I believed that Hole and P. J. Harvey stories were just a few anecdotes away: that these were women whose lives had changed as a result of being around other strong, orginal, hip female role models.

It was February 1997. Women in rock had become a marketing niche, but through the course of the evening I realized with some disappointment that they had not become a topic of inspiration or even of discussion among these industry women. The Cool Women spoke instead of the big money-making acts, the producer doing Madonna's next album, the ticketing conflict Pearl Jam had created. Penis talk. Mentions of gender, musical inspiration, or even art were noticeably absent from the industry news. I watched the canned hype, fueled by cigarettes and booze and industry intoxication, and felt cheated. I had had high expectations for a Girl Party. What electrical current had I expected to see running through conversation? Maybe one that would inspire a new layer of substance to rise to the top, as women in rock had used their individual voices to blaze their own trails into the public eye. I thought I'd find women here who lived by enlightened terms. Who had caught on to something I'd not yet found.

Then a woman entered the bar and caught my attention immediately. Her walk, slow and deliberate, did not highlight her figure or scream for attention, but simply got her from the door to the table. Her hair was its natural color, cut to her chin with bangs. She wore a suit, as if she had just come from her corporate job. Her makeup brushed her cheeks gently and I noticed that she was the first one of the women at the Girl Party to smile and make eye contact with all of us when she walked in. Her name was Beth, and I was glad when she sat across from me.

We began talking in sentences instead of expressions and phrases. Though she too worked in a hipster industry—documentary film—she had little to say about her "scene." I confessed to her my relief at conversing with someone about other things, and

I asked her how she kept her life from being monopolized by the industry. She told me she was in the midst of Shambhala training and that it helped her out a lot.

A fluid calm rippled across her face as the word *Shambhala* blew from her mouth.

"What's that?" I asked, though I had an instinct. I knew it was some kind of spiritual portal she had entered, one that had saved her, brought her back to her center. I'd become so familiar with spiritual people, I could sense their inner peace.

The skin around the corners of her eyes slackened as she thought. While she couldn't have been more than thirty-three, her expression said she'd lived with enough overstimulation to constitute an entire former life. She said, "I was caught up in the film industry once. For a long time I fed off excitement and stress, constantly socializing, drinking, extending myself. . . ." She paused. "Overextending myself. . . ." she continued, "for everyone else but me." Her explanation dropped off to vagueness. The chatter of the bar rose and fell in the dark and, in our silence. She was some distance from that time in her life, but she remembered.

"Everything I did and said was for my career. I reserved no time or attention for myself. Constantly doing became a habit, a way of life. Until I ran myself ragged, crashed, and burned." She described a life of rushing through her career objectives to work in film production, grabbing at any opportunity that might bring her closer to directing, dispensing all her time and leaving herself with nothing. She spoke of this former way of life almost as an addiction. Fortunately she'd found a way out of the grind in the nick of time. On the floor at a screening one night after everyone left, she found a book about Shambhala. The book's cover featured a yellow dot, the Shambhala symbol for the eastern sun. She didn't know then that in Shambhala, the eastern sun was a reminder that life is a never-ending vista of beginnings. She took the book home and familiarized herself with the principles of Tibetan Buddhism that had been streamlined into non-religious practice.

Buddhism has roots in India, China, Tibet, Japan, and Korea. A religion that presents a plan of human transformation, the many incarnations of Buddhism reach for enlightenment and happiness.

Theravada (Southern Indian and Southeast Asian) Buddhism pursues enlightenment through eradication of craving and attachment. *Zen* (Japanese) Buddhism presumes one's own nature is identical with the enlightened Buddha nature, and *Tibetan* Buddhism strives to clear the mind to a state of emptiness. Beth explained as calmly as the Buddha himself that Shambhala is one pathway based on Tibetan Buddhism's clarity, but one that is separate from the Buddhist practice. It is a path to spiritual illumination that is outside of the context of religion. The Shambhala practice taught her to nurture her individual self with respect. She mentioned the yellow dot, the rising sun, as a mirror for self. The few inches between us seemed like miles. I thought about the dot—plain, uncomplicated, somehow commanding of honor—and saw a trace of how one might connect one's identity with such a pure symbol.

She spoke of the Shambhala training fondly—the workshops, the teachers. Her words, even her cadence of speech echoed other spiritual awakening stories I'd heard. She'd begun by finding a moment of peace in the insane circumstances of her life, and recognized herself at a crossroad. She could not proceed along the same professional tract, with the same personal habits of disrespect any longer. With change inevitable, she synchronized her entire self—not just her fractured career-oriented and social self—but her entire physical and mental self with a solid pathway, clear of illusion, that appeared before her. She began to understand how life should *actually* be lived, once she saw a clear route and heeded its beckoning for her to begin. Once again I was face to face with a woman who had blazed a trail. Change sounded so easy.

I felt covetous of her forward movement, her bravery in identifying the trail as the one she needed to change her life. I sat listening, but was distracted by the colorful industry girls. Their chattering presence easily overwhelmed Beth's, whose peaceful existence in an environment filled with smoke, loud music, alcohol, and "cool" people told me her discovery was authentic. She needed no "look" to provide insight into her state of being. Beth had an inner calm, but no scent of sacrifice wafted around her. I wanted to know how she did it. What was the catch? Did she have to give up sex, or Sundays spent hung over, or devote a few days a week visiting other states of consciousness? Did she miss the time and lifestyle she sacrificed? Blazing a trail meant trading in a part of one's life in exchange for something better. Expending effort on the faith that it will be worth it. Did she feel the loss of the former life? How long did it take before she knew it was working?

All of these questions flooded my mind. I couldn't figure out a graceful way of asking without sounding like a complete skeptic. My skepticism was out of place in her presence. Beth sat across from me comfortably grinning, rock solid. She took a sip of her beer, enjoying the pause that to me felt abysmal.

After a few moments of just sitting with her, I received a push across the abyss. The body of spiritual knowledge I'd been carrying around suddenly kicked into gear. A soundless voice relayed what I knew to be an accurate interpretation of Beth's state: peace. Her tranquility illuminated that I was coming from a place of loss. I was someone who wanted something, anything—a clue, a line in to peacefulness, a role model, a Barbie. Beth, on the other hand, possessed the calm of gain. She wanted nothing, had already found it. I watched her sip her beer again. Perplexed, I sipped my own beer, then cut to the chase, asking her what the basic principle was that she found most accessible, the line in.

"Gentleness," she'd said. "I never knew how much gentleness within yourself could change your life."

I finished my beer and left the Girl Party. On my way out I noticed Beth's gentleness against the backdrop of the cool women, who seemed hardened by comparison. I knew I was just as hardened. Gentleness, if I could reach inside and find it, was something I might actually use. I felt as though someone had just handed me the sporting equipment from the back of the closet, the gear I'd been meaning to dig out all along.

The next day, I bought the book with the yellow dot. *Shambhala: Sacred Path of the Warrior* by Chögyam Trungpa Rinpoche himself. I read to chapter 2, the part about meditation instruction. I read until I reached the kernel of the practice, the explanation of gentleness. Remembering Beth's noticeable sense of center, I read the words:

By simply being on the spot, your life can become work-
able and even wonderful. You realize that you are capable of
sitting like a king or queen on a throne. The regalness of
that situation shows you the dignity that comes from being
still and simple.

"Being on the spot" was a curious phrase. I thought of Beth at
the bar among the pulse of entertainment talk at the Girl Party, of
her "non-look" of calm, and how it kept her in one focused place.
I looked at the yellow dot on the cover of the book, representing
the eastern sun, and began to see how Beth and the spot shared a
similar nature. Beth looked to the yellow dot on the horizon; by
practicing meditation, she had begun to free herself from illusion.
She had changed herself to one "sitting like a king or queen on
the throne." She had refined herself to "being on the spot." She *was*
the spot.

Being on the spot. I extracted the phrase, swallowed it down
with the rest of my spiritual info, but kept it on the front burner. I
took note of the book's suggestion to pursue one-on-one instruction in order to proceed with Shambhala training. I found out
where the local New York Shambhala center was located, and considered what it might be like to lead a Shambhala existence: individual, uncomplicated, alone.

○ ○ ○

Chögyam Trungpa's controversial teachings grew out of his auda-
cious assertion that the spiritual path was not a safe journey but a
running battle. He was the first Tibetan teacher to write for
Westerners, and his messages of goodness in the world, warriorship, and bravery caught on among people who were looking for a
ladder to higher consciousness. Trungpa began the Naropa Institute, a school in Colorado that features spiritual teachings as a
complementary discipline to formal higher education. Naropa
attracted free thinkers—among them, the poets Alan Ginsberg and
William S. Burroughs, who began a school of writing within
Naropa. Although a variety of spiritual teachings now define
Naropa's curriculum, Shambhala became the spiritual system that

lives on in book and lecture form, as well as in Trungpa's many students.

Shambhala, he said, is a way of living in the world with fearlessness and without destroying one another. It is a system of warriorship, a sense of self that helps individuals move through life with dignity. The Shambhala training process takes an individual through five levels of education, bringing the individual metaphorically into the kingdom of happiness. But beyond individual spirituality, Shambhala has another vision—to bring the world into community. The purpose behind practicing self-realization, Trungpa wrote, is to inspire a collective of realized individuals who understand the world could be changed—awakened—with their good efforts. This enlightenment would actually recreate the kingdom of Shambhala in the form of consciousness, in which all could live happily, gently, forever.

Curiously, Trungpa himself led a notoriously reckless personal life, filled with car crashes, sexual relationships, and a drinking habit that eventually killed him. Clearly the teaching was more important than the teacher, since it was still living long after he died.

○ ○ ○

I knew another individual who was committed to Shambhala. Coincidentally, I'd met her years before, at college. We'd never befriended each other even though we'd studied in the same program. A talented poet and a thin, attractive woman, she always appeared so distraught that I was hesitant to approach her. Her face had a sad beauty, and she wore intensity and brilliance like a suit of armor. My most significant memory of her was the moment before she received her diploma at graduation. Proudly gliding across the stage, instead of stretching out her hand to meet the dean's extended own, she ripped open her gown to expose her bare, skeletal body, a small, bright orange bikini clinging to her flesh. The effect was more shocking than sexy, exactly as she intended.

It was just by chance that the New York Shambhala center put me in touch with this woman when I asked to speak with a veteran practitioner. Years had passed. I didn't recognize the relaxed

woman I met now as either the orange bikini type or the distraught poet. We spoke as if meeting each other for the first time.

Sophie was twenty-nine, originally from France, but had lived
in New York on the Upper West Side since she was twenty. Her
studio apartment was strikingly clean and spare. A low coffee
table, futon couch, and a wooden desk where she regularly conducted her French tutoring sessions filled the space. A dry warmth
maintained by a low-powered air conditioner blew into the studio
like calm breath. She greeted me with a smile, quickly resuming a
peaceful manner. Her noticeably muscular shoulders held the
spaghetti straps of her sundress. Like Beth, Sophie's appearance and
manner didn't present her as a particular "type." I wondered if she
was hiding her former bikini-wearing self and her somberness.

When I asked her to describe her perspective on warriorship, I
expected her to dodge the question. Nothing about her made me
think of a warrior, at least not the kind of warrior I knew from
films like *Spartacus* or even from *Xena the Warrior Princess*. I had the
wrong idea of warriorship, as it turns out. Shambhala training does
not view warriorship as aggression but as personal heroism. "This
warriorship asked me if I was brave enough to stop everything
that I was doing up until now, and just sit," she explained quietly.
By sitting, she meant meditating. Her comfortable, straight posture
indicated a body accustomed to relaxation.

The warrior tradition of pre-Buddhist cultures in China,
Korea, and Tibet likens the individual to a brave soldier who walks
toward the most daunting challenges with calm. Each effort to
meditate requires bravery. The calm gained from sitting still, not
thinking of stories or fantasies, suspending identity, and halting all
activities surrounding that identity settles the mind. Once the
mind settles, Shambhala says, spiritual illumination is possible. But
fostering the bravery, Sophie said, requires suspending all pre-
dictable behavior.

"I was completely irritated, jumping out of my own skin,"
Sophie remarked, remembering her first sitting session. Once she
focused on sitting, however, her mental hyperactivity faded away
and a state of calm surprised her. "I had a feeling of wholeness, and
relief from all of my past, and all of my hope for the future. Sitting

brought me glimpses of 'Wow, there's not just what's going on in my head—there is something else.'"

As she told me how Shambhala appeared in her life, I saw flickers of the old, morose poet return in Sophie's disposition. Her voice grew soft, and a distraught look came into her eyes as she remembered her unhappy condition. But that former identity did not remain. A stronger Sophie retold the story of how Shambhala helped her address her true identity. Because I had seen this young woman at a vulnerable time in her life, I was impressed now with the strength in her presence. She had become a dramatically different person.

As a twentysomething living in New York, Sophie had been a fully functioning woman, working, going to school, trying her hand at an acting career. But she was deeply troubled. She had been plagued by bulimia since age sixteen, and a self-hating mentality for as long as she could remember. Like any New Yorker, she eventually took herself to therapy. Therapy sessions, though instrumental in combating her problems, did not provide an ongoing sense of well-being. The understanding that the world was "fundamentally good" did not ring true with her, even though her recovery from bulimia was well underway. That she herself was "fundamentally good" felt out of reach.

Sophie reluctantly attended her first Shambhala training seminar in 1996. She insists she wasn't "looking" for Shambhala training. The workshop was suggested to her at a time when she was recovering from a heartbreak. She was twenty-eight and no longer with the person whom she was certain she would marry. The rejection from the first person she trusted, her first true love, devastated her entire concept of herself. "I had thought we would go for a long time. I had all the fantasies," she said. She'd had another relationship before, but this most recent one had become her foundation—her main system of support during the years of her recovery, and her line to the future as a healthy, happy person.

"My understanding of myself as a healthy person was rooted in my identity with my ex. Now that he was gone, I needed to develop self-esteem, to get to know who I was on my own, and realize how afraid I was." Fortunately, her recovery from bulimia had embedded itself deeply enough in her identity so that she didn't have a relapse. When Shambhala entered her life, she was able to recognize its potential.

The first level of training consisted of two days of sitting at the center. Beginning on Friday night, Sophie received instruction from Shambhala teachers who guided her through the learning process, a step-by-step lesson in what seemed like the art of doing nothing. "At least that's what it feels like at first," Sophie said. "It's actually a very active training, as active a training as an athlete's." But the activity is internal; the discipline is to sit quietly in a room. Instructors encourage the practitioner to sit with a "light touch," meaning that if the sitting gets too intense, the individual can notice the intensity and pull back or even stop if necessary. Snapping themselves out of it was allowed, even advisable. Neither a psychological discussion nor a "no pain, no gain" mentality accompanies the sitting. "Holding the mind still is enough of a challenge," Sophie said.

This first night is a bit of a test for the new Shambhala student. If on the first Friday evening of Level 1 training the student "connects" with the teacher—that is, the teacher establishes trust and sincerity with the student—the student feels comfortable enough to return the following Saturday and Sunday. On those days, teacher and students continue to sit for intervals of twenty minutes at a time. Hour-and-a-half lunch breaks, ten-minute walks, and thirty-minute discussions punctuate the sitting. Issues like "Why do I want to fall asleep while I meditate?" and "It feels static," or, "I feel bored," or, "I keep having these fantasies," are discussed in between sitting. Without getting too involved in the whys of these questions, the instructors provide guidance that brings the student back to the focus of the Level 1 experience: sitting still doing nothing all day. This is the first step a warrior on a spiritual path must take. It sounded maddening.

Sitting demands so much concentration, Sophie said, that a lot of people don't want to return after the first weekend. She nearly didn't. The dare to step outside of her personal world of pain was almost too demanding for her. Pain was familiar and safe, whereas changing her entire structure of thinking—her entire concept of herself—was frightening and threatening to her already fragile condition. The inspiration to return, however, came from an insightful teacher who had said at one point during the weekend, "We are brought up in a way to think that there is something wrong with us." Sophie ran the phrase over in her mind. It rang true. Having spent years feeling that there was something inherently wrong with her, Sophie was ready to spend time with a teacher and a system that would cultivate a change in this line of thinking. At that moment, she committed. She was receptive to the training, she says, because she sought to change her reality.

"After only two days I got a glimpse of who I truly was—and realized the sum total of who I am is not anorexic/bulimic. It may be part of who I am, but perhaps, I thought, I don't have to define myself that way entirely."

The glimpse that first weekend of meditation and Level 1 training brought Sophie into contact with a sense of basic "goodness"—that people's natural essence beneath every situation was positive, and therefore she didn't need to be embarrassed about who she was; her true nature, like everyone's, was "good." The idea that she could ask the basic goodness within herself for the help that she needed—recovery from heartbreak, from recurring bouts of underlying self-hate—delivered her from feelings of helplessness. She had a breakthrough immediately. After being entirely estranged from her family since leaving France, she was able to phone them after the first weekend without experiencing a debilitating mental conflict. "I realized my mother and father are not just my mother and father, they are also Loic and Joelle. Other people."

Understanding of these truths, she said, was rather mundane. She didn't dwell on the connections as if they were miracles. She didn't feel as though she had "seen the light." Trungpa explains that discovering basic goodness is not a particularly religious experience. The idea that the world is a good place rings true to us because, as human beings, it is our basic nature to go along with the goodness of situations. Waking up to the Shambhala vision, as Sophie did, is understanding that goodness can happen to us, and in fact already *is* happening to us.

Simple objects and operations in Sophie's life became charmed with clarity. "A table was not just a table, a glass was not just a glass, but objects people worked to create," she explained. Sophie connected these isolated items to the fundamental ways in which things work. "The fact that I can walk, that cars go up the street and stop at red lights, is proof of function in the world. There are things that can go wrong. Accidents happen but, basically, things work."

Goodness in Shambhala is basic and unconditional. Sophie learned this axiom first. Once she was able to glimpse the goodness of simple things, Sophie stopped seeing daily life as obstacles or sources of irritation. "Waiting for the subway no longer became waiting for the subway. I no longer thought, 'I can only live when I am at home and at my destination.' Rather, being on the subway was just as valuable as being at home."

Sophie took meditation by storm. She meditated each day for fifty minutes—forty minutes sitting, the other ten walking—a schedule, she admitted, that fed her unhealthy tendency toward perfectionism. But the details of her heartbreak drove her to seek comfort in structure. She took Level 1's insight and applied it to the dynamics between herself and her ex: If she worked on herself, was good to herself, within five years the goodness would pay off and her ex would return. Of course, this thought was a form of denial, but it kept her going through the Shambhala training, like a prize for "behaving" in a healthy way.

The simple, carefree discussions in Level 1 became intense and difficult experiences in Level 2. As though waking up to the reality of her pain and predicament, Sophie realized she'd been kidding herself about her ex-boyfriend; they didn't have a chance. While getting help and wading through her breakup with a fantasy timeline of a reunion in five years, she was shocked to discover that her former lover was already involved in a new relationship. From beneath the mental trick she'd played on herself rose the raw pain of delusion. This delusion in Shambhala is called a "Cocoon," the place where a person goes in reaction to fear. Some people seclude themselves, while others dress in bright colors and socialize constantly. Sophie shut down, turned off to all people around her.

Dealing with attachment to the Cocoon is a process Trungpa calls "softening." "Softening" occurs within the heart through meditation. Much like the Sufi pays attention to the heart, and the yogi recognizes the fourth chakra as the emotional center, Shambhala encourages the practitioner to sit and connect to the heart, developing a genuine sympathy toward herself. This process of softening the rough edges and the knee-jerk reactions allows the practitioner to see her behavior and get to know the Cocoon that keeps her captive.

Doing her best to keep in mind the warrior mentality as she meditated, Sophie challenged herself to be brave enough to feel the pain. "Looking at it from a warrior's point of view, the warrior who is brave enough to sit through whatever comes up, and to dare to be yourself, to go beyond your usual cocoon behavior, and maybe even have a sense of humor about it, is the bravery I sought."

This time period marked Sophie's entry into a phase where she became a "conscientious warrior." The urgency with which she embraced her life sounded similar to that of a nonsmoker who was reclaiming a smoke-free lifestyle. "I started dressing differently, making my space soft and available for people, making it a little more abundant with flowers and teas and food." She entertained more often, offered her apartment as a place for visitors to spend the night, shared her belongings, her services, and herself with others in her life. She used this conscientious warriorship in order to muster the bravery to move forward with her artistic aspirations by creating an experimental performance piece with two other women. The process of working with other people to create something genuine and original opened her mind. Life was full of potential. She could truly feel her strength as an artist, as a young woman, as a warrior. She nearly forgot her misery. For a while she experienced life as tremendously fun.

Alternately, she said, she had cried a lot during Level 2. It wasn't heaving, sobbing crying, but an intimate connection to herself as a vulnerable human being. "In Shambhala they say that when you are feeling your heart, you are feeling something that is very soft. Crying is very natural when you feel your heart for the first time.

There no storyline attached to it anymore. No 'reason' why you are crying. It's just the experience of being alive, having a full heart, and, sometimes, feeling pain."

Sophie continued to see a therapist throughout the Shambhala training. Shambhala teachers don't claim that they have the solutions to everything. "When I've had bouts of feeling self-destructive, more than is normal, I've had Shambhala teachers say, 'Maybe this is something a professional should handle.'" Her therapist, who saw changes in Sophie as she proceeded with Shambhala, was very supportive.

But her recovery via therapy and her work in Shambhala training did not blend seamlessly. For all of Sophie's connecting to herself and the painful past, she still withheld opening her feelings toward other people in recovery meetings for fear of them not understanding her pain. In theory, the practice of Shambhala has tremendous societal implications, in that if one eliminates one's own convictions, his human experience can enliven others. Discomfort with her own process, however, kept Sophie from sharing her experience. "I didn't bond with anyone during those meetings. I didn't have lunch with people; I was still holding onto pain in a way. I didn't want people to help me. When I realized [my ex] was seeing someone else, I stopped going to recovery meetings even. But I was still sitting everyday, attending the Shambhala sessions." Sitting in solitude provided the privacy she needed to face and even befriend her Cocoon of isolation. Befriending the Cocoon is the first step to letting go of Cocoon behavior. It was a painful period of meditation.

Level 3 emphasizes immediate perceptions. That is, looking beyond what one thinks upon one's first impression. In Shambhala training, Sophie remembers, they stressed the vibrancy of colors, the sounds in the environment, aromas in the air, and other sensual information. The Level 3 course is taught over one weekend, skips the workweek, and then resumes the following Friday and Saturday. It is split between two weekends, so that after the first weekend of instruction the practitioner might exercise her new understanding of how to experience the world. The following weekend, practitioners regather and reflect. Appropriately, this level is called "Warrior in the World."

A warrior in the world is urged to befriend his fear. Trungpa asks the participant to do so by embracing the concept of renunciation; that is, to renounce anything that acts as a barrier between the practitioner and others. The idea is that by renouncing one's sense of privacy, one's Cocoon, the practitioner consequently wants more involvement and contact with the world. "You get a sense of opening to other people, you get over your ego, your selfish need for immediate gratification," Sophie explained.

At Level 3 the practitioner is urged to take on a meditation teacher in order to begin the process of interviews. Interviews relieve the practitioner from experiencing the Shambhala training alone, in her own head. They take place when a Shambhala teacher taps a sitting practitioner on the shoulder, inviting her to talk privately. The practitioner then has the opportunity to discuss with a sympathetic, trained respondent the thoughts coming up in her mind. Unlike a psychotherapist, who delves into storylines deep in people's psyches, Shambhala instructors are attuned to techniques and details that characterize the physical process of meditation. The Shambhala instructor does not discuss the practitioner's personal material but rather the way they respond to the meditation process.

At Level 3, Sophie's Cocoon was still dictating her actions. She did not choose to work with a meditation instructor. In her mind, working by herself through the levels was preferable. She wanted to succeed on her own, without the help of others, and did not see how this egotistical decision was a way of shutting herself off from others, reinforcing her Cocoon of fear. When she attended the Level 3 session, she experienced a profound moment of pain. It was inspired by an orange banner hanging in the Shambhala center. Upon looking at the banner, she began to cry and she knew her tears came from her sensitivity to the honesty of the rich orange color. She knew this because she had had a similar reaction a month before, equally emotional and unexpected. It happened when she was first struggling with the new predicament of her ex being involved with another woman. She fled New York City to a friend's country home. Autumn had begun to change the colors of the trees and, walking outdoors, her eyes fell upon a small sapling whose leaves had already turned a deep, ruby red. So sensual and rich was the color, that Sophie felt a stirring in her heart that moved her to tears. She knew then, as she did now, that her sensitivity to vibrancy in the world was a sign of her intimate connection to all living things. She began to question the positivity of undergoing pain alone.

Level 4 is called "Awakened Heart," which means letting go of the storyline one attaches to life's events. Sophie's entry into this phase of the training corresponded with meeting her ex-lover's new girlfriend. "She made me deal with awakened heart. This level asks you to go deeper, and in my case that meant looking at the quality of jealousy. Going beneath the storyline. The more I did it, the easier it was to look at the reality behind the story. By the end of each day, my own and everyone's behavior is clear."

Sophie began talking with her ex-lover's new girlfriend in order to face her own jealousy. In doing so, she realized they could actually be friends. At first her feelings of resistance manifested as mistrust in her own judgment. How could I like this woman? she thought. She is the enemy. But soon after, she broke through feelings of betrayal and protectiveness. She saw the woman as a person separate from the situation. She saw herself as separate as well. "I started to feel a sense of history behind me of other people who had undergone Shambhala training. I had a tremendous respect for all people who have ever sat before me and had learned the awakened heart." For Sophie, the realization that she and her ex's new lover could coexist on the same planet, perhaps even in the same city, corresponded with Trungpa's explanation of "letting go" as a warrior. He talks about contacting energy of the windhorse, an ongoing source of energy in one's life that can be ridden. When you contact the energy of the windhorse, you can naturally let go of worrying about your own state of mind, he says. Sophie caught the windhorse and rode it during this period. She was even able to apply this philosophy to a visit from her mother. Approaching her life with an awakened heart allowed Sophie to handle a visit from her mother with grace and skill. "Instead of me thinking, my mother is going to pull me in to all of her neurotic stuff, instead, her neuroses just stopped. Because it didn't have me to bounce off of, it stopped pouring out." Dealing with her mother was a notable success for Sophie.

Level 5 is called "Open Sky" and designates the completion of Shambhala training. It is the recognition of the dot, the eastern sun the practitioner always looks forward to, and therefore always sees. "Like when I see my mother and I'm not going to get involved in her history, I can actually snap my fingers mentally, envision the 'dot,' and she will stop. She stops because I've stopped." A vast visibility for Sophie appears every time she catches those dot moments. She has framed a print of this yellow dot; it hangs prominently on the wall of her studio. Upon entering level 5, she also began feeling attracted to other people. "I didn't know people had seen how I had changed. Until a fellow practitioner told me, 'The best part of this level is seeing you smile.'"

Since beginning Shambhala training Sophie never encountered a problem that kept her from moving forward. Where she was scared to go, confronting her mother and her neurosis, for instance, or even talking to her ex-lover's new girlfriend, she would bring in a smile or a sense of humor. Shambhala stresses the practitioner's acquaintance with humor. Trungpa writes about humor, "Life is a humorous situation, but it is not mocking us. We find that, after all, we can handle our world; we can handle our universe properly and fully in an uplifted fashion."

Confident in her ability to handle life no matter what hand it chose to deal her now, Sophie considers Shambhala principles among the most valuable of her beliefs. She recommends that I learn to go where it's uncomfortable, into the source of my fear. "Because that is why we are here. It is really scary, sometimes you go and then you come back. But you go there, then familiarize your self, then go through it and move on to the next level. That's the warrior path."

I identified with Sophie and her suffering enough to see how surrendering to Shambhala required an enormous act of faith. To go from constant introspection to self-acceptance and acceptance of all things—even the subway—was quite a journey. Her current state of calm and happiness encouraged me. I began thinking of the act of surrender, and decided that starting small with meditation might do me some good.

○ ○ ○

It happened spontaneously when I awoke alone one Sunday with a new sense of readiness. My boyfriend had gone away for a weekend gig. I didn't think the empty space next to me in the bed would make as much of a difference as it did. There I was, faced with space. The dot, the eastern rising sun, slid to mind easily. I mentally held on to it before the stack of things I might like to do on a Sunday began filling up the space. I lay under the covers and could see out the window, the canopy of trees, the sky, a cloud creeping by. How long could I remain this wakeful, this aware of life, nature, the dot, before the mental listing of errands, plans, and chores eclipsed the clarity? Still staring, I had an image of myself walking through the day with the sky and the cloud guiding me rather than following slave-like behind the confines of my everyday mind. Walking around this way felt like a dare.

I left my bed and moved through the apartment. It seemed insignificant, my container for world objects, my drawer for myself. The place was a mess, my books, papers, clothes piled on top of each other. I detached myself from the nuisance before the impulse to clean grew too large. Quickly I entered the shower, impressed for the first time that Brooklyn water, though overexposed to chlorine and city pipes, still maintained an essence of cleanliness. I let it drip down my face, a testament to things fundamentally working. The dot returned and, as if hovering above me, bestowed a transparent clarity like a path before me. I didn't know if imagining one's own clarity and gentle disposition was exactly what Beth had meant, or what Shambhala intended, but here I was, suspending my ordinary routine, grasping unencumberedness.

Fear, in Shambhala, acts as a mirror for our feelings about ourselves and about the world. "When we are afraid of ourselves and afraid of the seeming threat the world presents, then we become extremely selfish. We want to build our own little nests, our own

Cocoons, so that we can live by ourselves in a secure way," Trungpa writes. I couldn't help but think about the smallness of the world I'd created for myself in the apartment. The place was all but wrapped in silk and hanging from a tree branch. Our nest protected my relationship. Was even that a Cocoon? With my boyfriend—roommate, protector, and lover—out of town, what did I have representing me, really, but a dark messy apartment? I thought about the dot, how it might expand my sense of self now that I was completely alone. Why was this something I could only do alone?

I moved beyond the dirty dishes, unsure of where to place their significance, and glided out the door. On the train I observed the others around me. Most of the twentysomething hipsters were in that Sunday morning state. Their messy hair and rumpled clothing from Saturday night gave away their disorder, their wild energy moving outside the lines of dot-ness. I felt contained by comparison. But was I restrained? I thought about the dot, about whether or not it was just another Cocoon, a way of obscuring objects in the world with "clarity." Was this clarity really liberating, or was it a type of restriction? Looking again at the partyers in my subway car, most likely on their way to brunch, I felt a pang of longing. It'd been a while since I'd been out partying, stayed the night somewhere random, and then miserably met other hung-over friends for coffee and eggs. It seemed fun now, as I glimpsed it from afar on my way to try out another way of life. Why did I feel like I was giving something up?

Then I remembered Sophie's words about staying strong throughout the training in moments of weakness. "Shambhala is about making a connection with yourself. If I've made a connection with myself, it doesn't really matter what is happening around me. I used to be extremely threatened, and sometimes I still am, by thin people or anorexic people around me. But once I remember I have made a connection with myself, it doesn't matter so much." I thought about the dot, about the sun, and silently celebrated when the hipsters on the train faded into the back of my mind. My day's agenda to open my mind emerged and I relaxed. This dot-consciousness might be the very ticket to freedom. I arrived at

26th Street, in the doorway facing a panel of buzzers—dots. I pressed number 6, to the New York Shambhala Center.

Riding up in the elevator, I applied the Shambhala definition of warriorship to my present state. This morning, I dared to listen to my own needs. Addressing the peripheral things in my life before addressing my own needs was my habit. This morning, though, addressing myself had been easy. But would it be so easy when my boyfriend was back? It would be hard to resist our routine that had no connection to dot consciousness. Now as I spent my day alone I felt so close to this new sense of self, I wanted to restructure every relationship I had around it.

The bell of the elevator sounded, a single dot of song. The door slid open, welcoming me to an expanse of space—carpeted, clean, and spare. Little in the central room indicated spiritual activity. On the right, an organized desk where no one sat was stacked with brochures, papers, items for taking. Framed drawings of Asian landscapes and a giant yellow dot painted on canvas acted as a mirror, a model for my sense of self. I checked for signs of phoniness—fashion statements that might distract me from meditation, but found none. Only four banners hanging flag-style from the wall, among them the orange banner that had made Sophie cry, dubbed the space a Shambhala center. The loft space was just that—space. To my left a closet without a door held a rack of jackets hanging over rows of shoes. I kicked mine lightly next to the last pair in line. Shoeless, I padded forward. Adjacent to the closet a room with red square cushions with yellow borders awaited people who would arrive at the scheduled time.

At 11 o'clock instruction and introduction to meditation would be given. I was early. I scanned the area for a sign, a place where I should go. A vase of flowers on an end table caught my eye. I sniffed their dampened scent just short of fragrant. Then a murmur of voices drifted in from an adjoining room. I saw people gathered around buckets of flowers, listening to a speaker. He was an instructor giving Japanese flower arranging classes. I entered the room, curious to see other spiritual people participating in life.

The gentle crowd of Sunday morning flower arrangers may have otherwise been churchgoers. Instead of praying they silently wound their hands around leaves, wires, and green Styrofoam blocks floating in small trays of water. Instead of absorbing a liturgy, they trained themselves in an art made of beauty, nature, and grace. I hovered behind them watching their efforts to balance "man" with "earth" with "God," three important elements in Japanese design. What was I doing in there, among the floral parishioners? I observed, precariously standing in the space in between involvement and detachment. The pans of flowers under construction looked as though they were reaching for balance. Wax flower bending from the back of the arrangement forward. "With that branch are you signifying God touching the earth?" the instructor asked a student. The student nodded. "Perhaps make it less desperate," the instructor suggested. The student nodded, letting the instructor reorient the stem. The rest of the students, some studiously, some playfully, crafted their vision. I was on the lookout for frenzied or frenetic characters who did not belong, folks who might expose the place as a house built of cards. But the flower-crafters held concentration and were noticeably calm. The spiritual principle of "being on the spot" looked as though it had transcended theory into activity. I saw it with my own doubting eyes.

When a man approached me to ask if I awaited meditation instruction, I wondered if he saw me as a dot. He looked more weathered than wise. A messy tousle of gray hair patched his head. He had not shaved that morning, but his clothes were clean. He didn't seem like a dot himself, but was well acquainted with the state of mind. I answered him as he gazed into my eyes intently, as though he understood before I even gave an answer. I inwardly groaned, recognizing a look I had not seen on either Beth or Sophie. The look of someone who went too far. His smile seemed slightly mad. This man knew the practice, the routine, the style of "spirituality." But he unnerved me in his calm.

Nevertheless, I followed his hand, which guided me into the empty room with red cushions. I sat on one and folded my legs into a yoga position, with my knees lower than my hips. The man sat facing me, and shook his head gently. "That's not really necessary," he said. "This is not a discipline in the same way as other disciplines you might have studied," he said, carefully avoiding presumption. I knew he was talking about yoga, though. "Try to just sit comfortably, sit up straight. It doesn't have to be painful."

"I'm not really in pain," I said. "But okay." I loosened my position and relaxed into Indian style. A few others trickled into the room. A Puerto Rican man with a muscular build, as if he'd recently come out of the military. A young brown-eyed woman with naturally curled hair, wearing a sleeveless sweater and a flowing skirt. She hunched her body but smiled continuously, an effective shield from attention I'd used before. The Puerto Rican man stood straight and held his face sternly. Both assumed seated positions. The three of us sat there looking at the instructor. He spoke tentatively. "Well, here we are, I guess. Welcome to Shambhala training. The woman who is supposed to be teaching isn't here, so I guess I'll fill in with some history. . . ."

I knew Shambhala instructors were all volunteers. They rotated shifts frequently in order to accommodate each other's schedules and lives. But did volunteering introduce a flaky and uncertain element to the transmission of these teachings? I hoped not. I didn't want to be involved with any spiritual teaching that attracted even tangential flakiness. Before I had a chance to sigh, a thin, weathered woman swept into the room gracefully and moved to the front of the room. The uninspired substitute seemed relieved. He stood, gestured to the cushion on which he sat, indicating that the newcomer, the proper instructor, should replace him. The overt graciousness between them embarrassed them both. Neither of them was entirely comfortable with this custom of generosity, still.

The male instructor bumbled out of the room and returned with a glass of water for the female instructor. She sipped, gratefully. This exchange worked a little better. The woman took on a subtle authority, noticeably setting aside the previous circumstances that made her late by looking at all of us pointedly.

"So," she said. "This is a meditation instruction. This is not Shambhala training, but knowing how to meditate is an aspect of the Shambhala training process if you are interested in pursuing it." She sighed, I couldn't tell if it was a sign of relaxation or fatigue.

"So, meditation is a way to clear the mind. We try and do it in a quiet place like this, or anywhere you feel you can relax. You don't need a shrine or a special room to do it in, although," she specified, "you can certainly have one if that's how you work." She indicated the cushions. "We sit up straight on a cushion, comfortably, not rigidly. This is a relaxation for the body and the mind." Her effort to emphasize relaxation was a bit of a paradox: why she didn't simply present the practice in a relaxed manner eluded me.

"Meditation is a stilling of the mind. So what you do is lower your gaze to about four or five feet in front of you, pick a spot on the floor, and keep it there. You are just sitting, keeping aware of your out-breath. The out-breath is your exhalation."

We centered on the exhalation because during the process of meditation thoughts will begin to cross through the mind. "Stuff will come up," she said. "Your mind will wander away from clarity, to what you were just doing, something someone said to you five years ago, the dinner plan for later." She sighed heavily. "That's the practice."

"Be sure not to reprimand yourself mentally, though. No association is made to the thoughts that distract you, except for one. You simply think the word, *thinking* every time a thought enters your mind. Then use the out-breath to bring yourself back to clarity. That's it really," she said, almost bored. "Let's try it."

I sat up straight, inhaled deeply, then heard her voice interrupt me. "It's not necessary to inhale deeply," she said. "Just breathe regularly. We are just sitting." I suspended my irritation, permitting the teacher to invade just this once. If I wanted this taste of structured guidance, I might have to get used to someone else being part of the process.

I shut my eyes, then remembered we were supposed to keep them open, partly, resting them four or five feet in front of us. I rested them on the toe of the instructor's shoe, scuffed brown leather. I exhaled, squinting my eyes a little, trying not to exert too much effort. The shoe stared back at me. I used to have shoes like that, I thought. Then I remembered, no thinking. "Thinking," I said mentally, and then exhaled, sending the ideas of the shoe out of consciousness. For a minute the thought disappeared. The space in my mind was clear.

So this is meditation, I thought. It's not the easiest thing in the world. It's not that fun. I wonder if I'm one of the only people feeling this way, right now. I felt a heaviness creep in, the kind that kept me from getting up in the morning. I recognized this gloom as the kind that accompanied my thinking about life's isolation rather than feeling its unity. It often appeared when I didn't interact with enough people, and I didn't really know if anyone actually felt the same way. Despair flooded my mental space quickly. How the hell does meditation work anyway? I whined mentally. Don't people vanish into oblivion when they meditate? Wait, I thought, and the flood stopped as if I'd put my finger in the dike. "Thinking," I said, then exhaled. I felt relief wash over me; this wasn't my ordinary state of being, I didn't have to swim through it. "Thinking," I repeated, exhaling. The despair was gone. Clarity remained.

My body wanted to move, just to check and see if everything was still there, in place, not dead or asleep. Especially my shoulders, back, and spine. I remembered reading Trungpa's writing about posture in meditation, that slouching was a sign of giving in to neurosis. I straightened my spine, surprised to feel the lengthening. I stopped my fidgeting, trying to feel the same comfort in my new position. I wondered if I looked relaxed like I was meditating, or if my half-open eyes looked indecisive, like I wasn't concentrating. Was I concentrating? Somewhat. I'd had a little success chasing away the despair. I'd felt a moment of clarity. "Thinking," I said immediately, exhaling. That was the end of that dialogue.

"Okay," the instructor interrupted. "How did that go for everyone? Would anyone like to share?"

I didn't know if I wanted to share or not. I was exhausted. The effort it took to sit still was magnificently larger than I'd thought "doing nothing" would be.

"It's not like doing nothing," I volunteered.

"No," the instructor sighed into my eyes. "It's not. It's definitely not doing nothing. It's hard work," she said, then caught herself, then caught herself catching herself. Was there no end to this process of clearing one's mind of compulsion? "What I mean," she launched into even more explanation, "is that it's not supposed to be hard work, that's why we practice—so that it is effortless. But getting to the place where it is effortless takes effort," she said. "That's why it feels like such hard work." She smiled weakly, drained by the conundrum.

The other two people in the room volunteered comments that told as much about their state of being as mine did of mine. "I just got really uncomfortable," the brown-eyed young woman said. "My body started to hurt, my back especially ached. So I sent my breathing to the pain."

I recognized her language from yoga instruction, what you're supposed to do when pushing your body becomes painful. The instructor furrowed her eyebrows. "You're not supposed to be in pain," she said. "Do you have back pain usually?"

"Only when I sit still for too long," the young woman said. Then after thinking about it, she said, "I guess five minutes is too long for me to sit." She smiled at answering her own question, though it was an unsatisfactory conclusion.

The man among us presumed a distance that I first thought was a sign of previous involvement with a similar tradition, maybe a traditional branch Buddhism. "If five minutes is too long, that's something to learn about yourself," he said. Then he said, "It takes a while before you become comfortable with just sitting with your mind." Even though he said it as though he knew what he was talking about, I didn't get the sense he actually knew. Neither did the brown-eyed woman. She nodded politely with an unconvincing smile of thanks.

"Have you done this before?" the instructor asked the man.

"I've done a good amount of other things," he said boastfully. "I've meditated in other practices." He named one or two teachers he studied with in New York. The instructor nodded. "But the thing to focus on is not focusing," he said, giving me and the other woman a nod. "It takes a while, but you'll get it." He was trying to be supportive but he sounded slightly pretentious.

The session was over, and I returned home a little more with my body in the mind of the dot. I felt whole, somehow, freed from indecision, from confusion about God, and less wanting of a higher system of learning. Meditation, I decided, was my system of learning, right now. It was something I could come and go to quietly, without pantheons, other worlds, ceremonies, or social restrictions. If I wanted to, I could pull all of those elements into my life, but still take time out for sitting and meditating whenever the urge struck me.

Sitting required that I do the opposite of what I had been doing on my spiritual quest: seeking, searching, and testing external systems. To my frenetic self, shifting behavior seemed stagnating and counterproductive. At the same time, I knew the change would satisfy me, as it had already begun to. Sitting was an active practice I could employ without ceremony or other people, and yet feel intimately connected, like I had traveled far and arrived somewhere within. I wouldn't worry about anyone—either a human teacher or a God who was watching—seeing my progress or my backsliding. I didn't have to explain it to anyone. It was mine, all mine.

For a month I went to a writers' colony in Vermont, where a meditation room was at my disposal. Though it took a few days for me to venture in, the loneliness of one rainy afternoon led me behind the herb garden to the small wood hut. Inside, everything I needed to practice meditation lay before me. On the bark-colored carpet, nine red meditation cushions faced the low table against the far wall. Pillowed wicker chairs in the back of the room offered the option to sit or slouch, or maybe read a book from the vast selection on the Kabbalah, Hinduism, a Jewish interpretation of the Quran, a book of Gnostic verses. A skylight high on the wall kept onlookers curious while allowing light into the one-room hut. Though I was completely alone, something about the preconceived activity of the room encouraged me to relax into the empty space. These qualities were a guarantee that I'd be in good company. I removed my shoes, obeying the note tacked on the Japanese wood-carved wall, and took my seat in the center of the room.

I faced an eye-level wooden table stocked with incense, a meditation bowl, and candles. Above the altar a print of the yellow dot, the eastern sun, caught my attention and invited staring. I was glad no one else was in the room with me. Someone else's posture, or breathing, or outfit surely would lead my concentration astray.

The same thing happens at the gym when I'm looking for a distraction from abdominal exercises. But by myself it was easier to remain in my own state of mind, to stare without focus. I lit the candles. The smell of burned wick made the air familiar and confirmed my presence there.

I did a last-minute check around the room, glanced at the time: 1:50 P.M. How long would I be gone? As though preparing to climb aboard a space shuttle headed for the moon, I felt apprehensive about closing myself off from the world. Was it the fear of leaving my familiar state of mind, or fear of arriving in the unknown state I sought that bothered me more? I didn't know. Half-lowering my eyes, I felt most of the room go dark but for a tiny slit at the base of my eyelids, an opening. I sat as still as I could, slowly descending into a place where random thoughts, concerns, and ideas simply passed by as if behind a pane of glass.

Sounds outside the window—feet crunching on gravel, wind kicking up in the treetops—kept my mind from fully engaging with the empty space that Shambhala people insist is always there. I tried tuning out the sounds, reaching for the white space that seemed just out of my grasp. I could see it; even feel extended moments of its stillness a little easier these days. But detaching fully did not come with ease. Not at all. The mental impulse to think seemed physical, and my body desperately wanted to move, twitch, or tense up. I floated through the flickers of frustration. The minutes passed. After a while, I didn't hear sounds, or notice the bit of light at the base of my eyelids anymore. When I opened my eyes fully the clock said 2:10. I put on my shoes and left, feeling like the world was a little larger.

Meditating feels like flying. The material world disappears and, as if on a hot air balloon, the vast expanse of sky becomes the only truth. Landing back down on Earth brought increments of self-understanding within a month of regular practice. It reminded me of when I first started dating my boyfriend, the sense of calm walking home after a date, feeling as though I'd met the right person. If someone had only said that meditating was like love without the grief, I might have tried it a long time ago.

CHAPTER SEVEN

The Act *of* Surrender

For as long as I can remember, my recurring image of spiritual experience looked like this: I am standing outside in the country, surrounded by trees, or on top of a mountain, dazzled by the sunset forecasting the last moment of a moment. No ceremony marks the beginning or end of this moment, but a distinct sense of timelessness exists in the atmosphere. I fall into union with an interior self that I can only describe as pure, untouched, and deeply connected to all of existence. The environment inside my body and outside my body is the same. There is no me; there is only everything.

That was the recurring fantasy. In reality, my union with this interior self was fleeting and imprecise. It was as hard to enter the spiritual state of being as it was to enter a dream on demand. I wondered why it wasn't possible to access that state of being all the time, but secretly I knew the answer. Union with the interior self requires an act of surrender, and I didn't want to commit such a grave act alone.

From my tour of practitioners and their practices, I noticed surrendering to a tradition by oneself—not in the company of others—was how each woman had found her interior union. But was it the only way? Could one surrender in the company of others and find a collective path, a shared interior union? Though I had only met women who had individually surrendered to their chosen spiritual pursuits, my belief in the possibility of a collective spirituality available within the larger, public, outside world was still unshakable. Perhaps I simply hadn't found the proper road or the ultimate event yet. I read books like *Life after God* by Douglas Coupland, watched conspiracy-theory TV shows like *The X-Files,* and attended large group meditation gatherings in Central Park in search of a massive merging of group consciousness. I gravitated to any sign of kinship among people my age in mainstream culture, hungrily. These events were athrong with hip, young New Yorkers, and though I returned home from each feeling charged and exhausted, I did not necessarily feel unified with the other participants, or with myself. For some reason, concrete evidence of public unity in the media or in mainstream culture overrode the significance of my own path and precious moments of interior union and spiritual awakening. Like teenagers who flocked to Woodstock '99 to share ideals of hope and freedom with others their age, I wanted public events to provide size and dimension to the largeness of my desire. I wanted a soundtrack, like the perfect song playing on a car stereo during a drive out of town. I wanted company. I didn't want the union to simply lie within me. That seemed too solitary and lonely, and the wrong match for my dream of being one with all.

Part of me knew that I needed to tune in, that it was necessary that I surrender on my own to some spiritual path or amalgam. I meditated in the morning, practiced yoga in my apartment and as often as I could in Uma's class, which now attracted more than fifty people a session. These practices suited me. But the notion that somewhere, *out there,* a more cohesive American community with an intrinsic understanding of unity awaited me kept me from fully entering any of these practices, for fear they wouldn't be perfect, that I'd expend effort—self-indulgent effort— for nothing.

Just as I had searched for the perfect job and kept working to make mine the perfect relationship, I wanted the perfect group of people to tell me, "You can stop searching now, you've found us. We are the right people." When it came to spirituality, I refused to believe there was no such thing as perfect.

In retrospect, my wanting more than just those fleeting moments of interior union denied their individual potential and power over my consciousness. The craving distracted me from milking those moments for their worth. But, hungry for social reinforcement of a free-flowing spirituality that existed in the everyday, in a part of every person's society, I continued looking for other experiences, for other means to get inside of myself and at the same time feel more connected to the outside world.

Externally searching nagged at me, though. It was the same kind of nagging as when I would be attracted to an item while shopping because I couldn't get the song from the commercial out of my head. After years of living in a society where advertising sold me what I wanted, I wanted to be sold a unifying myth, a sense of security. I wanted the fulfillment religion had promised me but had never delivered. The urge to search externally was maximized during those times when I stayed away from yoga for too long or skipped a few days of meditating. Sometimes the warm interior space faded almost completely when my boyfriend and I floundered in the conventions of couplehood or when my job didn't fulfill me creatively. I couldn't tell if the job or the relationship faltered because I stopped my practice, or if my practice faltered because the relationship and the job were taking their toll. Where did spiritual structure fall as a priority in my life? Why was maintaining a spiritual focus so difficult? The up and down was as annoying as quitting smoking when the urge to light up would not dissipate. I tried to ignore the tendency to stop practicing meditation or yoga. I knew I'd be better off—happier—if I stuck to it, but pretty soon I gave in to the urge to look outside again.

A few tried-and-true methods of consciousness-changing were close at hand. Raves, the dance parties of the '90s, speckled with drugs like Ecstasy and K, continually drew thousands to participate in massive rhythmic movement to the automated, unstopping beats of Techno. Combined with the speed and high of the drugs, raves drove the individual into atmospheric spirituality. The atmosphere drew a scene, and a scene always created a sense of community (like those drawn by the Grateful Dead, or hip hop). Should I pursue the atmosphere? Would it be enough? Spiritual atmosphere was not the same as spiritual experience, but the former would at least lend an opportunity for the latter to occur. I was undecided. But my options were running out. The other possibility for consciousness-changing was an extreme activity like sky diving or resting in a flotation tank. Both physically augmented the body's adrenaline levels, not to mention its position in time and space, thus inducing a change in consciousness. Oooh, experimental. Experimental as they were, these options seemed dated to me, like I'd already outgrown them and their quick fixes. I didn't just want a change of consciousness, I wanted to face the risk of surrender and have it be worth it, too.

Then I heard about an event that combined all three extremes—risk, festivity, and change of consciousness. Burning Man.

Burning Man has several creation myths. One says it began on a San Francisco beach in 1986, when one man burned an eight-foot wooden model of a stick figure to commemorate the summer solstice. Another says he burned the model in order to rid himself of a broken heart (and the man he used to be). For whatever reason, he'd invited twenty friends to participate in the loose, spontaneous ceremony. The ceremony became an event, and the event became one of those impossible-to-plan landmarks of fun. Each year the number of people doubled, the stick figure and the fire got a bit larger, and one man's ritual became a yearly party for hundreds, then thousands, to express themselves. In the early '90s, as the festivities beckoned more participants and solicited many artists to display their creativity, the police moved the fire from the beach to the desert in Nevada.

Many acquaintances of mine had been going to Burning Man for years. They described it as a debauched Olympic event. They came home from the desert after Labor Day weekend with a West Coast glow—a combination of a healthy sunburn, protein deficiency, and a new optimistic view on the meaning of life. This change in attitude remained noticeable in their disposition for a few weeks. They talked about the crowds, their bodies baking in the sun each day, the pure bliss of walking around naked with strangers, of building and taking part in art projects, productions, dances, and concerts day and night. They spoke as though they'd seen a new, successful model of society. As though they'd had a taste of living a better way.

Their enthusiasm resembled intoxication. Burning Man fulfills a dramatic urge, provides a rush of life, challenges the participants' very survival, they said. But it also fulfills a spiritual purpose, one friend told me. "It's spirituality for Gen X," she said. How so, I wondered, thinking about how my isolated, independent spiritual practices lacked glue to my generation. "Burning Man is very cyber, which is what bonds our generation more than anything else. You have all these individuals coming together and maintaining their individuality, yet connecting through a lattice. It has all the liberation and independence of cyberspace, but all the promise of community. It *is* a community," she said excitedly. How the community was spiritual, though, I didn't know. I believed all communities had the potential for spiritual connection—if everyone shared in consciousness. But I didn't feel consciously connected to other people when I cruised the Web. As it stood now, I found cyberspace as spiritually promising as suburbia.

Yet live, visible evidence of Burning Man's bonding power appealed to me. So many of its strengths pulled at my desire to unite. It had an exotic location, in the highlands of the Nevada desert, and was celebrated at a convenient time on the calendar: during the first week of September. It had a gloriously destructive goal: burning a fifty-foot neon wooden stick figure (the man) loaded with explosives and fireworks. Much of its exclusivity lay in the danger/discomfort factor: Burning Man was not an event for creatures of comfort. An extensive warning on the ticket reads YOU VOLUNTARILY ASSUME THE RISK OF SERIOUS INJURY OR DEATH BY ATTENDING THIS EVENT. It escaped the trappings of mainstream society. No participant works a job at the festival. There is no money exchange. All commerce is based on what the founder calls a "gift economy." The attendees are generally of the same socioeconomic background. The crowd is young, white, and middle-class, and packs more men than women. Nearly 22,000 people attended in 1999. These five points gave Burning Man coveted status in my mind as a cool, albeit elitist, thing to do, like getting a summer Eurail pass to Europe between years at college. Besides the exotic cool, however, the event possessed a dark coolness. It was realistic in its destructive power. It was a dangerous vacation among familiar faces with a built-in purpose. But was it a spiritual experience that could change my consciousness? Friends insisted it could and would.

As with my pursuit of other spiritual experiences, drawbacks were necessary considerations, and Burning Man had quite a few. It costs a bundle. One must rent or bring a car, since the closest city and airport are in Reno, three hot desert hours away. One must buy or make desert camping gear, including a lean-to–like structure to shade you from the harsh climate that includes scalding sun, dehydrating dryness, violent wind and sandstorms, and extreme temperature drops at night. The cost of a ticket for the event in 1999 is upward of $65. In 2000, it is close to $200. This amount defrays costs of renting land from the Nevada Bureau of Land Management, hiring park rangers, an ambulance corps, a staff of people to clean the porta-potties several times a day, everyday, and a small fire department from a neighboring town. In addition to transport and ticket prices, there is the cost of bringing in a week's worth of critical survival needs: ice, sunscreen, food, and water, first aid, bathing and cooking facilities, anything you'd need on a camping trip, plus two wardrobes; one each for temperatures that go up to 110 and down to 40. If you didn't bring what you needed, you couldn't simply run out and buy it. One of the few rules of the event was a prohibition on selling. All exchanges are in the form of food or gifts.

A friend of mine had attended Burning Man for the past two years. So excited was she to coax me into experiencing the "temporary community," she offered to set me up with practical needs at the festival—like a space in her camp, food, friends, toiletries, and all other necessities—if I bought myself a ticket, some water, and got myself there. After all of my pining for a spiritual community, hers was an offer impossible to refuse. I decided to keep an open mind—it wasn't hard, I wanted Burning Man to be the generational community I sought—and leaped at the opportunity.

I flew to San Francisco. Via a Burning Man listserve, I found a woman who was looking for another solo traveler on her way to Black Rock City, the festival's desert location. She offered the passenger seat of her car in exchange for sharing gas expenses and good conversation. Caravaning with a stranger carved out my first point of entry into the Burning Man community. It recalled the carefree days of college, when I took a ride with anyone going the same way who looked my age and had the right smile and an Earth Day bumper sticker on their car. We began our six-hour drive. She was going to Burning Man because she believed that a spiritual community was not only possible but necessary. Not the philosophy of your typical Hanger-On. We became acquainted quickly. She was courteous; she offered to buy me water since I was flying in from the East Coast and presumably wouldn't have had a place to store it. Her silver hatchback, loaded with my water, her water, and both our gear, sagged slightly. She agreed to haul a second mountain bike on the back of her hatchback for another woman—someone she never met—because she had the means to do so. She was responsible; she worked for a nonprofit IPO. She'd had a few significant relationships but now lived the single life. Professionally, financially, and emotionally secure, this woman was politically active and aware. She filled me in on San Francisco politics over the last few years. I thought her a perfect product of her Virginia Protestant family, attending Burning Man like a conscientious volunteer of a church group. Escaping mainstream society for a long weekend was not the sole end of her action. Rather, she hoped to grow in the company of others.

Her path to growth included one method I would not take part in, which made me wonder if I'd miss out. She planned to camp with a friend of hers who agreed to bring her a supply of recreational drugs. "I don't do this kind of thing often, but I think its important to take opportunities to expand, especially with good people who are coming together for a common purpose," she said. We talked about drugs for a while. I was of the teetotaling opinion that if the event had any kind of backbone, I wouldn't need drugs to see it. The common purpose should be visible to anyone, no matter their state of mind. The sun darkened into purple hues as we sped through the desert. Our expectations about the festival, the society it purported to create, and its common purpose dotted our conversation. I told her I had very few expectations beyond the hope of massive unification among people our age. She told me she expected it to be an explosion of possibility for community and culture.

I'd done a little homework and skimmed the copy of a speech the founder of Burning Man gave in 1998. It talked about culture as a natural process. "Culture," he said, "is a naturally occurring phenomenon. It just happens. You can't plan it, and you can't control it—any more than you can control the flow of a river or the growing of a blade of grass. It's something that we as animals are adapted to do, and we spontaneously do it under certain social conditions. It ain't going to happen in an elevator, though. Culture isn't going to break out standing in line waiting to get a ticket to some event."

The idea behind the culture portion of the speech was that Burning Man attendees would have an opportunity to create an original culture. I guess I'd see once we got there. Certainly, we were all young humans taking a vacation in the same desert, under the same sun. That one truth alone held promise of a naturally occurring phenomenon. With or without drugs.

Nightfall, we knew from previous attendees who advised us to arrive in the cool temperatures of dusk, signaled the beginning of the festival's activities. We were anxious to get there in "time," though for what we had no idea since the festival continued twenty-four hours a day. We snaked along the one-lane local road until we caught up to the end of a line of red taillights glowing in the darkness. We turned off our engine: traffic had stopped dead between here and the playa, the five-mile plateau of desert. Crawling along the road, the windshield slowly filled with dust over the course of an hour. Here we were, parked in line, waiting to get a ticket to some event. The last place, according to the founder, where culture could spontaneously occur. Contrary to that notion, elements of festival culture passed by. We watched individuals walk from car to car, their flashlights and their headlamps illuminating the empty expanse of dry, hard ground. The moon lit the surrounding landscape. In the distance, jagged rock scraped the sky. At the foot of the mountains lay the "city" with makeshift shelters speckling miles of desert ground.

Neither of us spoke during the wait, perhaps in attempt to ignore the mundane reality of such a large event needing some sort of institution and structure. While we waited, one of the wandering individuals, a volunteer for the festival, stuck his head in the window of our car. His face was painted with neon designs and he wore an elated expression. "Have you brought enough water? Have you brought food? Do you have plenty of sunscreen of at least SPF 30?" were his questions. This was his only job, to cartoonishly ask questions, to hear the answers and then admit us, or to send us away if our equipment was insufficient. The festival energy oozed from his presence into the stagnant car environment, and both of us perked up immediately. The festival was happening, suddenly. We had arrived. Hearing that we had come prepared, the greeter delightedly handed us a packet of information—a map, a newspaper issued by one of Black Rock City's temporary presses, and a list of where we might find our camps. He slapped the side of the car and yelled, "Well, Happy Burning Man. Have a great time, be safe, and make sure you PISS CLEAR the whole time!" "Piss clear" would be one of the most repeated slogans: an important reminder to drink plenty of water to avoid dehydration, one possible scourge of the event.

We pulled into the temporary parking spaces beside a herd of message boards. They stood like caribou, covered in bright construction paper, upon which messages for newcomers were scribbled. Among the open invitations to sushi dinners at various camps, ads for performances using dead animals, and personal notes from friends, cousins, and lovers to latecomers giving directions to their camps, I saw no note from the friends I was to meet. Nor did my ride. We entered the information booth, conveniently positioned beside the message boards. Burning Man was organized, if not sophisticated. Inside we consulted the rolodex and found the

address of each of our camps. A giant map of the "park" covered
the wall and captured my attention. It was loaded with toothpicks
and flags sticking out of various locations, resembling a UN strat-
egy for attack. The theme of Burning Man this year was "The
Wheel of Time," referring to the moments before the millennial
turn, a countdown that participants couldn't help but live with
consciously because of the design of the "city." The city plan took
the shape of a crescent moon, with streets and avenues running in
a grid. Avenues were named after planets in our solar system, and
streets were named according to fifteen-minute intervals within
the hours of the clock. In the epicenter, a crude image of a stick
figure stood alone, separated from activity. It was the "man"—the
effigy whom we had come to burn. His tiny image mirrored my
own sense of place. He represented the individual. He represented
the species. He represented energy that would burn under the
right conditions. He seemed strangely desperate. I had come all
this way to burn him with friends. Was there a higher purpose?

I remembered another part of the organizer's speech that
touched on a sense of mission, though it resembled more of a
mythology. He spoke of the displaced human condition. It had to
do with the birth of mass production in England, 200 years ago.
Once merchants realized that with machines they could create
textiles at an incredible rate, they usurped common land shared by
everybody and sold it as property. "Suddenly they created,
overnight, a class of displaced people, who'd lived in the country,
who had a culture that went back hundreds of years, that connected them to each other, and connected them to the land. . . .
This class of landless people became what Marx finally called the
Proletariat. These were people who'd been deprived of their folk
culture, deprived of high culture, they'd been deprived of everything. And they turned into the trash of the world."

Was this the motivation behind Burning Man and my participation in it? Was I reclaiming the land with my displaced proletariat generation? Were we the trash of the world, and Burning the
Man who displaced us in retaliation? It was hard to thoroughly
embrace the anti-establishment implications. After all, working for
the man was how we all could afford to get here.

Camp locations in mind, we set off driving slowly, obeying the road signs to keep more dust out of the already thick air. Rows of U-Hauls and minivans parked haphazardly along the streets gave us an idea of where one camp ended and the next one began. I could see people hanging out in their shade structures, makeshift desert housing made of drapes and poles. They barbecued, slouched on their couches and chairs with drinks in hand, wore boots and wool sweaters. I presumed my friends would be doing the same: settling down before evening events in the communal space, sharing in the Burning Man environment like Sufis shared their living space, like Shambhala practitioners shared a meditation room, or yogis shared the sound of "om." All spiritual experiences I'd witnessed so far offered unification through sharing, which was usually symbolic of a higher purpose or ideal. Burning Man participants shared everything—space, food, tasks around camp. Sharing seemed to be the ideal in and of itself.

People at our camp had already built our shade structure out of an army parachute stretched over a half-golf ball-like structure made of plastic piping. It looked a lot like a small, unfinished Epcot Center. In the row of other similar shade structures, some more crude, others impressively conceived, it resembled a lively home on an avenue of a post-apocalyptic Levittown. In effect it was a giant tent of the bigtop variety. I acknowledged the tent as my home for the next four days.

I peered in from my seat in the car. Glow sticks hung from the ceiling inside our home like neon worms, illuminating only the fact that we had insufficient lighting to see the various things littered across the imitation oriental carpet: makeup bags, paper towels, coolers, water gallons, dirty socks, canned goods, Band-Aids, shoes. The place was already more trashed than a college lounge on the weekends. It smelled like sunscreen. The Who blasted out of a nearby car stereo. No one was around.

I was slightly horrified, suddenly realizing that I'd be surrounded by desert dust and camp clutter for the next four days, probably unable to shower more than once. It wasn't unsanitary, the tent, just without order. This was the reality we'd be sharing. Were chaotic and dire living conditions elements of unification

here? Was uncleanliness the risk we sought? I couldn't believe it
was. But how to justify this extremity as a necessary bond with my
generation wasn't yet apparent. Ignoring cleanliness told me
everyone was thinking about something else, presumably something more worthy. Camp was just a repository for basic human
maintenance. Unlike real camping, living off the land at Burning
Man wasn't possible: the playa was dead; no babbling brooks or
rivers offered their services. I knew we were not at Burning Man
to be one with nature. Maybe marginal living was akin to breaking
boundaries of comfort, in order to get in touch with our true
selves. Like sitting in an uncomfortable asana in order to feel the
divine. Yes. That must be it, I reasoned. Otherwise we'd have a
camp of dirty, angry, and depressed people. And like I said, no one
was around.

○ ○ ○

Upon closer look, figures moving in the shadows told me our
camp was not empty. Two men, tall, thin, and accessorized in
feather boas, facial glitter, blue lipstick, and bindis across their
cheeks emerged from the back of the shade structure and
approached the car. They greeted me effusively, taking my bags
without my having to ask. They offered me food, beer, and
cigarettes while I waited for my friend, who would be back in just
a few minutes, they said. I sat in one of the lawn chairs under a
purple glow stick, and watched them strut around camp to "Going
Mobile." They looked fabulous, like two glam rock stars primping
before a performance.

I barely recognized my friend J., usually a blonde, bookish-bor-
dering-on-librarianesque beauty, in her Burning Man gear—
motorcycle boots and pants with an Indian silk sarong wrapped
over them, an old pullover sweater, cowboy hat, loads of glitter
makeup. Feeling underdressed, I could see that costume played a
role at our camp. We headed out into the desert, J., myself, and one
of the glam boys who rode a bicycle. The three of us wove
through the streets already crowded with costumed partyers
enjoying the ultimate blowout. Everyone looked spectacular, as
though dressed and primed for a giant show. But there was no

show. We were walking through the show. The next three days were to be a show. If I wanted, I could be part of the show, too.

I heard pulsations of massive sound systems pumping out ambient electronic music. Some of the best DJs in the world hauled in their equipment and set up raves all across the playa, J. told me. Raves? In the desert? The more I walked around, in fact, I saw that many modern festivities had been transported here and had become tools of transgression—elaborate orchestras of handmade instruments, desert dancing, drinking, debauchery, and lots of drugs. These were typical means of escape and enjoyment in everyday society. But here, where everyday society was replaced by an escapist's paradise, the trangressive elements functioned more as a challenge than recreation. Trangression was the main thing; it was what people were to do for the next three days. Trangression would motivate our exploration, permit us to express who we truly were. Handling the volatile trangressive devices, in either creative or destructive ways, was the game.

The organizer of Burning Man had talked about creativity as a way to liberation. He even said, "We've given you all the chance to live like artists out here. Everyone of you can live like an artist. That means you can give everything away and live on the edge of survival. Just give it all away and live on the edge of survival, 'cause that's how artists live. . . . And what's happening is that people are coming back from Burning Man and beginning to live like Burning Man in their daily lives. I mean, this event doesn't really mean a whole lot if it's just an entertainment event, a way to blow off steam and then go back to what we call reality. What they call reality really isn't going to be reality in the future, and it never really was."

I walked out into the reality of Burning Man to see how people gave themselves away. The open playa glowed with recognizable elements of modernity but set against the empty space, the objects and events lost their everyday definitions and took on new ones. Like art. The red and orange neon outline of the man stood auspiciously aloft in the emptiness, an icon selling nothing. Airline runway lights circled the man in a fifty-foot perimeter. Outside of his area, art installations, fantasy camps, and outrageous activities sprouted up haphazardly. A field hockey rink, lit by stadium lights and emceed by a referee in a black-and-white striped jacket, held twelve lithe young men wearing dust masks as they played a full game. Desert cars roared passed us across the open space. Each was gutted and refashioned with tractor wheels or bicycle wheels, was often doorless, or was covered in stainless steel to suit the demands of the playa.

We turned right at the Man, toward the pulsating music. No rules or restrictions on behavior so far. Police, park rangers, ambulance crews, and fire departments had been enlisted for the event. Their presence was so well cloaked, however, that people could walk into Bianca's Smut Shack, watch others have sex, and enjoy a grilled cheese sandwich without feeling like a raid was imminent. While the combination of lawlessness and indulgence was not "spiritual," as I knew it, it certainly liberated the spirit. But could liberating the spirit necessarily facilitate spiritual living?

A distant sculpture of three daisies, easily twenty feet tall, marked a dance area. Soul music blasted into the night and elaborately dressed club kids kicked up desert dust as they danced. We dragged ourselves there and danced until I couldn't breathe any more. Green laser beams streaked overhead onto the side of the mountains, vibrating in unsteady patterns. The wind kicked up. I was nearly out of water. We weathered a dust storm home.

I barely slept at night. I was the only one at camp who actually tried. The drum circles and the beat of the raves did not stop until after the sun came up. During the day, the desert heat was dry but deadly. I tried connecting with people around me, for a walk, a chat, a hang, but found myself with little energy for others. People walked around looking much like I felt, alternately exhausted and exhilarated. Hot, happy, flummoxed, fried, drunk, dehydrated. Roaming the streets, visiting theme camps like the Temple of Reformed Hedonism for free margaritas and scalp massages, and Camp Sunscreen, where teams of naked people massaged sunscreen onto your naked body, threw me into the community. The atmosphere encouraged anything and everything. The pulse of the scene was everywhere. It never stopped. I felt constantly drawn out, and I found myself craving time to retreat within. But I couldn't find it. I tried meditating in the tent, giving up when it became too stuffy and unpleasant. A few mornings I awoke and did some yoga under the sun before it got too hot. Before privacy was disturbed. After a while I gave up. I could not resist the drive to extend myself in as many directions as possible. To overexert. I succumbed to the undertow. During the days I explored the desert and the temporary life thrust upon it, as though we were in the last days of the world.

I boiled down each day, little by little. Biking from camp to camp, wandering the sights on the playa, I moved around as much as possible in effort to utilize the constant stream of energy. I had little energy to intellectualize or even enjoy the art—stimulation overload prevented me from processing beyond acknowledging the sheer spectacle. A man, known as "tesla coil man," had dressed in electricity-bearing materials in order to allow volts of electricity to shoot through his body. His purple electric silhouette impressed me, but I wondered if I needed a similar contraption in order to endure the full capacity of Burning Man. Then I remembered, most people here were on drugs.

Though exhausted at night, the roving urgency of others took hold of me, and I seemed to awaken when everyone's drugs kicked in. Though I couldn't imagine being on drugs here, since the random occurrences already challenged ordinary comprehension, accompanying someone on drugs for the evening gave me focus, a sense of mission in the wake of myriad distractions. I welcomed the opportunity to be someone's grounding force. It was the one way I could participate. The only way I felt comfortable giving. The second night I walked with one of my campmates while he tripped on Ecstasy and mushrooms. We hiked toward one of the many bonfires in order to warm up in the 40-degree weather. Soon enough, a larger crowd formed, and a parade led by a neon school of fish headed our way. That's right, fish. We may as well have been in the ocean. The school consisted of a dozen people on bicycles that had glowing neon fish attached above the bike seats, hovering over the cyclists' heads as the bikes glided by. The fish circled in toward the fire, and soon other neon figures appeared, monstrous skeleton puppet people in top hats, butterflies, and insects. A life-sized tree made out of old animal bones floated in from somewhere on a wheeled platform, with a Moses-like figure standing on its roots, shouting words. No one was listening, I was sure, because fantastic costumed figures were appearing now in a steady stream. Everyone followed them as they moved in a line. My campmate and I were swept up in the chaos, unable to find our way out. The neon parade carried instruments, small keyboards with preprogrammed electronic music, gongs, cymbals, and drums. The music emerging from their instruments blipped and beeped, honked and crashed. My campmate and I both roared at the awkward hilarity of the parade's movement and sounds. We roamed with the cacophonous crowd in no particular direction until we couldn't take the confusion anymore.

We walked across the playa. Lasers shot overhead, the sounds of the parade behind us echoed off the mountains, the shrieks of happy ravers rose and fell. Are we just two more in the festival of freaks, he wondered? I wanted to say yes, that we'd somehow caught on to a giant festival of wackos who just don't fit into the mainstream. But I knew it was untrue. That these were normal everyday people taking full advantage of a wide open space to do anything and everything they wanted. None of us fit into the mainstream. We belonged here to protest and celebrate that truth as much as anyone.

The third night on the playa was the Burn. A flare went up into the sky thirty minutes before the burn commenced, signaling all participants to gather. Fire burned everywhere at the foot of the Man: dancers performed with it, circus people ate it, and four flame-throwers positioned around the ring belched huge flames into the sky. The Man stood unlit. I loved him. I hated him. Three days of overextension had charged me with base emotions—the only kind that could survive in such a climate. Technical difficulties with the wiring, the neon, and the explosives were causing a delay. Glitches in the system prevented the Man's arms from raising above his head. Instead they remained at his sides, the yellow and red neon flickering from short circuits. The crowd grew impatient. The flame-throwers spit more fire into the sky, and the descending heat caused the crowd to take a step back every few minutes. We were all positioned dangerously close to the man. If something disastrous were to occur, if people were to catch fire, there'd be no preventing further chaos. Security—police, fire department, and ambulance— might easily be overwhelmed by one too many complications. I knew I was in danger just by standing here. That was the thrill, though. This was the high. Walking the line between potential danger and euphoria raised the stakes, and everybody knew it. Nothing was secure. The desert environment could turn on us any minute, the drugs people were on could bring psychotic darkness into the mind, the crowd could segment into violent factions—for all anyone knew, aliens could land.

I realized that this desperate reliance on each other's good spirit was overwhelmingly spiritual. When life or death was at stake, relying on love truly was the only option. If I were on drugs, I might have had greater trust in the fact that others would resort to love, not hate, in the case of an emergency.

Something went wrong. The man burst into flames without warning. Flames and fireworks shot out from the center of his body toward the crowd. People started yelling, deep, guttural sounds that mimicked cries of war. The hay bails on which the man stood caught fire as flames dripped down from his heart. The fire blazed. Constant yelling now. Flame-throwers erupted violently. People's arms were in the sky, fists clenched, their faces tense in blissful frenzy. Everywhere I looked fire reached into empty spaces. Group rage seemed imminent. In this desperate moment, I remembered another portion of the organizer's speech that catered to a sense of powerlessness, and saw this climactic burn as a frightening response to the kernel of truth.

"We've created this world in which they do these demographic studies, and they find out what people think they want, and then in a kind of séance they summon up before you the Ghost of Your Own Desire and they sell it to you. And it doesn't connect you to anything. It connects you to your own individual desires, and then it turns out, as it often does in life, that what you wanted wasn't what you needed. So we spend all our time now consuming stuff, consuming these dream images that nourish us spiritually like Styrofoam pellets."

After years of eating Styrofoam pellets, we needed to burn the man. We needed to see him go down. When the Man broke in half and fell, black smoke clouded the sky. This apocalyptic moment, at a ceremony built around a kind of apocalypse, was the most unnerving experience I hope to ever have. Because suddenly it was over. What we'd come to do—burn the man until its presence literally turned to ash—was done. But the crowd's energy was still pitched higher. People were still haunted by the Ghosts of Their Own Desire. They'd still led a life of consumption all year in order to fully release that reserved, unused, unrecognized, neglected energy, and by George—I felt this way myself—they'd be damned if the self-expression, the revenge, was already over now. It had just begun.

This was the moment, my friend had told me beforehand, that the crowd rushes forward and races around the Man a few times, creating both climax and closure. Sure enough, bodies around me surged forward and I lost most of my campmates, except for one who was just beginning to trip on his drugs. We walked slowly on the outskirts of the crowd, watching. Glowing cinders blew into the air as the wind kicked up, landing on people's bodies and in their hair. Excitement had reached a blinding height, but not enough to distract me from the impending fire hazard. My campmate and I moved away from the crowd into the emptiness of the playa. We watched the post-ceremony rage. This is what we are, outside the parameters of families, cubicles, and commodification, I thought. This is the human species at its critical mass. Given only three days of freedom to make what we can with our modern technology, our ideas, and our effort, we created a place in which to desperately, violently, release our souls.

The days after my return from Burning Man I could do and say little. I ate a hearty diet of eggs and bacon and cheese, showered for several hours, pulled clumps of knotted hair from my head, and coughed up several ounces of phlegm and dust. I wondered if I'd found what I needed at Burning Man. Never had I witnessed such intense connection with people my age and to the time in which I live. The people with whom I camped, and their friends and acquaintances, were responsible for that sense of unity. Perhaps if

I'd taken lots of drugs, I too would have trusted the other 20,000 participants enough to feel fulfilled and heartened by the chaos we created in the name of self-expression. But I didn't.

I was surprised not to have benefited more from the extreme spiritual experience of Burning Man. After all, I believed in the value of a space where people could leave their regular selves, or rather, get in touch with more intimate parts of themselves. I believed in any step people took outside of their ordinary lives in their office cubicles or their family roles or their social structures. I even believed in doing these things communally. Like the carnivals of the European Renaissance, Burning Man provided a structure outside of conventional society for social and political transformation. It was weirdly regenerative in that I was given a new look at my peers, what we had in common, what separated us. Somehow, in a way I'd not yet experienced, Burning Man was spiritual by default. It ridiculed modern society, and in doing so exalted all elements, thoughts, and behavior that fell outside of social convention. But it did not provide a visible, positive system within which I could grow. The experience was way too based on fantasy for me. I needed a system that would mark progress, where self-discovery was grounded in something besides the structure of self-expression. The gift economy prevented the event from becoming a disaster like Woodstock '99. But a gift economy was just an alternative to the economy we have now. It was still commerce. It still held the society together.

Part of the Burning Man experience was the art of survival; it was a place where self-expression was as crucial as water. In the process of surviving, however, I got sidetracked from spiritual growth. Even the night of the burn, when people came together to experience the euphoria of the ceremony, I felt the desperation, the nonverbal excitement, but not an accessible collective state of consciousness. And more than feeling the rush of a community of people in various states of need, I longed for the rush of a community in a collective state of bliss.

But plenty of people left Burning Man with their minds opened and elaborate plans made for the next year: to build a better shade structure, create a more festive costume, to bring their

friends to the camp so that the experience might be more personal, more intimate, more connected to their ideal. Even I entertained the idea of returning, but if I did, it wouldn't be for spiritual
community. The interior space I'd worked so hard to cultivate
shrunk in the presence of too much activity. Burning Man satisfied
my need to know that many humans shared an urge to transcend,
and that, if necessary, I could survive in the desert for a few days
on little more than blowpops and beer. But that was all.

It was a relief to admit: There was no big connection out there
that I could get in one weekend, as immediately gratifying as taking a spaceship and landing on the moon. The connection I
needed was ongoing, like the hours of the day, like breathing, like
housework. Daily maintenance was required to fill the gap, like
working a job or nurturing a relationship. As for community, I was
sick of hunting outside of myself and meeting with some group
that didn't suit my needs. I was willing to continue meditating,
practicing yoga, and expanding the little understanding of personal
growth I had at the rate that it came. Like the day I stopped cram-
ming myself into bars on Saturday night in the name of fun, I was
now willing to chill out on my own, surrender quietly to the
desire I had for spiritual union.

Revelations

It's been ten years since Cindy the God-girl forced herself and her friend Jesus into my thoughts. It's been five years since I started exploring spirituality, to my own surprise, and about three years since fully engaging on a spiritual journey where I sought an individual sense of the divine. During all this time, I've refrained from telling people about most of my forays. I've clung to the conventional wisdom that spirituality, like religion, is a deeply personal, private matter that shouldn't be discussed openly. Even though religion was not the same as spirituality in my mind—one depended on institutions; the other, experience— I still adopted the same protective rule of secrecy I had been taught: Don't talk about religion. The secrecy acted as a shrine for me. It kept me separate, as though I lived a life removed in a monastery I'd built out of odd bricks and found objects, like a nomad builds a shelter during his life of wandering. All this time, I've been dwelling pensively within the protective shell. I knew that in this shell my exploration would be safe. I'd be free from ridicule, criticism, sarcasm, conservatism, or any of the thoughts that would harm my fragile hope that if I sought the divine, I would find it.

Conventional wisdom, and my protective shell, were also their own tomb, however. Keeping my spiritual experiences under wraps seemed to defeat the purpose of that very journey, which was to explore options, find a foundation on which to stand, and presumably grow further into the world, closer to people I knew, and strengthen our human connection. In my silence, I was still harvesting the fruits of the journey. I'd certainly explored. And grown. I'd moved beyond being angry at my dissatisfying Catholic experience. I could even forgive the nuns. I'd been brave enough to make myself vulnerable to other traditions. I'd learned to appreciate people who assumed nun-like positions in those traditions, and learned to recognize them as teachers. Why wasn't I brave enough to discuss my exploration, to share the fruits of my journey with friends and family? I was a wuss.

In part, I kept to myself because I still didn't know which path I wanted to take. I'd decided nothing. I hadn't gone back to embrace my former Catholic or even Christian identity, though I no longer had a problem with Jesus. Nor had I gone forward and adopted any other spiritual discipline enough to say, "I practice X," though all of them might have suited me just fine had I been slightly more . . . what? Committed? Confident? Religious?

At the same time, I was no longer comfortable saying, "I'm not religious." My former spiritual frustration at feeling disengaged from the world seemed to be waning. I no longer felt like a frenzied shell of a person working endlessly to make sense of professional and personal life, without any sense of interior self. I had gotten involved with processes of transcendence; I had experienced unforgettable rituals, trances, and ceremonies in which I had shifted into a spiritual state. These had changed me.

I'd reached a few definite conclusions. Catholicism, for me, was the wrong route for religion but the right route for revolution: it had catapulted me into a crisis. I was forced to notice my lopsided sense of self, my uncertain sense of place, as a young woman expecting to grow freely. Before about age twelve, I didn't know that throughout society, women's desire for growth had been considered subordinate to men's. Nor did I know that a giant leap would soon be required of me in my Catholic education, from feeling shameful for ruining paradise to feeling beatific as I embraced motherhood, with no plotted path for growth in between. That was the problem. There was no plotted path. No wise women foretelling future events or remarking on the past, or dispensing advice that I could live by. No women sitting at the table at the Last Supper. No scene of them in the kitchen cooking the food, even. They didn't exist. Until my twentysomething quest, I didn't know how alienated I'd become, how much leaving behind the scrap of spiritual identity I'd begun with had amputated an arm of my growth. I wasn't the only one who had made this decision. So many women I knew had inflicted the same amputation upon themselves. We all thought it was a good idea. We were certain that a more personal, flexible, and productive system of growth that took into account who we truly were would come along at some point. We'd know it when we saw it. Ten years later, still a spiritual adolescent, it hadn't come along in the right package. I needed examples of women who had discovered their true natures and had begun to take this part of their identities back on their own.

Finding them helped me reach another conclusion: Personal spirituality was practical. Each woman flexed her spiritual muscles when deciding where, with whom, and how they lived. Arianna's decision to divorce came about through her contemplation and summoning of fire energy. Lisa's decision to live in a house full of Sufis rose from a deep place of nonsexual, spiritual love. I saw the same devotion that propelled these women forward in their spiritual lives—to take shamanic journeys, or meditate, or pay tribute to a pantheon of gods—emerge in their personal lives. And it helped them find a way to live in which they could continually honor their total sense of self. I sucked up their examples, correlating what had become their everyday lives with my newfound impressions of compassion, healing, warriorship, surrender, rebirth, and universal awareness. These were underdeveloped but growing at hormonal speed.

I bought into a dream. Choreographing my journey around other women's spiritual lives served a different purpose than I'd originally thought it would. So awed was I by their real, live, active spirituality, I treated these ordinary women with allegiance I'd previously reserved for the Bionic Woman and Charlie's Angels. I looked to them as though they were archetypes themselves. Live heroines. Just like on TV, but bigger, and better. The size of God. Initially, I was certain that clicking into their lives meant I'd be admitted to a sisterhood—a special series of divine secrets stored in some cave or frozen inside giant glaciers, divine secrets that were guarded by priestesses and reserved only for us. Chosen us. With my admission, I'd come away with a separate set of beliefs that exalted women to their true divine seats in the universe, that moved them past the mundane and even denigrating places in society that had been appointed to them, to a place of pure divine femininity. But as I got to know their spiritual truths, this particular initiation did not happen. Nothing happened until I'd experienced spiritual living myself.

Yes, I found female archetypes like Yemaya and Kali—Mother of the Sea and Mother of the Earth. They provided me with supernatural notions of my divine self as it exists in an earthly female body. But those archetypes were more passageways than endpoints. They acted as conduits to the sense of self that is without gender. The archetypes helped pull me into the spiritual dimension, but once I was in, issues of gender were nearly moot. From a spiritual perspective, I neither had to flaunt nor hide my identity as a woman. Spiritual desires transcended manhood and womanhood. My experience in this world as a woman was equivalent to my experience in this world as a person with a mouth, or with one leg, or with the ability to calculate the number of minutes it would take to walk to the moon. Every tradition I examined held gender to be a gift; the body, like the mind, was a tool but was not the sum total of self. My body influenced my experience, but spiritual peace actually dictated my experience.

Of course, I couldn't ignore my female physical reality or the important role played by feminism in balancing the power between the genders. I was outraged that throughout history, cultures had used religion to oppress women. When suffragist Elizabeth Cady Stanton wrote *The Women's Bible* in 1895, she voiced the same inequality I had felt in Catholic school but couldn't articulate as a teen, that "the chief obstacle in the way of women's elevation today is the degrading position assigned to her in the religion of all countries. . . ." Such degradation is spiritual oppression. Hundreds of years old, it still trickles down to women like me, and I can see now, by how much my consciousness has grown by chanting or meditating or journeying or praying outside of the Catholic institution, that as an adolescent I could smell the traces of spiritual oppression like a decaying corpse in the closet. Alas.

Even if I weren't a woman, I might have rejected Catholicism. I knew lots of men who had abandoned their Catholic roots, too. The Catholic doctrine I'd absorbed in school just didn't touch me individually as a young person trying to live bravely. The teachings seemed canned, like no one had considered how to present them cogently to young people at a time when we were increasingly aware of ourselves as media targets, as points of economic interest, as a workforce, and as other societal vessels that would make the world work. Young women and men have been abandoning institutional religion for years. Evidence is provided not only by the fact that religion was all but banished from our social vocabulary, but was proven in American statistics. Seeking religious alternatives is an ongoing trend. A 1997 Gallup Poll measuring teenagers' (ages 13–17) interest in faith reported surprising interest in Native American spirituality (44 percent) and Paganism (22 percent). In casual conversation, alternative forms of spirituality as they exist visibly in the world have become familiar topics. Burning Man has made it to the Travel Channel; the Dalai Lama attracted thousands of people to his talk in Central Park. Fifteen-year-olds rap along with the Beastie Boys' song *Bodhisattva Vow*. Madonna's *Ray of Light* unabashedly expressed spiritual emotions. Spiritual life for young people has become a hip and acceptable fashion. Women wear saris over jeans. Men wear Tibetan friendship bracelets. This spring, I saw a white woman in dreadlocks wearing a pro-Rastafarian T-shirt with Prada shoes. One night I passed an art gallery full of men with shaved heads wearing Burberry plaid shirts. They were sipping wine in front of a mural that read Hari Rama Hari Rama Ram Ram Hari Hari. Yet on a one-to-one basis, shrouding one's feelings about spirituality in mystery—or mockery—is more socially acceptable than actually discussing them.

My hiding of my spiritual experiences echoed this trend—I was still treating spirituality like religion, a sign of weakness in a hip twentysomething—though the powerful practices of transformation I'd found paled in comparison to my Catholic experience. I didn't often tell people that I took shamanic journeys during times of need. In fact, I *never* told anyone. But when problems turned over and over again in my mind, problems that touched a deep chord of conflict or survival, I would lie down, play my drum tape, and take a quick trip to the turtle. I asked her how to ask for a raise at work, or how to balance personal time with relationship time with my boyfriend, or how to remain calm when I became upset. I asked her how to stay happy. She always met me on the beach, patiently listened to my problems, and sent back information that broke open my cycle of worry and contemplation. The trance allowed me to see truth outside of my perceived reality. It tunneled beneath the surface of life, and left me calm for the rest of the day.

Nor did I tell others how often I chanted aloud during the day, chants to Kali or Durga, Sita and Rama, that asked for protection from fear, for internal union when I went on job interviews or felt myself in the presence of unpleasant people or even visited family. I didn't tell because I felt vulnerable—and with good reason. People my age—people I respect for their thoughts and convictions—generally treat the subject with suspicion and distance. "Did you meet any Wiccans?" one man asked me, mocking his own interest in my search for spiritual traditions. "Yes," I answered. "Those Wiccans—I just love them!" he said. "They're so . . . witchy!"

I laughed at his comment at the time, since I knew the man was trying to convey a genuine admiration despite the backhanded presentation. But underneath I wondered, Why do we do this? Despite my daily spiritual practices I was still roped in by suspicion and distance. My exploration of different beliefs did not calm my lurking fear of what people might think, what stories of my journeys and observations would sound like coming out of my mouth. I was still equally suspicious. Even though I had seen a handful of positive examples, I wasn't positive that a spiritual foundation was strong enough to live by—truly live by—in the modern world. If spiritual centering was considered valid in the twentysomething's world, as was cynicism and ambivalence, *how* valid was it? My peers saw spirituality as a far from legitimate way to pass one's time. As one friend said, "I resent this talk of spirituality: people pawn it off as a substitute for thought." Paradoxically, this was the same friend who brought me to Burning Man. But what if her sentiment was correct—that I and others were just looking for an easy way out, something to take care of us as we faced the authorities in the world that we had been groomed to despise? Among twentysomethings, there seemed to be a divide between those who considered spirituality a subject worth delving into and those who dismissed it with disdain. The divide plagued me.

The word *spirituality* is itself a buzzword, and not everyone understands it the same way. One twenty-eight-year-old who lives in the Midwest immediately questioned the word *spirituality* with, "You mean L. Ron Hubbard [Dianetics] or Tibetan meditation?" Knee-jerk mistrust. Because he came from a nonreligious background, he said, spirituality was not a comfortable topic for him to discuss. More than likely, if someone brought up the subject, he'd steer the conversation to, "Well, I saw the movie *Dogma* last weekend." To him, too much openness to spiritual matters was a sign of fanaticism, a "cult mentality."

I could relate. I too feared encountering cultish people, who might be blind to my desire for spiritual growth and were intent only on influencing my thinking according to their needs. The fear of surrendering to a larger, more powerful force in hope of deepening autonomy but instead losing it was embedded in my approach, too. Perhaps because I was very young when my parents shared stories about the Manson murders or crazed leaders like Jim Jones. Or perhaps I was too conscious of David Koresh and the Heaven's Gate commune. Or perhaps because I watched too much TV that was riddled with advertisements. I easily surrendered hours to that institution for the hope of unification, but ended up, ultimately, losing fractions of autonomy. It wasn't religion, but it was close.

○ ○ ○

Deep down I knew that twentysomethings weren't spiritually devoid, but somehow acting as though spirituality were an alien or fabricated human ideal was easier for us than acknowledging its significance. No one saw proof of spirituality in society, so we denied the possibility. The denial actually created a bond among many of my acquaintances. I knew, because on each occasion that my spiritual experiences "came up" (people seemed interested enough to ask me about them, or to tell others I had done such things), we ended up bonding over the "weirdness" or "edginess" of each experience—not how we could relate to it. The story of Uma, for example, who pursued her spiritual path full force without regret, shocked my listeners instead of inspiring them. One woman responded uncomfortably, "Wow, she sounds a little lost." "No," I said, "she is totally found." "But to go that far," my friend tried to justify, "seems a little extreme. But I guess that's cool," she decided. Yes, I allowed. Extreme is cool. But is that really why Uma's story makes sense to my peers? Because it's extreme?

My friend seemed to miss the point, but then I couldn't really articulate what that point was. She didn't want to hear it, and I feared sharing my spiritual conviction; I didn't want to come off as a prose-lytizer. On the other hand, sealing my lips seemed equally weak. Perhaps I should treat my searching as an extreme sport, like an epic trek up Machu Picchu alone in winter. I looked at the spiritual land-scape on which my friends stood, or at least said they stood, and saw rows of twentysomethings standing with smirks on their faces, wait-ing to be either impressed or disappointed. Though people were educated enough to respect Uma's choices, curious enough to inquire about it, and even savvy enough to be dazzled by her hipness, they were unable to act in response to it. I too, in part, was behaving like an audience member. As though I had no frame of reference.

Building my own frame of reference was only the first step. The next was to act bravely, and each time I attempted to do so—that is, to pursue one form of practice or another—I resisted, hesitated, and repeatedly had to justify my efforts to myself. The solid sense of place I got from meditating clashed with the social conditioning that told me my sense of place was grounded in peers, career, consumerism. The sources of this conditioning are amorphous, but I'd venture to say they are media-based. So much media projects images of young people as consumers and producers. Very little mentions that just being human has significance in the real world. Every time I sat to meditate I thought, Is this a waste of time? Will I get where I want to go? Will I be late for whatever I had planned afterward? It wasn't until I persevered, remembering to label this mind activity as "thinking," that I was able to settle in and see my doubts and distractions for the idle activity that they were.

I couldn't even enjoy reading Sufi literature. I first had to justify to myself the beauty of surrender to a guru. It took pages of reading for me to reconnect to the peace Lisa and my cousin Mary felt from living within the Sufi community, from surrendering themselves to part of a larger, functional consciousness. It was as though I suffered from some syndrome, some impulse that mechanistically would doubt anything that uplifted the soul or would continually critique any comfort in the spiritual world I desperately wanted to enter.

But I had already entered. Six different ways. I had seen with my own eyes and felt with my own body the beauty and benefits of shamanic journeying, of yoga, of living with a guru, but my instinct to mistrust won out every time I left each world. Yes, I absorbed the information. I even accepted it on some level. But on another level—the one I shared with my generation—I mistrusted the truth I had experienced.

Gen-Xers have a natural mistrust of authority. The government is an authority that we believe is completely out of touch with our needs. Working for "the man," signing one's life away to a full-time job, implies surrendering one's own authority to a larger, evil system. Freedom from authority is what matters to us. Taking too much advice from parents or committing to a mate compromises autonomy. Yet we exist in these systems, if only half-heartedly. Plenty of us have functional relationships with parents and lovers. Plenty of us shop at commercial chain stores like the Gap or

Starbucks, subscribe to America Online and prefer to use PCs. Many of these things I did with regularity, but on some level they invoked traces of shame: Weren't we just letting large corporations dictate the way we look or influence the coffee buzz we experience? What about the individual? Who was looking out for the preservation of the individual? Anything other than self-authority over personal, economic, or social well-being was a young person's demon. It was certainly my demon, and religion was the mother of them all.

To me, religion fell into the same category as other archaic authorities to which I felt some obligation to surrender. But religion demanded an even higher commitment to the soul. To surrender one's soul, the very nest of faith, is the ultimate surrender to authority. I knew from the Catholic example that in order to fully "see" God, one must follow scripture, understand the commandments, and adopt the Catholic view of the world. Wandering off the path on your own was not a choice, it was a sin. But it saved me.

Many scholars of religion look down upon personal exploration as a means to spiritual security. One scholar even called exploring "cafeteria spirituality." I say, exploring is a lot more like bringing your own lunch and swapping with a friend. Exploring granted me the freedom to get off the path, look around, think about what I had seen, and truly taste spiritual activity. Though fraught with doubt most of the time, I eventually recognized the possibilities a conscientious spiritual life offered not just me, but all people. Once Ava Kay and the Sister showed me how to cultivate strength, and that nothing could shed the theological binding but my own hand, the amorphous outside authority I despised disappeared. I saw that my path—whatever it turned out to be—was really in my own hands. It always had been. It always would be. The truth was, a type of surrender was always necessary in order to glean spiritual benefits. In order to lead a spiritual life, one had to believe that the self had a true nature, that the world worked according to certain universal laws, that there existed a path to liberation and that these three elements composed a type of reality. Spiritually, this surrender led to freedom, not punishment. Gain, not loss. I saw access to a trouble-free consciousness, to a divine order of cause and effect in which I was intimately involved, to camaraderie with others. Somehow, religion as I first learned it did not explain that "surrender" is really a surrender to self. Spirituality, on the other hand, gave me proof that surrender to self and experience was the only way to see the divine.

So why was I still blocked from fully devoting myself to a path? Commitment problems and cold feet left me wanting to jilt myself, leaving me standing at the altar. I was still uncrossing my wires between notions of religion and spirituality, making sure spirituality wasn't the same scam with a different name. Also, it was hard to make the switch from being committed to nothing to being committed to one's True Self. Spiritual living involves changing habits. Devotion takes discipline. Discipline takes time.

An on-target assessment of why time for spirituality was so hard to come by came from a hipster Renaissance man I knew, who dabbles in Web education, music, and writing. He said, "I have a curiosity for [spiritual] things. But the pace of my life leaves me little time to explore the matter. Spirituality is about 'being.' My life at the time is too full of 'doing' to actually be."

Such is the nature of our age and the time in which we live. We all "do," in order to fulfill our ambitions, our responsibilities, and our desires for happiness. Learning how to "do" is imperative to making a living, developing social skills, and completing an education. Yet "doing" pervades all of our activities, it seems. Even when I embarked on my quest, I approached each tradition from the perspective of "doing"; in all of them, there were rituals or practices to "do." I did the shamanic journey. I did yoga. But doing wasn't how I gained significant knowledge. Doing was merely the doorway. The moments when I suspended my doubt and allowed myself to "be" was when experience actually transcended into meaning.

At its worst, spirituality looks like a distraction from doing. "Doing" is not only fashionable, but, in the case of work, doing makes the world go faster. We create more product, we raise more money, we buy things that make us go faster. The tragedy of my generation, and the hope, is that despite how fashionable it is to lead a frenetic life, we still have an instinct to just "be." Maybe it's a rebellious instinct. Maybe it's a natural instinct. Maybe it was a self-indulgent habit fostered by seeing so many media images of ourselves, or because we grew up listening to *Free to Be. . .You and Me,* and because many of our parents in the '70s were involved in health food and yoga, the Kabbalah and Eastern mysticism. Or maybe it's because we have high levels of education and know, deep down, our chances of living harmoniously amid a developing global economy, worldwide struggles for human rights, gender equality, and racial and religious tolerance depend on our efforts.

Yet, I agree, visible examples of just "being" in our society are creepy. Being, to us, looks passive. Living in a competitive, free society where we have the privilege to do exactly as we please, doing dictates our sense of value. We've seen lots of pictures of people "doing" things for the good of the environment, or the labor unions, or foreign relations, or the local YMCA. But pictures of people "being" happy are less common and therefore less attractive. Also "being" does not make our earth turn economically. One twentysomething arts and crafts teacher remembers cynically her mother's ventures into a phase of just "being" in the '70s. "At that time, every Jewish woman going through a divorce went to the local ashram. She dragged me along and we just hung out there. After a while, they realized life was passing them by, and they moved on." A coworker of mine spoke with similar misgivings of a colleague who had found solace in the Virgin Mary. My coworker said, "She's clearly so much happier with Mary in her life, but that glint in her eye really bothers me. It's so obvious she's found God and it just freaks me out." She was freaked by the woman's stillness, her calm, her lack of motion that was the essence of being.

I too still have the urge to think spirituality will take away from the things I must do. And that being will turn me into a softie, a flake, a person who contributes nothing to society. A person who doesn't get it. Yet I cannot go back to being spiritually inactive. Like crawling back into the womb, it is no longer an option. I've been shown too much experience and information; too many people have shared with me their understanding of God. However reluctantly, I have received the understanding that spirituality is active, and I have been trying to tailor it to my own life. It's taking a long time.

I feel obligated to learn how, though, now that I've asked for the teachings. People I asked made themselves vulnerable to me in order to explain their reality. Their vulnerable honesty was more truthful than anything I'd seen in years. Explaining the bliss and comfort that they feel helped me feel its promise, too. Their dispensing of knowledge was a type of initiation. It primed me for experience. Even though I've refrained from committing fully, I've largely altered my life.

I tell myself to stay on track, practice meditation to remain in the dot consciousness, practice yoga to move with the breath, read Sufi literature to understand the full dimension of life lived according to love. Because, I tell myself each day, these things are true. These practices work. But I still have to practice, which is a bit of a drag at times. I hope that at some point I'll just do it, like taking a shower in the morning. I've grown comfortable using the word *spirituality* to describe a personal sense of God. This God is an interior sense of love and bliss and belonging. It's a knowing—a consciousness—that every person has. It's like a portal that occasionally opens and closes. People either jump through it or they don't.

It would be nice to have more company. Rationally, I know I can't be concerned with whether everybody else has gone through the portal yet. Or whether they even want to. It's like the decision to save money or run up debt or just waver in the middle, living hand to mouth. Everyone lives how they want to live. I remember thinking the very same thought when I snapped at the God-girl's desire to include me. I would still freak if a zealot approached me too aggressively about their path, today. I understand the lack of restraint. Taking a path and walking alone is disheartening. Your solitary commitment gets even stronger when others who are like-minded join you. It's like any army. There is strength in numbers. But I had no interest in joining a spiritual army. Armies tend to ignore the universal spiritual principle of respect for all beings everywhere.

Now that I'd had a look around at the spiritual landscape, I didn't mind walking alone. I've already found an assortment of possible places where I might end up. They all seemed pretty much the same, in the end. Putting faith into action is like turning on a flashlight in the dark, or having night vision. I see that any road I take is safe as long as I walk with my mind in a state of devotion. Devotion, I'm happy to reconfirm, is holy: it's another word for *brave*.

This is not to say that the urge to roll my eyes when someone talks too enthusiastically about karma has completely left me. That impulse is part of my shame as a fairly liberal, spiritually educated person. The belief in something invisible is unacceptable among my generation. But my personal quest and the women I met on it have given me reason to believe we will all tire of the despair we feel at not seeing a direct connection to something greater than ourselves, to each other. Maybe then we'll begin moving from the outside in.

Acknowledgments

Many people have supported me from the first day I invited this book into my life. I am grateful to Allison Draper for planting the seed, and to Barbara Seaman for nurturing its roots. My gratitude to Dave Isay for helping me reel in my thoughts, to Felicia Eth and Mary Jane Ryan for sharing my vision and helping me realize the book's true voice. I thank the astute women and spiritual elders who granted me their words, thoughts, and beliefs in interviews that never made it into these pages but are imbedded in my mind. I thank my friends who never doubted me, and my writing group for reading every chapter and commenting with candor. I thank my parents and brother for their love. I thank Nick for his faith in me and his years of irreplaceable love and support.

I thank and honor all of the women in this book; they are all my teachers.

I thank my grandmother, Elizabeth Keeley Clores, for talking to me every day.

TO OUR READERS

CONARI PRESS publishes books on topics ranging from spirituality, personal growth, and relationships to women's issues, parenting, and social issues. Our mission is to publish quality books that will make a difference in people's lives—how we feel about ourselves and how we relate to one another. We value integrity, compassion, and receptivity, both in the books we publish and in the way we do business.

As a member of the community, we sponsor the Random Acts of Kindness™ Foundation, the guiding force behind Random Acts of Kindness™ Week. We donate our damaged books to nonprofit organizations, dedicate a portion of our proceeds from certain books to charitable causes, and continually look for new ways to use natural resources as wisely as possible.

Our readers are our most important resource, and we value your input, suggestions, and ideas about what you would like to see published. Please feel free to contact us, to request our latest book catalog, or to be added to our mailing list.

2550 Ninth Street, Suite 101
Berkeley, California 94710-2551
800-685-9595 • 510-649-7175
fax: 510-649-7190 • e-mail: conari@conari.com
http://www.conari.com